CONTENTS

Acknowledgements

A book like this is the work of many hands, and this one in particular has been helped by a large number of people. It was the original suggestion of Mr Douglas Walshe (formerly of the Cork Public Museum) who, several years ago, prepared a document based on the extensive contemporary clippings files assembled by the family of Sir Edward Fitzgerald and held by Cork Public Museum. It was Douglas who fired an interest in International Exhibitions in us. Aside from Douglas, Ms Stella Cherry (Curator) and her colleagues at the Cork Public Museum; Messrs Mathew O'Herlihy, Charlie Davis and David Donovan, along with Ms Rita Buckley, provided encouragement and understanding for this book, since we embarked on it in the summer of 2011. Mr Dara McGrath was also extremely helpful in photographing documents and memorabilia in the museum's collection.

At an early stage Mr Kevin Terry (ret'd) and Ms Valerie O'Sullivan of Cork City Council pledged their intention to support this project as part of the restoration and improvements to Fitzgerald Park in 2013/4. Their colleagues Mr Liam Casey, Cork City Council Parks Department, and Mr Liam Ronayne, Cork City Librarian, were also key in arranging the funding grant.

Furthermore, we would like to thank the following for arranging additional book sponsorship; Mr Neil Kenefick (DOSCO Ltd.), Mr Brendan Murphy (CIT) and Ms Carol Quinn, Archivist (Irish Distillers Ltd.).

Other council employees helped also, with their time and advice, including: Mr Kieran Burke and Mr Paul O'Regan, Cork City Library, Local Studies Department for supply of images and documents, Mr Pat Ruane, Conservation Officer, for his insight, and Mr Conor Sullivan, Cork City Council Parks Department for arranging access to the Fr Mathew Memorial Fountain. Mr Brian McGee and staff of the Cork City & County Archives Institute were helpful as always.

In addition to this, we were aided by several professional historians in the preparation of the manuscript namely: Dr John Borgonovo for advice on the text, Dr Donal Ó Drisceóil for helping us to focus our ideas and Dr Stephanie Rains who read an early version of the manuscript. Dr Alicia St Leger and the Cork Literary & Scientific Society invited us to talk to them in January 2012, and this provided an impetus for the research for this book. Chapter

6 is based on a paper delivered to the inaugural conference of the All-Ireland Architectural Research Group in Dublin in 2012, which was organized by Messrs Noel Brady and Brian Ward.

As you can tell from the object you are holding, illustrations were very important to this project, and many people aided us in tracking down images which have not seen the light of day for many a year. The Directors of the National Library, and especially the National Photographic Archive, were most helpful sourcing images from the Lawrence Collection, as well as other material. In addition the National Archives of Ireland were a great help, especially their online Censuses of 1901 and 1911. Messrs Michael Lenihan and Niall Murray allowed us to use images from their collections, without which this book would be all the poorer, in addition Ms Tracey Walker, Manchester Art Gallery and Mr Tim Craven, Curator of Art, Arts and Heritage, Southampton City Council allowed us access to images in their collections. Mr Bob Montgomery, Royal Irish Automobile Club, helped with the 1903 Gordon Bennett races and Mr Colum O'Riordan, Irish Architectural Archives, provided some striking images. Mss Nicola Russell, Fiona Neale and Fiona Laird, University of Glasgow Library, Special Collections were most helpful in sourcing images of the Glasgow 1901 Exhibition which so influenced Cork's. Dr Robert Treharne Jones of the Leander Rowing Club, Henley aided with the illustration of the Cork International Trophy. Images were also sourced from The Science & Society Picture Library, the Ronald Grant Archive and the Scottish Screen Archive (National Library of Scotland) and UCC Library, Special Collections.

We would like to acknowledge in particular the following people who aided us in tracking down some unpublished images: Mrs Myrtle Allen, Mr Timothy Allen and Dr Dagmar Ó Riain-Raedel, University College Cork, were a great help with Arthur Hill's work on the Exhibition. In addition, Messrs Michael and Declan Ryan, provided information and images relating to their grandfather, Michael A. Ryan, who worked at the Exhibition. Mr Jack Lyons provided information about his grandfather, Jonas Wagner, who was also there, and thanks also to Mr David and Mrs Anna Cooke, Auckland, New Zealand, for allowing us to quote from the recollections of William Levingston Cooke.

Local historians are always helpful with a project such as this and (as usual!) Mr Ronnie Herlihy provided invaluable suggestions and background knowledge, Mr Pat Poland was helpful in relation to Cork's fire services, and Mr Patrick O'Donovan and Dr Conor O'Riordan shared their enthusiasm for all things relating to the Exhibition. Mr Brian Gabriel and Mr Richard and Mrs Sylvia Bolster of the Blarney & District Historical Society and Sir Charles Colthurst of Blarney, provided interesting information on the links between that village and the Exhibition. Messrs Tom Walsh and Anthony Duggan and Br Ned Hayden, Community Leader, Christian Brothers (North Monastery) were most helpful on the relationship between the North Mon and the Exhibitions. Mr Walsh also provided invaluable translations.

Further afield, Ms Jo Brock of the Fulham & Hammersmith Historical Society provided information on John McManus & Co. and Ms Megan Butcher and Ms Alexandra McEwen, Library and Archives Canada, Ottawa, diligently tracked down references to Cork in their archives.

A number of people were extremely helpful in tracing the influence of the exhibition of Cork's domestic architecture, namely: Mr Denis Kennedy, Mr Dom Daly, M et Mme Arnaud Disant, Mr Paddy and Mrs Adie McKeown (neé McCarthy) and Mr John McCarthy for sharing their records and stories, Mr and Mrs G. Fitzgibbon and Mr and Mrs D. Swinburne. Mr and Mrs Des Ryan lent us a useful print of the exhibition site, and thanks also to Mr Jason Byrne, Ms Billy O'Flynn and to Ms Teresita O'Callaghan, Lee Rowing Club.

Our commissioning editor, Ms Lisa Hyde, and Mr Conor Graham of the Irish Academic Press were invaluable for their advice and guidance, and we thank them for having the vision to take this project on, when others were sceptical; our thanks also to Mr Stuart Coughlan at edit+ for the beautiful design.

On a more personal note, Tom Spalding would like to thank to Mr Guy Briggs, and also Ms Catherine Bates and Mr Patrick Flynn are to be thanked for accommodation at short notice and his wife, Ms Aideen Sullivan, for her usual fortitude and love.

Daniel Breen would like to thank Messrs Patrick Gillen and Joseph Jolley for reading early drafts of this book. He would especially like to thank his wife, Ms Carola Murphy, without whose love, support and patience, this book would not have been possible.

Authors' Notes

Due to its encyclopaedic nature, the study of International Exhibitions calls on knowledge of many fields, from politics and international relations, to technology, sport, architecture and art. It is therefore inevitable that a book such as this would touch on all of these areas, but it is also evident that only a very particular blend of talents would be capable of doing all of these spheres full justice in the printed word. Whilst we have endeavoured to cover as much of this multi-faceted event as humanly possible, it is likely that some readers may find that we have underplayed the importance of their particular area of interest, be it temperance, Gaelic games or classical music; for that we apologize. We were lucky to have an extensive archive of contemporary newspaper clippings and reviews to call upon, but this in itself is a two-edged sword; one gets the immediacy of an eye-witness account, but one is also conscious of a certain over-enthusiasm amongst the correspondents and of hobby-horses being ridden. There is also the fact that the press in Ireland was divided between nationalist and unionist organs, even in Cork: the *Cork Examiner* taking the former view, the *Cork Constitution* the latter. In addition, certain events (the Royal Visit of 1903 and the international rowing and yachting events come to mind) loom very large in the reports of the media of all persuasions, and overshadow other, perhaps more long-lasting, phenomena visible at the Exhibition, such as the Gaelic Revival or the under-current of criticism of the event by 'advanced' nationalists.

In terms of currency, we have generally used the costs in 1902 terms, with conversion from 1902 Pounds to Pounds Sterling in 2013, using a factor of 100. This is based on work by Jim O'Donoghue, Louise Goulding and Grahame Allen, in their paper 'Consumer Price Inflation since 1750', *Economic Trends*, 604 (2004) and their further work. From 1826 to 1979, and thus for most of the twentieth century, the Irish Pound (Punt) was equal to the Pound Sterling, and Irish money was minted in England. Readers in the Irish Republic or other Euro areas can multiply figures by a factor of *c.*120 to get a feel for historical values at 2013 levels.

Tom Spalding and Daniel Breen
Cork, March 2014

Introduction

Daniel Breen and Tom Spalding

Coming out of the Shadows

From May to November 1902, Cork City played host to one of the most significant events in its entire history: the International Exhibition of Manufactures, Arts, Products and Industries. It spanned a 44-acre site not far from the city centre, encompassing an area on the Mardyke that now includes the Cork County Cricket Club, the Sunday's Well Boating and Tennis Club, Fitzgerald Park and the University's Sports Arena. The exhibition grounds were elaborately laid out and had several large halls and pavilions as well as an assortment of smaller buildings including tea houses, restaurants and kiosks. Irish and foreign exhibitors, some from 'exotic' locations such as China, Russia and Turkey, filled these halls and pavilions with exhibits and demonstrations for all to see. The exhibition also boasted the most up-to-date amusements and attractions that guaranteed 'something for everyone'. Indeed it was visited by over 1.8 million people and enjoyed a profit of £6,500 (c.£650,000). All this was achieved on a budget of £100,000 pounds (c.£10 million) and completed within the staggering timeframe of fifteen months. In fact, it proved such a popular and commercial success that the decision was made in late 1902 to re-open the event as the Greater Cork International Exhibition in 1903. Thus, for two years, Cork city and its exhibition was the centre of national and international media attention, yet today the event remains largely unknown, consigned to be remembered only by a small group of local historians.

It would be unrealistic to claim that the 1902/3 Cork International Exhibition had the same global impact as the great expositions held in London in 1851, Paris in 1889 or Chicago in 1893. After all, these exhibitions collectively cost hundreds of millions of pounds, were visited by over sixty million people, and gave us the Crystal Palace, the Eiffel Tower and the Ferris wheel, respectively. It would however also be a mistake to downplay the event

1.1
View of the Grounds from
Beneath the Portico of the
Industrial Hall.
© NLI

as a merely provincial endeavour, as this would do a great disservice to the impressive scale and influence of the project. There are many events from Cork's historical past that have now faded from our memory, but the Cork International Exhibition is by far the most neglected of the early twentieth century. Occurring as it did between the turbulent nineteenth century and the frenzied formative years of the Irish Free State, it is no wonder that it has by now slipped from popular remembrance.

In a letter written to *The Times* in London some months before the Exhibition opening, prominent Cork businessman and owner of the *Cork Constitution* newspaper, Mr Henry L. Tivy, expressed the view that:

> So much is heard in Great Britain of any political disturbances which occur in Ireland and so little, by comparison, of the many peaceful social and industrial movements in this country, that perhaps you will please allow me to mention some of the circumstances attending the Cork International Exhibition, which is to be opened on 1 May (*1902*).[1]

Mr Tivy went on stress that, although he was an Irishman who held his country's welfare close to his heart, he was 'a loyalist, Imperialist, Conservative, and entirely opposed to Home Rule'. He was quick to follow this declaration by saying that he had spent a year working on various organizing committees, three quarters of which were made up of nationalists, some of which were of the 'most advanced type'. Yet he did not suffer 'any remark offensive to me on political grounds'. The letter went on to highlight the eager and enthusiastic involvement of all political and social classes in making the Exhibition a reality. He emphasized the non-sectarian nature of the Exhibition, saying that its success could only be achieved 'by united and harmonious effort'. He was concerned about the manner in which Irish affairs were reported in England, and he closed his letter by asking the editor if he would 'bring these facts about this peaceful and useful Irish project under the notice of your readers…'[2]

This book is an attempt to re-fulfil Tivy's wish and to again 'bring these facts' about the 1902/3 Exhibition to the attention of a modern readership. Tivy's viewpoint that the contemporary English media were only interested in political and social unrest still rings true today for modern historiography, as it is rare to find a book on early twentieth-century Ireland that does not explicitly deal with political or military conflict. Here we attempt to re-address this imbalance by asserting that the Cork International Exhibition proves an ideal and useful medium through which we can glimpse a 'snapshot' of what life was like in Edwardian Cork. By shining a light on a period so often neglected, we get to experience a growing and motivated city attempting to take a giant step towards becoming the modern place we know today. By utilizing various primary sources, we will see firsthand how impressive Cork's accomplishment really was by learning what it took to organize, fund, lay out and eventually construct such a major undertaking. Tivy's claim of cross-political and religious co-operation on such a large project is a unique aspect that also warrants closer examination. In an era when political tension could easily disrupt any public undertaking, we will see how Cork's exhibition promoters helped to neutralize any potential threat to a successful outcome. Though it would be foolish to claim that this was the only event in twentieth-century Ireland that garnered such wide and universal support, it was certainly one of the most substantial. Tivy's strong desire to promote the exhibition to his English audience was a clear attempt at selling an image abroad of a city of potential and optimism.

After the difficulties and general industrial malaise of the nineteenth century, Cork's citizens were ready to work together with their fellow countrymen in bringing economic and social betterment for all.

The Ireland of the early Edwardian period is a fascinating place. In ways it is very familiar: it is just over the horizon of living memory, and hardly ancient history. For example, many of us today could sing a bar of 'Daisy Bell (a Bicycle Made for Two)' or 'I do Like to be Beside the Sea-side', products of the mass entertainment in music and drama which was a feature of the period. The music of John Philip Sousa and Edward Elgar was also popular, and can still be heard on classical music stations daily. It was a great time for children's literature. The first of Beatrix Potter's *Peter Rabbit* stories was published in 1902, and two years later J.M. Barrie's *Peter Pan* appeared. *Wind in the Willows*, which dealt with the impact of new technology on traditional life, was printed in 1908. Many of the buildings in which we live and work were similarly a product of the early 1900s. Much of the infrastructure of the modern world was already in operation, or soon to arrive. One could go as far as to say that the key ingredient missing compared to the present day was computerization. Cork was becoming recognizably 'modern': a place of electric light, the telephone, cinema, mass participation in sport and mass literacy. Coverage of international sporting events between Ireland and other countries was a regular feature in the city's three daily papers. Women had the vote, albeit only in local elections, and could be seen in public, out on bicycles or (scandalously) smoking. Gaining the local vote in 1898 had emboldened female activists to demand further rights for women. There was a rising popular pride in the Irish language and things Irish, but mass emigration, much of it to other parts of the Empire (Canada, Australia and New Zealand) was the option chosen by many.

National and international tourism was an important industry; the resort hotels in Killarney or Glengarriff for the wealthy and the sea-side boarding-houses in Bray, Tramore or Youghal for the workers were all connected by one of the densest mass-transit systems in the world. The advertising industry was in its infancy, but its paraphernalia abounded. The streets and hoardings in the city featured large posters and coloured enamel signs and its influence was felt in the establishment of brands which became household names then, and remain household names today. Cork had a modern tram system that was the envy of Belfast and Dublin and it was intimately interconnected with global affairs, business and innovation. Refrigeration, radioactivity, X-rays, the motor car and the aeroplane (not to mention the existence of electrons, viruses, enzymes and blood groups) were recent or emerging technologies and they would change peoples' lives forever. It has been written that 'you'd have to be pretty brash to claim that [scientific developments in recent decades] were noticeable more glittering' than these.[3] Vanity, silliness, bravery and imagination were (of course) as prevalent then as they are now.

In other ways, the country was a very different place. Reading accounts and documentation relating to the exhibition, one is frequently struck how the event was an All-Ireland event, taking place in the context of a thirty-two-county kingdom. We are not dealing with 'Ireland' as we generally find it today: a twenty-six-county republic, with a six-county 'statelet' adjoining it. However, despite the ecumenical tone of much of the coverage, and as we shall see the good showing of northern firms at the Exhibition, this was not a united island. The dominant political ideology in the south was nationalist and (what may seem to us) contradictorily loyal. In the north traditional unionism held sway. Those wishing for a wholly independent Ireland, to be achieved at the barrel of a rifle, were a hardline fringe in 1902. The Irish Labour movement was small and weak. The island was often referred to in the newspapers as 'the kingdom' as opposed to 'country' or 'nation', and when the King came to Cork, he was welcomed by the bulk of the community. The country would strike a modern visitor as unfamiliar in other ways too. Even allowing for the fact that much of western Europe was also heavily militarized at the beginning of the twentieth century, Cork was notably a place of soldiers and guns. Its harbour included some of the largest naval fortifications in the British Empire, as well as a system of barracks throughout the county and an armed police force. Catholic Irish men made up a disproportionate draft of the Army, whose upper echelons were dominated by other Irish men, Protestants from Ulster. Again, like much of Europe at the time, the country was heavily class-bound, but it had also retained elements of the semi-feudal arrangement of landed estates and landless peasants. The level of poverty and misery in Cork's dilapidated Georgian tenements and the 'courts' off the Main Street might shock a seasoned visitor to today's Third World slums. At the other end of the spectrum, the names of the aristocracy and gentry of Cork filled several pages of the street directories; gaining their support for a new venture, or royal approval for your product, could be of major assistance. The population's deference to 'one's betters' would be out of place today, but a popular deference to the Catholic church is well within living memory.

A visitor would also have noticed the bustle and smell on the city's quays. Live and dead animals, butter, beer and whiskey were loaded up, whilst coal and chemicals, fruit and vegetables were imported. Though our marine trade is still important, it has become less visible. Looking down the streets from his hotel room, a guest would notice the bustle on St Patrick's Street and the other main thoroughfares as people shopped daily, instead of weekly as they do now. There was extra excitement in the air however, as Cork was holding its third, and most ambitious exhibition since 1852.

Over the coming chapters, we intend to look briefly at the origins and history of the International Exhibition tradition, and to trace its development from the mid-nineteenth century to the early years of the twentieth century. We will illustrate how the organizers of Cork's Exhibition were very much aware of international trends and were more than willing to embrace these influences in order to make their venture both memorable and successful. For any reader of *The Times* who wanted to visit the exhibition, they would find themselves, according to Tivy, 'in pleasant surroundings and among a genial, kindly and inoffensive people'.[4] The 1902/3 International Exhibition has, for far too long, been left in the shadows. When it emerges, it shows itself to be a most remarkable project that deserves to be celebrated and understood as a landmark in Cork's civic achievements in its pre-Free State history.

Notes
1   *The Times,* 3 May 1902.
2   Ibid.
3   N. Calder, *Magic Universe: A Grand Tour of Modern Science* (Oxford: Oxford University Press, 2003), p.202.
4   *The Times,* 3 May 1902.

2.1:
Visiting Civic Dignitaries. Two carriages belonging to the Lord Mayor and councilors of Dublin Corporation making their way down Patrick's Street. Note the elaborate and stylish costumes of the footmen. (© NLI)

OH! THE EXHIBITION

Oh! the exhibition / Is in grand condition,
Ah' we're celebratin' the openin' day.
Shure we're decorated / An we're titivated
For the big purcesshun marchin' all the way.

But I won't be wastin' / Yer time from tastin'
The grand enchantments that are to be there.
So take a mission / To the Exhibition
For 'tis open now in our city fair.

– *Anonymous,* The Cork Examiner, *1 May 1902*
(Should be read in a Cork accent!)

2
Opening Day – A City on Display

Daniel Breen

'If fair skies favour today's comprehensive function, it should be a joyous as well as a memorable day for Cork and her myriad visitors', enthused *The Cork Examiner* on the eve of the opening of the city's International Exhibition of Manufactures, Arts, Products and Industries. However 'fair skies' seemed an unrealistic prospect on the morning of 1 May 1902, as rain clouds appeared above the large crowd that had gathered at Parnell Place awaiting the beginning of the 'big purcesshun'. The day had been declared a bank holiday by the

2.2:
A City on Display.
At the centre of the bunting strung across St Patrick's Street is the banner proudly emblazoned with 'Success to our Exhibition'. There are also national flags fluttering in the strong breeze, including the Union Jack, the Stars and Stripes and the French Tricolour. Such a display underlined the desire to illustrate the 'internationalism' and inclusiveness of their endeavour. (© NLI)

city's civic and business leaders, allowing the thousand-strong gathering to join in the civic parade. In all, thirty-nine trade unions and societies were represented in this memorable event. The majority of marchers were suitably dressed, displaying the official sashes, flags and banners of their individual groups. The presence of twelve local brass bands would have only added to the already simmering sense of excitement and anticipation (Appendix 1). As the procession of workers and musicians began to move off, shortly after 11 o'clock, it did in fact begin to rain. Thankfully, the threatening turn in the weather did not continue, and by the time the procession had arrived at the exhibition grounds two hours later, the light drizzle had stopped, having 'effectively kept down the dust' kicked up by the marching Corkonians.[1]

A second group of eminent marchers had gathered inside the vestibule of Municipal Buildings on this overcast May morning. These included dignitaries from across the country, such as the Lord Mayor of Dublin, the Mayors of Waterford, Derry and Limerick, the Aldermen and councillors of Cork Corporation, as well as other invited civic and political leaders. The President of the Exhibition's organizing committee and patron of the entire undertaking, Lord Bandon, Lord Lieutenant of Cork County and the instigator of the entire project, Alderman Edward Fitzgerald, the Lord Mayor of Cork, were the most prestigious members of this distinguished gathering. The two groups were unable to set out together from the Municipal Buildings since some of the processional banners belonging to the trade unions were too large to fit underneath the overhead electrical wires above Parnell Bridge. As the worker's procession departed from Parnell Place, on the far side of the River Lee the assemblage of dignitaries began to cross the bridge to join their fellow processionists. They, however, would not be making the journey by foot, but instead utilized various modes of horse-drawn transport, ranging from elaborate state carriages to simple Hansom cabs, that had been put at their disposal. Despite the obvious differences in parading methods, men and women of all social classes, as well as political and religious persuasions, were coming together to celebrate and support a worthy venture.

A serpentine processional route was planned so as to encompass the entire city within the opening day celebrations. This was a 'demonstration on a stupendous scale', which would make its way via the South Mall, Grand Parade, St Patrick's Street, Pope's Quay, North Main Street, Great George's Street (now Washington Street), Western Road and onwards towards the

Exhibition Grounds located on the Mardyke.[2] Homes and businesses along the route were lavishly decorated, signalling a concerted effort to show the city in its most favourable light. Indeed, the Lord Mayor, at a Council meeting a few weeks prior to the opening, remarked how the people of Cork had answered the call to paint and brighten up their city 'most cheerfully and loyally'.[3] Their efforts did not go unnoticed. The correspondent from the *Cork Examiner* gushed compliments about how beautiful the city looked: 'the streets presented the most abundant tokens of the universal rejoicing and the old borough wore a garb of brightness and gaiety such as never assumed from the time its charter was conferred till the present day. Bunting and banners were everywhere displayed, and in many streets green boughs were generously bestowed, while from all the larger houses in the principal thoroughfares flags waved'.[4]

The hosting of this exhibition was a prestigious international event for the city. It would potentially not only attract a local and national audience, but would also draw attention, and hopefully tourists, from foreign shores. The nineteenth century had seen rapid improvements in transport and people could now travel long distances in shorter periods of time. International Exhibitions proved to be extremely popular destinations for tourists, and they acted as catalysts for the emerging tourism industry. In Chapter 8, we will examine more closely the symbiotic relationship between International Exhibitions and the tourism industry, but it is important to note at this stage that Cork's organizers were all too aware of this relationship and were more than willing to exploit it. On the Saturday prior to the official opening, a 'press day' was held at the exhibition grounds, where journalists from Ireland, Great Britain and America were given a special 'pre-opening' tour by the Earl of Bandon, Lord Mayor Fitzgerald and other organizing committee members. They were then treated to lunch, at which Lord Mayor Fitzgerald praised how the 'friendly, cordial and sympathetic' support offered by the press to the enterprise from the very beginning 'was one of the reasons why the Exhibition had attained its large proportions and considerable success'.[5] He hoped that the reporters would 'herald to the world what they had seen that day'.[6] This public relations event was important in helping to promote Cork City and endorse its exhibition in the hope of attracting as many foreign and domestic visitors as possible. By the opening day, the auspices looked good. Special trains had already conveyed 'thousands upon thousands' of visitors to the city

2.3:
May Day remained popular well into the twentieth century. This Cork Camera Club photograph was taken at an unknown location sometime between 1915 and 1920. The decorated Maypole, the young girl's white dresses and the gathered crowd of onlookers in the background highlight the celebratory nature of the day's events.
(Cork Camera Club © CPM)

from around Ireland, with many more arriving from Britain and America.[7]

The opening day also happened to be May Day, coinciding with the pagan Irish festival of 'Bealtaine' that traditionally marked the beginning of summer. This festival emphasized renewal and rebirth, as pre-Christian communities throughout Europe celebrated the end of winter and the promise of a good harvest brought by the warmth of the summer months. These celebrations proved particularly boisterous in the eighteenth and nineteenth centuries, when rioting between different factions became normal practice and often resulted in serious injury and even death.[8] On one occasion the Mayor of Cork had to intervene in an attempt to stop the 'mischievous and disgraceful custom' of striking people, especially females, with nettles. He promised that he would 'punish with the utmost rigour, any person detected in the commission of this savage offence'.[9] Despite its unruly and colourful history, May Day continued to be celebrated right up into the twentieth century in both rural and urban areas throughout County Cork (2.3).[10] In the city, people used the opportunity afforded by the day to spruce up their homes, streets and workplaces. Shop fronts and the city's trams were decorated in green and gold foliage, while boughs made from beech garnished the harnesses of the city's working horses. According to one source, groups of girls would stroll through the city in the evening singing an old song with an Irish refrain:

> The girls of Boyce's Street [*off Blarney Street*]
> Beat the boys clean,
> Tugamair féin an Samrad linn
> [*we ourselves brought the summer with us*]
> With their piggins of buttermilk
> And cakes of oat meal.
> Tugamair féin an Samrad linn.[11]

On the first Sunday of May, Glanmire traditionally hosted a procession of artisans and tradesmen who would spend the day participating in sporting and dancing events.[12] Nineteenth-century writer Francis Tuckey noted that 'dancing, prize-fighting and running in bags' took place in the Mardyke fields as part of the May Day celebrations in 1781.[13] The most intriguing evidence about May Day celebrations in Cork however, can be obtained from pre-nineteenth-century maps of the city where Evergreen Street, on the south side of the city, was once called Maypole Lane. The subsequent use of 'Evergreen' is a clear reference to the flora imagery and motifs championed during May Day celebrations once held in that area of the city. The decision therefore to host the opening day of the exhibition on May Day appears to us to symbolically link the upcoming exhibition with the promise of industrial rebirth and economic renewal.[14] There was also historical precedence at play, as the majority of International Exhibitions, including the 1851 Great Exhibition, were opened on 1 May or as close to that date as possible.

Images from the Lawrence Collection of historic photographs in the National Library of Ireland reveal the sense of occasion and excitement felt on the city streets on the morning of May Day 1902.[15] The procession which brought St Patrick's Street to a standstill wound through a throng of waving and cheering spectators (2.1, 2.2, 2.4). Bystanders packed either side of the parade while many others watched on from the windows and roofs of nearby

Preceding page
2.4:

Opening Day Parade on
St Patrick's Street.
Members of the Union
of Operative Tailors and
their 'Garden of Eden'
tableau marching down
'Pana'. Thousands of
spectators lined the
streets while others
crowded the overlooking
windows to get a better
view. Stationary trams
were used as makeshift
viewing platforms. Note the
premises of Thomas Cook
Travel Agency in the centre
of the photograph. (© NLI)

buildings. The city's tram service ceased for the duration of the procession as onlookers filled the top decks of the trams, turning the static vehicles into makeshift viewing platforms. Amongst the flags and bunting on display were numerous Union Jacks and Stars and Stripes adding life and colour to the event. The contemporary newspapers reporting on the opening day were eager to emphasize a city in celebratory mood, describing the day's proceedings with terms like 'spectacle' or 'pageant'.[16] Public demonstrations and parades were a common aspect of urban life in Victorian and Edwardian Britain and Ireland. They afforded opportunities for people to publicly display their political, social and religious allegiances. The inhabitants of Cork were no different and often used public processions to highlight political or social issues, for example during the unveiling of a monument or the visit of an important dignitary.[17] One of the most important days on the civic calendar in Cork was (and still is) St Patrick's Day, which usually involved a parade through the city as well as other traditional customs, like the wearing of shamrock.[18] However, with the rise of Irish nationalism during the late nineteenth and early twentieth centuries, St Patrick's Day became a key occasion annually for promoting and encouraging Irish independence and culture. In 1902, for example, the large St Patrick's Day procession that followed a tortuous route through the city and culminated in a large public meeting held in the Corn Market, where several nationalistic resolutions were passed. These included the reaffirmation of support for a free and independent Ireland as well as the continued promotion of Irish industries and culture.[19] Later in the twentieth century, St Patrick's Day was also the day chosen to unveil two of Cork's most prominent memorials, the National Monument (in 1906) and the Cenotaph (in 1925).

St Patrick's Day did not become a bank holiday until 1903, so many who participated in the celebrations prior to that year often did so at the loss of a day's wage. However this was not an issue when it came to opening the Exhibition, as a decision was taken to close the city's businesses and give a day off to the workers, which added greatly to the sense of a communal celebration. Since early morning, vast numbers of spectators gathered on the streets and at the Exhibition Grounds hoping to get an optimum vantage point to watch the unfolding festivities. They had 'discarded the signs of their profession and seemed bent on losing the cares of work in the general abandon to rejoicing which was everywhere'.[20] Indeed *The Times* mentions how a thousand inmates from the Cork Workhouse were permitted to join the throng of sightseers while emphasizing that there 'was much enthusiasm and no unpleasant incident to mar the effect of the display'.[21] The success of the opening day is due in large part to the presence and involvement of so many of the city's population from all social strata. This is perfectly illustrated in one of the Lawrence images, where a banner emblazoned with the phrase 'Success to *our* Exhibition' hangs proudly across the city's main thoroughfare. The exhibition was conceived and implemented with the intention of belonging to everyone (2.2).

Captured in Time: Mitchell and Kenyon in Cork

As historians studying the Victorian and Edwardian periods in Ireland, our work often depends solely on written sources. These are occasionally supported by photographic or figurative evidence, but by and large we are forced to try and visualize the events for ourselves from the descriptions found in newspapers, letters or books. However, when it comes to studying Cork's International Exhibition, we are extremely fortunate to have another invaluable resource at our disposal. This is a series of thirty-three films shot in Ireland by travelling cinematographers from England in 1901 and 1902, collectively known as the Mitchell and Kenyon collection. Of the surviving Irish films in the Mitchell and Kenyon collection, the majority (twenty-two) were filmed in Cork in the late spring and summer of 1902 in conjunction with the Cork International Exhibition. Glaswegian, George Green, one of the most influential fairground showmen of the late-Victorian era, was given sole rights for exhibiting the cinematograph at the International Exhibition in February 1902. Though we will deal in greater detail with Green's cinematograph in Chapter 8, it is important to note that Green's first contractual obligation was the filming of the opening day procession.[22] The surviving footage provides the viewer with an unparalleled and unique view of the social and cultural lives of our Edwardian ancestors that is often unattainable from the usual primary sources. Our forefathers come alive and appear more tangible when they are released from the historic restraints of the printed word.

The film showing the opening day events is titled *Trade Procession at Opening of Cork Exhibition*. The majority of the action takes place on the Western Road where the camera, an unwieldy and cumbersome piece of apparatus known as a Prestwich Model 4 (2.5), was positioned opposite the Presentation Boys School (now the UCC Archaeology Department). The high number of

2.5:
Cork City on Film.
The Showman (21 February 1902) stated that the maker of camera selected for use at the Cork Exhibition should have the 'satisfaction in knowing' that it had been chosen 'by one of the most experienced and practical operators in the cinematograph world (*George Green*)'. The camera was a Prestwich Model 4 camera, designed by Alfred Prestwich (1874–1952) and built by his company in London in 1898. This was the first camera to be fitted with detachable external film magazines. There were at least two of these cameras in Cork used in various locations around the city and county.
(©Grant Collection London)

filmed processions in the Mitchell and Kenyon collection as a whole supports the view that parades were universally popular and served as 'the outward expression of the rich mix of voluntary organisations, clubs and societies forming the social cement of the English [or in our case, Irish] town'.[23] There are four separate films that capture the bustling and vibrant exhibition parade. As early cameras were still relatively new and were largely unfamiliar to the public, it is no surprise that many of those passing by look into the camera with a somewhat suspicious and curious demeanour. A mix of joviality and purpose is written on the faces of the marchers and spectators alike as they make their way down the Western Road. The footage beautifully illustrates the complex social make up of the city, with a large and prominent working class (both as participants and spectators), a new and emerging middle class, as well as the ever-present aristocratic and Anglo-Irish ruling class. Gender roles are also highlighted in the film. The procession, like many aspects of public life, was male dominated. However, before we dismiss the Cork International Exhibition as a sexist affair, it must be noted that the Women's Section formed an integral and important part in both years of the enterprise (see Chapter 5). Apart from the obvious insights into class and gender on display, the Mitchell and Kenyon collection also captures the sense of adventure and excitement experienced by all those parading. Cork's processional footage captures forever on celluloid form an emerging modern city with an urban population united, however briefly, behind a common goal: the successful outcome of Cork's first International Exhibition.

It is apparent from the available sources that the trade union movement formed a substantial part of the day's celebrations, as they had done during the earlier opening day processions, though on a much smaller scale. At a meeting in early April the Cork United Trades Association had signalled its intention to take part in the opening day demonstrations.[24] Cork's working classes (and trade unions) had been represented by labour councillors on Cork Corporation since 1899 (3.3), and the Exhibition opening parade provided an ideal opportunity to show their new political strength.[25] Their President, Alderman William Cave, a staunch nationalist, had urged his fellow members that 'the occasion was one that should be properly and fittingly honoured by the trades and labour bodies, and he trusted that the various organisations would turn out in their full majesty, strength, regalia, and numbers to render the opening day one not soon to be forgotten in the city'.[26] This sentiment was

2.6:

Cork Masons.

This photograph of what appears to be a family of masons highlights the strong generational bonds forged in this union in Cork. The sashes and apron worn by the men are similar to those worn by marching trade unionists during the opening day procession. (© CPM)

echoed by the secretary of the association, Alderman J.J. Kelleher, who stated that there 'were occasions on which capitalists and the workers sometimes had differences, but during the coming time they should all work harmoniously for the one object of making the Exhibition a success, and sink all differences where the prosperity of the city was concerned'.[27] With these words of encouragement ringing in their ears the city's workers readily answered their president's call.

The majority of the participants marched in groups carrying placards and dressed in the individual aprons, sashes or other regalia associated with their unions (2.6). They can be observed in the Mitchell and Kenyon film marching with a dignified calm while the excited spectators hover around the edges of the parade. The large trade union banners were, by far, the most visually dominant forms of regalia on show that day. The banners on display during the opening day procession were designed to be eye-catching and visually represent what the members of each union stood for. The banners were very large and could measure anywhere from 10 to 20ft (3–6m) in height and required horse-drawn carts to transport them in the procession (2.7, 2.8). The Mitchell and Kenyon footage illustrates how a strong breeze could make these banners billow violently such that ropes were often used to control them.

2.7: above
The Mason's Union Banner.
This recently conserved banner was carried during the opening day procession and was no. 17 in order of participation. The reverse of the banner shows Grattan's Parliament and portraits of nationalists heroes like Daniel O'Connell and Henry Grattan. (© CPM)

2.8: left
The Procession Comes to an End.
This Cork Camera Club photograph captures the front of the parade at the west end of the Western Road after separating from the dignitaries at Donovan's Road. Centre, is the banner belonging to the Baker's Society, which had 200 members marching at the head of the parade.
(Cork Camera Club © CPM)

2.9a:
A branch of the Irish
National Foresters was
formed in Cork City on
the 21 October 1887. The
uniform and sash worn by
participants during the
opening day procession
are well illustrated on this
certificate. The Foresters
embraced Gaelic imagery
(wolfhound, round tower,...)
by other nationalist
organizations at the time.
(Courtesy of Francis O'
Connor)

Not all trade unions made use of large banners to publicize their cause. One group, the 'Shop Assistants and Industrial League', employed the services of a young woman, Miss B. Fitzgerald of Cash & Co., and a young boy, Master Shanahan, to lead them in the procession. Both were seated on ponies and acted as moving advertisements for the attractive clothes they wore, which were made of Donegal and Munster tweed. This is a small example of the important commercial facet to International Exhibitions which are dealt with in a Chapter 7. By far the most intriguing float, however, belonged to the

Tailor's Society, which depicted a tableau of Adam and Eve on either side of the tree of knowledge. Though this float is mentioned in passing in the newspaper accounts, without the surviving footage we would never have known that Eve's character was played by a man dressed in what appears to be a skin-coloured costume complete with fig leaves and wig (2.4)!

Of all the societies and groups marching on the day, the Irish National Foresters are by far the most visually arresting and interesting. They marched one-hundred-strong behind an impressive horse-drawn float decorated with the green Forester's flag, as well as an American flag. Preceding the float were four mounted members, in their official green uniforms with feathered hats, carrying ceremonial spears (2.9a, 2.9b). This flamboyant costume was called the 'Robert Emmet Uniform' in honour of the leader of the failed 1803 rebellion. At the opening day procession they were also given the privilege of providing an escort for Lord Bandon and Lord Mayor Fitzgerald. Eight members rode triumphantly on horseback beside their carriage, acting as both a bodyguard and a means of clearing a route through the increasing number of spectators.

It had been arranged that the procession of the city's working classes would come to a halt '100 yards from the new road' (Donovan's Road) to allow the invited dignitaries to move from the back and overtake the trade unions and societies.[28] There was now a sense of urgency, palpable from the footage, to get this important group to the exhibition grounds as the official opening ceremony was due to start as soon as Lord Bandon and the Lord Mayor arrived. The cavalcade of civic leaders moved swiftly past the patient marchers. It is very apparent that there was a genuine respect and appreciation from the crowd towards the distinguished visitors. It was reported that representatives of Irish municipalities 'were received throughout the entire way to the Exhibition with warmest testimonies of esteem of the peoples', while the Lord Mayor and Earl of Bandon's reception was 'of the most cordial and enthusiastic nature'.[29] All invited municipal authorities were represented by their individual Mayor or Lord Mayor as well as an entourage of aldermen, councillors, sheriffs and clerks. Sword and mace-bearers proudly exhibited their civic regalia as they sat atop

2.9b:
Detail showing an Irish National Forester in full uniform, and, below an Irish National Foresters sash presently housed in Cork Public Museum. (© CPM)

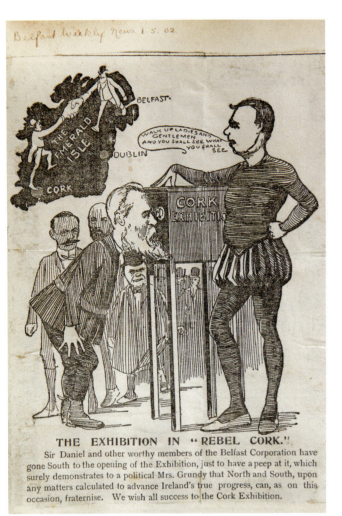

THE EMERALD ISLE

BELFAST.

WALK UP LADIES AND GENTLEMEN AND YOU SHALL SEE WHAT YOU SHALL SEE.

DUBLIN

CORK

CORK EXHIBITION

THE EXHIBITION IN "REBEL CORK."
Sir Daniel and other worthy members of the Belfast Corporation have gone South to the opening of the Exhibition, just to have a peep at it, which surely demonstrates to a political Mrs. Grundy that North and South, upon any matters calculated to advance Ireland's true progress, can, as on this occasion, fraternise. We wish all success to the Cork Exhibition.

2.10: Support from the North.
This quirky illustration from the Belfast Evening News captures Unionist opinion towards the 1902 exhibition. It was a mixture of genuine admiration and patronizing curiosity. It also testifies how organizers and supporters used the project as a marketing tool to counter the dismissive attitude of many 'Mrs Grundy' types who saw little purpose in promoting an 'all-Ireland' solution to the country's industrial and economic problems. (© CPM)

their carriages. One group that missed the opening procession was the Belfast Municipal deputation who had only arrived in Cork that afternoon. They hurriedly made their way to the grounds in a hastily arranged hotel omnibus. The crowds that gathered on the streets blocked their route, and had it not been for the actions of a local police sergeant who escorted and guided the delegation through the dense crowds, they would never have made the official opening ceremony.[30] The effort made by members of the Belfast and Derry Corporations to travel to Cork and help their southern counterparts celebrate the exhibition opening underlines an eagerness to put differences aside and make the Exhibition an all-Ireland endeavour (2.10). The reporter for the *Observer* noticed the suspending of the usual political animosity as he pointed out that 'The most remarkable feature of the show, from the social and political point of view, is the unanimity of sentiment which is behind it. North and South alike, Catholic and Protestant, Unionist and Nationalist, are all interested in its success.'[31]

Of all the delegations present, the state coaches carrying the Lord Mayor of Dublin, Timothy Harrington MP, and his corporation were the most impressive.[32] The ornate nature of the vehicles made them stand out amongst the other ordinary-looking vehicles. Add to this the stylish and elegant costumes worn by the foot-men and it can be said that the Dublin delegation brought a great deal of pomp to the whole occasion (2.1). The Cork City Fire Brigade under Captain Hutson also had a prominent part in the procession. The firemen in full uniform and helmets can be seen making their way past the camera in two carriages, while also parading an early steam fire engine.[33] In the final frame of the processional film, we catch a quick glimpse of the Earl of Bandon as his carriage moves past the camera. The genuine happiness etched on his face as he waves to the crowd highlights that he, like everyone else present that day, was pleased that the project had come to fruition, as well as being excited to see the exhibition grounds and buildings for himself. The last segment from the opening day film shows the arrival of the processional group at the exhibition grounds. It very much resembles a scene from *Keystone Cops* as carriages, horses, spectators and dignitaries form a chaotic throng around the Exhibition entrance.[34] Unfortunately, no film footage of the official ceremony in the Concert Hall exists. However, from the material that has survived, we are able to see Edwardian Cork celebrating one of the most important ventures undertaken in the city's history. Despite the many political, social and economic differences on display, we get the sense of a strong urban group coming together to support and celebrate this momentous event.

The Official Opening Ceremony

The arrangements in connection with the opening of the Cork International Exhibition tomorrow are now complete, and everything points to the occasion being a red letter day in the history of our city.

– *The Cork Examiner*, 30 April 1902

The celebrations now moved from the city's streets to the exhibition grounds. The Concert Hall hosted the official opening ceremony and much effort was expended to ensure the occasion passed smoothly. The organizers had decided to open the entrance gates early, at 10am, as they had anticipated a high attendance. They were proved right as a large crowd had gathered at the grounds early that morning and the 2,000-person capacity Hall had little standing space left by the time the ceremony started over three hours later. It had been reported the previous day that over 1,000 season tickets had been sold and all the best seats for the opening ceremony had already been

filled in the Concert Hall.[35] The occupants in the Concert Hall included the cream of local, as well as national, society. If the street procession had been a celebration of Cork's working classes, then the festivities at the Concert Hall were dominated by the political, religious, intellectual and commercial elite. These included the Catholic and Protestant Bishops of Cork and the Catholic Bishops of Limerick, Waterford and Cloyne, as well as the Right Hon. Horace Plunkett (Vice-President of the Department of Agriculture and Technical Instruction) and important business leaders. Irish society's female elite was represented by Countess Bandon, the Lady Mayoresses of Cork and Dublin and many other distinguished ladies. The beautiful costumes of both the civic

The Cork International Exhibition

and female attendees drew much praise while the interior of the Concert Hall created 'a most brilliant and attractive picture'. [36] (2.11)

All eyes were on the spacious stage from which the afternoon's ceremonies would be conducted. Seating on the stage was reserved for the visiting dignitaries, many of the organizing committee as well as the 500 members of the Exhibition orchestra and choir, under the musical directorship of Herr Theo Gmür. At the back of the platform, reaching 30ft (9m) in height, was the beautifully constructed Exhibition organ; a credit to its maker, Mr T.W. Magahy. In front of the platform all the regalia of the municipalities were impressively displayed on a large table. Finally, sometime between 1.15pm and 1.30pm (depending on what newspaper report you read), Lord Bandon and the Lord Mayor Fitzgerald took to the stage to commence proceedings. Their appearance 'was greeted with enthusiastic applause, the vast audience rising in their places and cheering vociferously'.[37] Positioned on the stage next to the Earl and the Lord Mayor were many of the important contributors to the conception, planning and creation of the exhibition. These included Mr Henry Cutler (City Engineer and Exhibition Architect), Mr William O'Connell (Exhibition Contractor) and Mr Richard Atkins (Hon. Exhibition Secretary). At either side of the stage stood a troop of National Foresters. Everyone was now in place and the scene was set for the ceremony to begin.

It was Richard Atkins, Exhibition Secretary, who started proceedings by directing an address to the Earl of Bandon, in which he congratulated him on the 'happy circumstances' under which he appeared before them that day. He thanked him for all his support and encouragement and hoped that the Earl would 'unite with us in the earnest hope that the Cork International Exhibition may fulfil our desires by stimulating the industrial development of the country and by leaving behind it many permanent beneficial results'(see Chapter 10).[38] As the applause abated, the Earl of Bandon strode to the front of the stage and delivered his address, in which he thanked the Lord Mayor and the Committee for their kind words and continued by stating:

> It has been a great pleasure to co-operate with the Lord Mayor and the other members of the Executive Committee in a movement which I believe to be of inestimable value in stimulating and developing the industrial resources of our country. This pleasure is intensified by the fact that a large and

2.11: facing page
Inside the Concert Hall, 1 May 1902.
This photograph of the 'official' portion of the opening day celebrations perfectly captures the excitement of the occasion. The audience, predominantly made up of society's elite, are focused on the Earl of Bandon, addressing them from the stage. The prominent place of the National Foresters on either side of the Earl of Bandon is an example of the complex relationship between Irish nationalism and the British Establishment.
(© CPM)

influential body of gentlemen, who represent the opinions of
varied political parties, worked, as you all did, with the greatest
harmony and unity. It was this happy circumstance, combined
with your earnest and devoted labours, which has crowned
your undertaking with such signal success.

He also echoed Atkins's sentiment by emphasizing that everyone there desired
that the Exhibition would help stimulate Ireland's industrial development.[39]
The final part of the Earl's speech was directed towards the Lord Mayor,
whom he recognized as the main driving force behind the entire project. The
Exhibition stood as a monument to the 'indomitable and untiring energy'
he showed in bringing it to fruition. He finished by saying that the Lord
Mayor 'recognized from the first the importance of enlisting the support and
co-operation of all classes of the community, and of bringing men of various
shades of political thought to work side by side in the effort being made to
promote what is so manifestly for the interests of the country'.[40]

The Lord Mayor was warmly received by the audience as he stood to begin
his speech. The opening paragraph of his speech is worth quoting in full as it
captures the feelings of satisfaction and achievement felt by the organizers and
promoters in the hall:

My Lord and Gentlemen, I find it difficult to give adequate
expression to the feelings of pride and pleasure with which
I take part in this inaugural ceremony, or to acknowledge
suitably the kind of address with which has been presented
me. This day's proceedings are the reward and crown of many
months of keen anxiety and ceaseless toil. But if the labour
was arduous the harvest was great, and as I face this splendid
assemblage and look about me at the result of our exertions,
all remembrance of the difficulties which we have encountered
fades from my mind, and I can only think and speak of the
wonderful success which has crowned our work.

Fitzgerald was quick to downplay his own 'humble part' in getting the
Exhibition off the ground and remarked that he would have been found
wanting as Lord Mayor if he had 'grudged whatever expenditure of time and

energy was necessary to secure the success of a project in which our city is so deeply concerned'. He wholeheartedly thanked the other towns and cities who had willingly and enthusiastically supported the project from the start. Fitzgerald also graciously gave the majority of the credit, and a great deal of thanks for the Exhibition's existence to his Executive Committee, especially Mr Atkins and Mr Cutler, whom he reminded the audience worked tirelessly for a year without fee or reward. Fitzgerald was keen to emphasize that all that had been achieved to get to the opening day could not have been done without the support and help of everyone involved, saying that 'what we have jointly accomplished no one man could have performed'.[41] Bespoke engraved gold keys were presented to both the Earl and the Lord Mayor and amidst the tumultuous applause, the Exhibition was proclaimed open (2.12).

With the formalities over, attention now turned to entertainment. Mr Osborn J. Bergin, a lecturer in Celtic Studies at Queen's College Cork (now University College Cork), was given the honour of reciting his Irish poem entitled 'Duan Oscailte an Taisbeánta' ('Ode to the Exhibition Opening').[42] Bergin had won first prize in a competition organized by the Exhibition's Executive Committee.[43] Bergin (in his Bachelor of Arts gown) stepped forward to tell his audience (the Irish people) to awake from the slumber of many centuries of economic and cultural malaise and feel the warmth of prosperity promised by the upcoming exhibition:

2.12:
An Opening Day Souvenir. Two keys made especially by Egans of St Patrick's Street that were engraved with the details of the occasion. This key was presented to Lord Mayor Fitzgerald. The second key was presented to Lord Bandon. (© CPM)

> Draw nigh, O ye hosts whose birthright it is to be Gaelic,
> Over great hill and plain, over narrow glen, over sea;
> Do ye feel the new pulse throbbing and leaping?
> The long sleep is breaking, and there is a sunbeam
> on the meadow.

As we shall see in Chapter 4, by the time of the 1902 exhibition, Irish audiences were well accustomed to the practice of closely tying Irish mythology to Ireland's nineteenth-century industrial identity.

Bergin, who would later become Professor of Early and Medieval Irish at UCD, and subsequently the first Director of the School of Celtic Studies at the Dublin Institute for Advanced Studies, utilized Irish Mythology to create imagery of a country and people who have endlessly suffered. Bergin exclaims that 'the enchantment that was upon us is broken forever' as Fodla's voice can be heard offering us counsel 'that would save us henceforth from sorrow'. Fodla was an Irish goddess whose name was frequently used as a literary name for Ireland.[44] He followed the lead of the dignitaries he shared the stage with when he lavished praise on the entire enterprise:

> Here are gathered in a fair lawn
> on the bank of Lee of the swans,
> In trim new halls, pleasantly, beside a grove,
> Every expert and excellent work devised by human ingenuity.

The Exhibition was therefore portrayed as a turning point for Ireland, the point from where Ireland could escape the torment of its mythological and historical past. The audience was encouraged to look to the future with optimism and to embrace the Exhibition and the modernity it stood for. Cork City was ready to welcome visitors and through Bergin and the organizers of the inauguration day, the message was loud and clear:

> Yes! Let them come gaily, both simple and gentle,
> Bearers of the burden of learning and men
> Whose work is with their hands;
> Here is an invitation for them and a summons:
> Let us go on together.
> To visit the feast that is spread before us.
> Let them gather, let them gather,
> We have pleasure in store for them –
> Our hearts are full and our doors are open.[45]

For many people present, the highlight of the afternoon's festivities was the performance of the choral work 'The Building of the Ship', a poem of 400 lines written by Henry Wadsworth Longfellow and set to music by the English composer John F. Barnett.[46] Longfellow wrote the poem in the aftermath of the American Civil War, and is best remembered for his poems 'The Village Blacksmith', and 'The Wreck of the Hesperus'. The poem details the story of how a master builder entrusts the building of the ship to one of his workmen, who on successfully completing the task would gain the master's daughter's hand in marriage. In his instruction to the workman, the master insists the ship be built from:

> Cedar of Maine and Georgia Pine,
> Here together shall combine
> A goodly frame, and goodly flame,
> And the union be her name.[47]

In the poem, the construction of the ship represents the re-unification of northern and southern states after the bloody and bitter Civil War. This symbolism would not have been lost on the Irish audience at the 1902 Exhibition opening.

Though this concluded the official aspects of the inauguration, the day was far from over. Due to the widespread use of electricity throughout the grounds, the Exhibition organizers were able to keep the Exhibition gates open until 10pm daily. Visitors on this first evening were both impressed and awestruck by the site lit in the glow of electric light. All the buildings were lit inside as well as on their exterior by 'myriads of small electric lights against the backdrop of a starry sky', producing an effect that one reporter termed as 'almost magical'.[48] Music filled the air as the Butter Exchange Band and the 1st Life Guards entertained the masses by performing a selection of Irish and classical music. There was even a repeat performance of 'The Building of the Ship' in the Concert Hall to a sold-out audience. This was the first real opportunity for visitors to stroll through the grounds and to move between buildings while experiencing the many exhibits, demonstrations and amusements on offer. In Chapters 5 to 9, we will be making our own visits to the Exhibition as we examine closely how it was planned, built and laid out, while perusing the range of exhibits and amusements that were on offer there, and we will ask ourselves whether it lived up to the auspicious unveiling it received on its opening day.

Conclusion

The first step had now been taken, and Cork's first International Exhibition was underway. The months of detailed and meticulous planning had been brought to fruition. Though the opening day was deemed a success, the organizers knew it would count for nothing if the Exhibition itself failed to match the expectations of the press and public. The opening day celebrations were specifically designed to be as inclusive as possible. This fact did not go unnoticed in the following day's *Cork Examiner*, when the reporter gushed, 'Of the many pageants that have been witnessed in the city, none was ever witnessed with circumstances that claimed general attention and participation in the degree that the proceedings yesterday demanded.'[49] Along with many of the other participants, he marvelled at how the entire day's proceedings enjoyed 'the support of every order of men, irrespective of social levels, religious differences, political bickerings, class animosities, or any of the many temporary prejudices which precludes one section from combining with another to add pomp and éclat to such occasions'.[50]

As with most public celebrations in late Victorian or Edwardian times, processions, speeches, poetry and song all played an important and integral part. Most of the larger International Exhibitions held before 1902 had impressive opening day ceremonies including large and vibrant processions with reigning monarchs, presidents or prime ministers as their guests of honour. There would be performances of newly composed poems or songs as part of the opening day programme. The British Poet Laureate Alfred Tennyson, for example, composed 'The Choral Ode' for the opening of the 1862 Exhibition in London, while the audience at the opening of the 1876 Centennial Exhibition in Philadelphia was treated to a 'Centennial Hymn' written by John Greenleaf Whittier. [51] The opening ceremony of the 1893 Columbian World Fair involved 13 contributions including speeches, orations, a performance of 'Hallelujah Chorus' from Handel's *Messiah* and a 'Dedicatory Ode' of over 300 lines.[52] Opening day celebrations therefore offered the organizers the opportunity to communicate the ideals, aspirations and goals behind their exhibition. The discourses, poems or music were all composed, not only in praise of the event but also to highlight and emphasize the virtues, wonders and benefits of the host city or nation and its exhibition.

In Cork's case, the procession, the speeches and the choice of artistic works were all designed to send a very clear message. The Exhibition, a beacon of harmonious collaboration, was to be a credit to the city and its citizens as the project willingly crossed social, political and economic divides. When you look at film footage and records from the opening day of the 1897 Stockholm Exposition for example, the lower social classes have no involvement and are reduced to the role of spectators, as the Swedish political and social elite dominated the entire event.[53] This was also obvious at the 1852 and 1883

Cork Exhibitions, where public participation was also limited to the part of onlooker. Mitchell and Kenyon's footage testifies visually to the involvement of all social classes in the 1902 project, while the speeches and the impressive choral performance re-enforce the notion that when it came to the planning and execution of this massive undertaking, religious and political views did not hinder progress. Matters of economic and industrial betterment were too great to allow the usual divisions to pull it apart. As the *Belfast Newsletter* remarked rather wishfully, 'Why should there be any differences amongst Irishmen on matters of this kind?'[54]

Overall, the entire day's proceedings aimed to show Cork as a modern city with the will and determination to make an exhibition possible, but more importantly with the people, infrastructure and political maturity to make it work. There was an overriding faith placed in the Exhibition by its promoters and the general public that it had the potential to act as a springboard for the future social, economic and industrial growth and development of Cork and Ireland. Promoters of exhibitions from all over the world have shared this belief. Whatever the special circumstances in Cork, it becomes clear that the 1902 International Exhibition was part of a much wider international tradition, and cannot be considered in isolation. With this in mind, the next chapter will also see us follow the origins and historical evolution of International Exhibitions from their inception in 1851 in London through to later examples held globally up until the outbreak of the First World War. In placing Cork's exhibition within a larger context, we hope the reader will appreciate the national and international character of the exhibits, amusements and buildings found on the exhibition grounds and come to understand that the undertaking of the 1902/3 Cork International Exhibition was far from parochial.

Notes

1 *Cork Examiner*, 2 May 1902. At the start of the twentieth century, Cork's streets were paved with crushed limestone, and it became necessary to regularly water the streets in the summer months in order to keep the dust down.
2 *Irish News (Belfast)*, 2 May 1902.
3 *Cork Constitution*, 18 April 1902.
4 *Cork Examiner*, 2 May 1902.
5 *Irish News (Belfast)*, 28 April 1902.
6 *The Glasgow Examiner*, 3 May 1902.
7 *Irish News (Belfast)*, 2 May 1902; *Cork Examiner* May 2 1902.
8 F. Tuckey, *Cork Remembrancer* (Cork: Tower Books, 1837 (1980)) details several occasions when violence and rioting seemed to dominate celebrations on May Day: pp.141, 144, 151, 162.

'I should have been wanting indeed as Lord Mayor of Cork, had I grudged whatever expenditure of time and energy was necessary to secure the success of a project in which our city is so deeply concerned.'

– Lord Mayor Edward Fitzgerald, 1 May 1902.

3

Timekeepers of Progress

The International Exhibition Tradition and the City of Cork 1852–1904

Daniel Breen

What the Olympian Games, and other public festivals of Greece, were to the poet, the historian, or the sculptor, of former days, the Exhibitions of modern times are to the inventor, the manufacturer, and the artisan.
– Mayor of Cork John Francis Maguire MP, 1853[1]

Cork is like a bee-hive full of life, expectation, energy, bustle, and business; a great impetus has been given to trade; human industry is awake and active.
– *London Illustrated News*, 1852

Cork City's Nineteenth-Century Industrial Exhibitions

Historically, Cork City has enjoyed a love affair with exhibitions, hosting four between 1852 and 1903. Though they differed in size, location and make-up, they all symbolized the city's willingness and desire to improve and progress. Internationally, exhibitions were the products of a new period of human existence, where technology, science, industry and urbanization came to shape and change how we lived, worked, socialized and interacted with the world around us. Exhibitions were like flashy billboards advertising the benefits and endless possibilities that this new world offered. They afforded politicians, businessmen and industrialists a platform from which to inform, educate and influence, ultimately helping to shape Victorian society. The organizers and promoters in Cork were no different, as they strived to ensure the city and its inhabitants could prosper from the latest advances in manufacturing and education as well as enjoying the latest in entertainment. And so it was that within a month of being elected Lord Mayor of Cork, Alderman Edward Fitzgerald presided over an important council meeting on 15 February 1901

3.1:
Lord Mayor Sir Edward Fitzgerald (1846-1927). He was Cork's first elected Lord Mayor and the successful outcome of the Exhibition ensured he was re-elected twice. His popularity in local politics failed to transfer to the national stage due in part to his perceived 'closeness' with the British establishment which did not sit well with the evolving hardening of Irish nationalism in the decade before the 1916 Rising. (© CPM)

at which he proposed Cork City should host its third industrial exhibition (3.1). The other councillors present unanimously supported his plan and it was decided that a public meeting needed to be called in order to discuss this grand project in greater detail.[2] The subsequent public gathering, held at the municipal buildings on 7 March, was attended by Cork's political, business and working classes, as well as representatives from Cork County Council, and major towns like Queenstown, Mallow, Lismore, Youghal, Clonakilty, Midelton and Fermoy. The following resolution was passed at the civic assembly:

> That it is desirable to hold an Exhibition of such Arts, Manufactures, Products, Machinery, and Appliances, as may be calculated to stimulate the growth and improvement of Manufacturing, Agricultural and other Industries and Handicrafts throughout Ireland; and that such an Exhibition be opened in the City of Cork, in the month of May, 1902[3]

By stimulating growth in agriculture, industry and manufacturing growth, Fitzgerald anticipated a boost in employment and Irish consumerism as well as helping to eradicate the scourge of emigration from the country. He highlighted tourism as a potential benefit of the exhibition as thousands of visitors were expected in the city and they (he hoped) would leave with a 'favourable impression'. The Exhibition would also serve as 'an educational institute', enabling local artisans to see the 'improvements that were made in the manufacture of industrial products' without having to spend their much-needed money on travelling abroad to learn this. Finally, and above all else, the 1902 exhibition would fall on the fiftieth anniversary of Cork's first Exhibition, and it afforded the 'opportunity of taking stock' as to how the city has modernized and improved in the previous half century.[4] For Cork's exposition organizers, the precarious nature of Cork's economic and social conditions was a constant concern that drove their desire to bring these events to the city. J.F. Maguire, in writing his history of the 1852 Exhibition, challenged anyone who did not see the worth in expositions:

> Is it of no advantage, I would ask, to awaken intelligence, to excite emulation, to impart knowledge? Is it no advantage to exhibit the gradual process of a nation in the arts of civilised

life, and urge the mind of the country to bolder efforts, and more glorious achievements?[5]

To understand the strong attraction Cork's civic fathers had for the Exhibition tradition, we must first cast our eye over the many challenges and transformations faced by the city during the nineteenth century, and how these struggles helped influence Fitzgerald and his colleagues in unveiling their aspiring project.

Nineteenth-Century Cork: Big Dreams, Small Steps

The city of Cork, so enthusiastically displayed during the 1902 opening celebrations, had undergone great social changes during the previous century. It was a period bookended by two very important pieces of political legislation, the 1800 Act of Union and the 1898 Local Government Act. Both Acts were London-directed efforts to help tackle Irish political grievances and neutralize any further threat of revolution. The last two decades of the eighteenth century had witnessed a form of limited self-rule in Dublin, today known as 'Grattan's Parliament', but any dreams of an independent Irish government was squashed by the 1798 Rebellion. Ironically, this rebellion hastened the development of the Act of Union. The major deficiency with Irish government at the time was that it favoured and protected Protestant and Unionist interests even when the majority of the population was Catholic. Discrimination was rife under the Penal Laws and Catholics were barred from voting at elections or even holding office.[6] Under the 1800 Act, the political, social and economic entity known as the United Kingdom of Great Britain and Ireland came into existence, further emphasizing Unionist control of Irish politics while strengthening colonial bonds with Britain. The next 100 years marked a concerted battle in local and national fora over a whole range of issues, including Catholic emancipation, agrarian and rural reform and Ireland's status within the British Empire, (collectively known as the 'Irish Question'). Home Rule was the political vehicle that dominated Irish affairs and influenced British policy towards Ireland from the 1870s until 1914. It articulated the desire by both nationalists and some unionists to repeal the 1800 Act of Union and re-introduce self-government to Ireland. Two attempts to introduce Home Rule in Ireland in 1886 and 1893 were both defeated by Unionist and Conservative politicians in London but it remained a realistic political goal of the majority of Irish nationalists until the 1916 Easter Rising.

In the eighteenth century, a mercantile class comprised of Protestants and Quakers had dominated Cork City socially and economically. Prominent Protestant citizens also controlled the city's political affairs, as Catholics were not allowed to stand in local municipal elections until 1841. This was in spite of the fact that many Catholic merchants were wealthier or better educated than their Protestant fellow-citizens. Catholics, however, who by the start of the nineteenth century made up 80 per cent of Cork's population, began to play a more prominent role in Cork's mercantile life.[7] The introduction of the 1829 Catholic Emancipation Act, the 1832 Parliamentary Reform Act and the 1840 Municipal Reform Act had a profound and lasting effect on the life of Catholics in the city. The traditional dominance enjoyed by Protestant merchants and politicians was now challenged by their Catholic counterparts, who under the new acts were granted gradual commercial, economic and political freedom. Organizations like the Trades Association and the Chamber of Commerce had given Catholic merchants and tradesmen experience and a voice in the city's commercial arena in the decades before municipal reform.[8] The powerful Protestant-controlled Committee of Merchants, which centred on the butter trade and its subsidiaries, coopering and tanning, would become three-quarter Catholic in orientation by the 1870s. After municipal reform, Catholics would also hold no less than fifty-two per cent and as high as seventy per cent of the seats in the corporation between 1841 and 1899.[9] Regardless of denomination, commercial interests (merchants, retailers and vintners) continually controlled fifty per cent of the corporation seats, thus confirming the powerful influence of the commercial elite. Throughout the mid- to late-1800s, strong groups like the vintners, larger shopkeepers and pawnbrokers formed themselves into burgess associations to act as a check to the larger and more powerful city merchants. Other groups of white-collar workers, namely clerks and shop assistants, also began to flex their political muscle.[10] The rise of unions for unskilled and semi-skilled workers and the emergence of labour as a new political movement meant that by the start of the twentieth century, mercantile concerns were giving way to working-class issues.

The reform of local government in the 1898 Act brought much-needed change and laid out the system of rural and urban governance that still exists (in modified form) in Ireland today. The new system gave greater autonomy in local affairs by increasing the franchise to ordinary Catholic workers.

This helped to create a native political class that wrestled dominance from the Protestant and Unionist clique and became a medium for proponents of nationalist, labour and liberal agendas. Popular and more radical nationalist movements like the Young Irelanders, the Fenians and the Land League had left their mark on Cork's political scene but by the beginning of the new century, the Irish Parliamentary Party (proponents of Home Rule), enjoyed the largest support within the nationalist community. The day-to-day running of the city's affairs was carried out efficiently, but underlying differences between members of the council caused friction when debating more sensitive national and international issues like the aforementioned Home Rule Bills or the Boer War campaign (1899–1902). Surprisingly, most of the political contests that occurred in Cork City's municipal battleground were not along the historic unionist/nationalist lines but instead seemed to fester within the nationalist and labour movements.[11] The split in the Irish Home Rule Party in 1891 was bitterly felt in Cork City and antagonisms 'were a long time dying'[12] (3.2).

Nationally, by 1902, there was an uneasy alliance in place between various nationalist factions, but remaining tensions amongst Cork City's home rule politicians regularly resurfaced.[13] In short, the nationalist movement in the city

UNITED IRISH LEAGUE CANDIDATES.

UNITED IRISH LEAGUE.
To the Electors of the South Ward

Dear Sir or Madam,
As the Selected Representatives of the above, and Supporters of the Policy of the Irish Party, we, the undersigned, beg to solicit the favour of your VOTE and INFLUENCE at the Municipal Election which will take place on the 16th January Next. If elected we will endeavour to faithfully serve the interests of the ward.

We are, yours faithfully,

For ALDERMAN: —
1. RICHARD CRONIN, T.C., P.L.G.
COUNCILLORS :
2. MATT O'RIORDAN,
Ex Chairman Co. Board G.A.A.
3. JOHN HORGAN,
U.I L. Organiser.
4. DANIEL CRONIN
5. SIMON MAHONY
6. TIMOTHY JOS. MURPHY
7. JAMES O'CONNELL

covered a wide spectrum of opinion, ranging from conservative constitutional politicians like Edward Fitzgerald and Augustine Roche to minority hard-line nationalists like Liam de Roiste and Terence MacSwiney.[14] The newly formed Labour movement also suffered from internal disagreements. Despite having contested the 1899 (3.3) and 1902 municipal elections and electing city mayors in 1899 and 1900, there was a constant tension between 'true' Labourites and those with more nationalist leanings.[15] Indeed, nationalist and labour politics in Cork during the early years of the twentieth century was divided along class and geographical lines, where 'political dynamics dictated that personalities rather than ideologies dominated discourse'.[16] Though Unionism had ceased to be a major player in the local politics, unionists retained a significant commercial and political power in Cork, as they often stood for local elections as independent or 'commercial' candidates.[17]

In the period before the Famine, all denominations had been willing to 'shelve' their differences and opposing ideologies when 'their economic interests were at risk'.[18] When it came to the organizing and promoting of Cork's exhibitions, a majority of politicians, manufacturers and commercial parties were willing to do the same. J.F. Maguire described the various political and social persuasions that rallied around the 1852 Exhibition as deserving 'the merit of hearty and fraternal co-operation, of untiring zeal, and unflinching perseverance'.[19] This was a sentiment echoed at Cork's second exposition in 1883, and as we have seen in Chapter 2, it was trumpeted again in 1902.

Economy, Industry and Urban Development

Notwithstanding a bright and positive start to the 1800s, Cork's industrial and manufacturing output fluctuated throughout the century, preventing any sort of consistent or long-term growth. The period of 1780 to 1840 for example, saw growth and expansion in many industries in the city like brewing, distilling, milling, tanning, papermaking, gunpowder, engineering and shipbuilding. By 1900 however, most of these industries had declined sharply or even disappeared altogether, resulting in high unemployment amongst the city's inhabitants, of which eighty per cent were working class.[20] Cork's economy was always in a state of flux, characterized by phases of growth followed by periods of decline.[21] The Great Famine cast a long shadow over Cork's economic development from the mid-nineteenth century, as it underlined the uncertain and insecure nature of the economy. J.F. Maguire, then Mayor of Cork, painted an extremely bleak picture of life for the majority of Irish people during the mid-1800s:

> its gentry prostrated beneath the weight of national ruin; its agricultural population rushing to its shores in affright, at the rate of a quarter of a million annually; its labourers driven to the workhouses, with their families, there to become victims to those various diseases generated even in the best-circumstanced institutions of the kind, or to remain a drag upon the failing industry and diminished means of the ratepayer; its cities and towns filled with the degraded and demoralised wrecks of the population, who had not means to emigrate, or who would not seek relief in a workhouse; its mind darkened with visions of ruin and disaster; its heart almost paralysed with terror and despair.[22]

Maguire, and other like-minded men, saw the improvement of manufacturing and industry as a necessary antidote in a country over-dependent on agriculture.[23] International exhibitions were believed to be ideal instruments to re-ignite confidence amongst an Irish population ravaged by the effects of the Famine. With this in mind, it was hoped that holding an exhibition in 1852 could act as a catalyst to put Cork and Ireland on the road to recovery by inducing 'every person who entered the walls of the Exhibition to resolve, within his or her mind, on doing as much as possible to give employment, diminish poverty, lessen taxation, promote happiness and elevate the moral and physical condition of the mass of the people, by the practical encouragement of the native industry.'[24] Despite the 1852 Exhibition, Cork clearly did not become industrialized like Belfast, and its manufacturing industries continued to decline throughout the nineteenth century. Many of Cork's most prominent industries during the eighteenth century, like butter and distilling, had stalled by the late 1800s due to a 'resistance to change, and a lack of entrepreneurial initiative'.[25]

This trend was counterbalanced, however, by the fact that Cork was fast developing into a very important regional centre, with a large increase in lawyers, banks, insurance companies, shops and warehouses providing financial, administrative and retail services for the city and surrounding rural hinterland.[26] The prominence of the city's professional classes can be observed by the number of solicitors, architects, commercial and insurance agents,

3.4:
Cork City in 1900.
These images of Cork City at the dawn of the twentieth century show a city that had already adopted the modern conveniences popular in other contemporary European and American cities. Many of the Cork-based businesses that exhibited in the Industrial Hall came from St Patrick's St and King's St (now MacCurtain St) (facing page). (© CPM)

The Cork International Exhibition

dentists and stockbrokers that worked from the South Mall by the end of the 1800s.[27] The period of 1841 to 1901 also saw employment opportunities increase in the public service and the burgeoning transport industry, while the number of provision merchants more than doubled in the city.[28] Despite these new industries, the reality is that by the beginning of the twentieth century the economic resources that Cork employed best were its rich agricultural hinterlands that allowed the city and county to successfully compete with other areas of the British Isles. Ultimately, the industries that managed to survive in the Cork region 'were generally those engaged in processing raw materials provided by the agricultural sector'.[29] J.F. Maguire's desire to lessen dependence on agriculture notwithstanding, it still remains a dominant economic sector in twenty-first-century Ireland.

The nineteenth century brought many changes to Cork's physical and spatial layout, as the city slowly began to take the shape of a modern European city (3.4). It was a period of consolidation, with the city fathers enhancing and surpassing the great reclamation processes of the previous century.[30] Since the mid-1700s, the medieval core of the city had not been adequate to support a city striving to modernize. Faced with this reality, a century and more of public and private building programmes was instigated by the resurgent and politically re-activated Catholic mercantile and middle classes,

aided by the old Protestant elite. These works were designed to develop the trading, industrial and social potential of the city, including refurbishing the city's harbour, its quays and bridges, its commercial market places, and most importantly, its transport system.[31] By 1901, Cork had a tram system and five train stations providing services from the city to areas throughout the county and further afield.[32] The building works encouraged the emergence of a vibrant and confident local community of architects, builders, artists and engineers, including Sir Thomas Deane and his brother Kearns, the Pain brothers and the Hill family. These architects heralded the 'first wave of truly accomplished interpretations of contemporary western architecture in Cork'.[33]

Under the stewardship of the Bishop of Cork and Ross, John Delaney (1847–86), the Catholic Church embarked on an extensive building agenda during the nineteenth century that included a cathedral (St Mary's and St Anne's) on the north side of the city as well as numerous churches and other religious buildings. Though the impressive Protestant cathedral, St Finn Barre's, was also built in this period, the explosion in Catholic building works signalled a departure from the previous century, which had been dominated by Protestant church building. City Engineer and architect of the 1852 Exhibition John Benson bequeathed upon Cork an impressive legacy, including modern landmarks such as St Patrick's Bridge, Berwick Fountain, and the Lee Waterworks.[34] Robert Walker, the designer of the 1883 Exhibition

3.5:
A Tram at the Douglas Village Terminus.
The introduction of the tram service in Cork City helped expand the city's boundaries enabling those who could afford it to move to the cleaner and healthier suburbs. (© CPM)

Douglas, CORK.

The Cork International Exhibition

building and one-time student of Benson's, also left an indelible mark on Cork's future skyline.[35] Both men were prolific in fulfilling the Corporation's desire to transform Cork into a modern metropolis, so it is little wonder they were charged with the task of bringing the city's exhibitions to life.

The nineteenth century was also an era of expansion in Cork, as new suburbs and streets were built, pushing the city's limits well beyond its medieval constraints. This process of sub-urbanization so fundamental to modern city living was propelled forward with the introduction of improved roads and the arrival of a tram system.[36] The tram service, opened in 1898, coincided with and facilitated the 'migration' of the upper and middle classes out of the city centre to live in newly developed and fashionable suburban environments (3.5). Judging by the *1891 Guys Cork City Directory*, the main streets of the city centre were beginning to take the form of modern streetscapes, with a high proportion of retail and consumer shops, small trades and businesses, and less emphasis on residential properties.[37] This trend was visible on many other of the city's main thoroughfares. [38] Moving to the cleaner and healthier suburbs was an option for the emerging middle class drawn from the city's professional and service industries.[39] Those who continued to reside in and around the city centre tended to be the poorest members of society. It has been estimated that as late as 1891, forty-four per cent of the city's population lived in over-crowded slums in deplorable social conditions with

3.6:
Apple Seller, Late-Nineteenth Century Cork. Though the nineteenth century brought many progressive changes to the city and its infrastructure, many of Cork's population remained in poverty, struggling to raise their families. At the heart of the international exhibition movement was a Victorian ethos and genuine desire to educate, enrich and improve the lives of the working classes. (© CPM)

little or no sanitation.[40] Like most other European cities at the time, Cork struggled to meet the demands of its population and facilities were often far from satisfactory.[41] This unceasing task was not made easy, as the city's social problems like high unemployment, poverty, inadequate housing, filthy streets, disease, prostitution and alcoholism continued to hamper progress (3.6).

An example of these social problems was the city's poor water supply. Though work began on Cork's first general water system in 1765, the majority of the city's inhabitants were still dependent on public fountains to provide their water supply throughout the early nineteenth century.[42] In 1866 there were 148 public fountains in the city.[43] During the 1850s and 1860s, an extensive network of pipes was laid across the city while new reservoirs and the city's first waterworks were built.[44] The water system required constant maintenance and repair as water shortages and wastage, through inadequate equipment or broken pipes, remained a problem. It was estimated in 1904 that the daily consumption of water per person in Cork was seventy-two gallons, of which forty gallons were wasted.[45] Despite the slow, gradual and very often-imperfect system, there was a realization that a healthy and sanitized city needed an adequate and reliable water supply. Architect Robert Walker, in a lecture given to the Cork Literary and Scientific Society, stressed that sanitation must be a feature of the city's future development.[46]

The Improved Dwellings Company (IDC) and Cork Corporation instigated various building programmes in an effort to house the working and artisan classes in better and more humane conditions. Indeed, in 1886 future Lord Mayor Edward Fitzgerald built Madden's Buildings in Blackpool, the corporation's first public housing scheme. Areas around Blackpool, Shandon and Barrack Street saw significant slum clearance projects in the late nineteenth century, with housing schemes given suitably inspirational names like 'Prosperity Square' and 'Industry Place', underlining the reforming philosophy behind them.[47] However, despite the best intentions and the clearing of over three thousand sub-standard houses in the city during the 1880s and 1890s, the plan to re-home all the former residents proved harder to realize.[48] On a positive note, the percentage of slum-dwelling families had however fallen from 44.1 per cent in 1891 to 12.6 per cent in 1901.[49] Extreme poverty, uninhabitable dwellings and disease remained serious issues for the working classes well into the twentieth century, as the city struggled to totally eradicate their social ills.[50] Cork Corporation was to the forefront however in embracing the 'electric-revolution' that was sweeping the world at the start of the twentieth century.[51] In a 1905 report, the then City Engineer J.F. Delany noted that the illuminating power of the city's lights in 1905 was estimated to be fifteen times stronger than it had been in 1900.[52] This was due to the gradual and increased usage of electricity instead of gas to illuminate the city's streets.[53] As the city's tram system spread into the suburbs, the Cork Electric Tramways and Lighting Company could offer to connect customers to the electricity network for a small fee. Though electricity would gradually overtake gas as the dominant power supply, gas lighting was still used in some parts of the city well into the 1930s.[54]

With this brief overview in mind, it is fair to say that during the nineteenth century the city had attempted to remodel itself as a modern commercial and trading hub. Though this process was slow and to a certain extent ongoing, it did signal a civic-mindedness amongst the city fathers to make Cork a convenient, safe and healthy place to live, work and visit. The city now had an influential middle class and a politically active working class that would play a greater role in putting Cork on a path to modernity. The 1800s had witnessed as one historian put it, 'the transition of Cork from a mercantile to modern city, a transitional period which saw the evolution of new structures and forms alongside the persistence of those of earlier times'.[55] International Exhibitions were one of the new 'structures and forms' adopted by Cork to show a national and global audience that it was ready and willing to learn, adapt and implement changes in order to take her place in this brave new world. To understand why the Cork organizers placed so much faith in these modern marvels, a brief exploration of exposition history will aid us in framing the city's continuing fascination within the context of a wider global movement.

International Exhibitions 1851–1914: Trade, Education, Peace and Progress
Industrial Exhibitions, Expositions or World's Fairs burst onto the scene in 1851 with the opening of the Great Exhibition of the Works of Industry of all Nations held at Hyde Park in London (3.7, 3.8). This exhibition was entirely contained within one building made of iron and glass, the aptly named 'Crystal Palace'.[56] The event attracted over six million visitors, made a profit of £400,000 and, according to historian J.R. Davis, 'acted as a superbly effective propaganda weapon in favour of modernity'.[57] It set in motion a movement that would come to command the attention of everyone from monarchs

3.7:

The Crystal Palace of the 1851 Great Exhibition.

Joseph Paxton acquired his experience of building large greenhouses on the Duke of Devonshire's Chatsworth estate. He used this knowledge to design and construct the Crystal Palace. It became a symbol of the British dominance in manufacturing and technical innovation. It also signalled to other would-be exhibition hosts that the design and lay out of the building and grounds were equally important as the material displayed inside. (© Science and Society Picture Library)

and presidents to the lowly working classes. Expositions were seen as 'the natural outcome of the Industrial Revolution' and became monuments to the perceived merits of a Victorian liberal ideology that encompassed and encouraged material progress, philanthropy, imperialism, capital and above all else, Free Trade.[58] The nineteenth century saw such advancement in all aspects of human existence that it was often daunting for peoples, cities and countries to keep pace in the rapidly evolving world. For many countries, expositions became a very important means of communicating and interpreting their position on the global stage, both domestically and internationally. Though the larger international events understandably dominate the historical record, smaller and more focused expositions exploring science, technology and art sprang up in cities and towns throughout the 1800s and beyond.

In modern times, when national and international conferences are held so frequently, we tend to under-appreciate the enormous impact

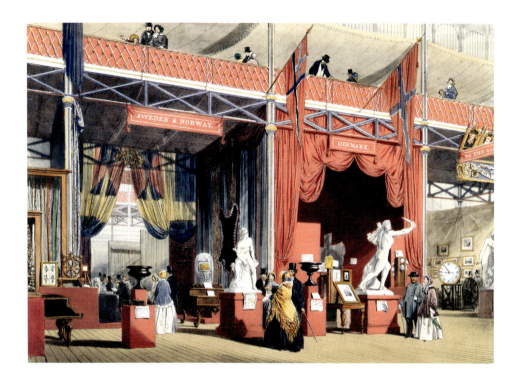

exhibitions had on the Victorian world. After their inception, exhibitions slowly metamorphosed from predominantly industrial and trade-related affairs into far more complex and multifaceted entities. By the beginning of the twentieth century, they had evolved into what can be described as part trade show, part museum, part department store and part themepark. They came in all shapes and sizes, with different agendas, organizational models and funding mechanisms, allowing for much regional diversity. Though the most spectacular and memorable of these World's Fairs took place in Britain, France and the United States, less powerful countries like Ireland, Australia or Italy readily expended vast amounts of money, time and energy organizing their own versions. These places used the larger expositions as blueprints on which to base their own unique interpretations. Despite the differences in scale, design and success, exhibitions were the first fora through which industrial, economic, social and cultural concerns were displayed, explained and discussed in an international context. These massive undertakings helped shape nations and mould international co-operation (and competition) in a

3.8:
Inside the Crystal Palace. The Crystal Palace was arranged such that countries displayed their industries, culture and artistic products side by side. Despite the hope that industrial exhibitions would promote 'friendly' competition between rival nations, by the 1870s individual nations had moved into separate Pavilions. However, the influence of the Crystal's Palace's layout is evident in all Cork's nineteenth-century exhibitions. (© Science and Society Picture Library)

range of issues including manufacturing, art, religion, sport, technology and science. In the process, they laid the foundations for the globalized society we are so accustomed to today. In a time before the invention of the internet, the formation of the United Nations or the beginning of the modern Olympics, expositions became models for globalization and helped give what the authors of *Fair America* have identified as 'form and substance to the modern world'.[59]

From the 1850s to the 1870s, exhibitions could rely on what Paul Greenhalgh has termed the shear 'novelty of their existence' to attract visitors.[60] During this period, Britain and France held alternate events in a tit-for-tat fashion. Paris hosted two lavish expositions in 1855 and 1867 while London followed the triumph of 1851 with the less successful 1862 Exhibition. It can be said that 1851 marked the pinnacle of the British Exhibition tradition, as it became obvious that France had a flair for expositions that left British examples in the shade (3.9). British organizers tended to be overly concerned with technical and industrial display and instruction while their French counterparts brought style and elegance. At the 1867 Exposition, France was the first nation to officially introduce entertainments and amusements as part of the experience. Though Britain had given birth to International Exhibitions,

their neighbours were quick to demonstrate 'that the key to material success lay in a blend of popular and high culture'.[61] The failure to grasp this meant British exhibitions became somewhat stale and predictable and thus less memorable.

As Britain's role in World's Fairs lessened, her place was taken by an emerging nation with an eye on becoming a global superpower, the United States.[62] A World's Fair was held in New York in 1853, but this occasion failed to generate widespread interest nationally and ultimately ended in financial failure. America's first triumphant exhibition was the 1876 Philadelphia Centennial Exposition, which they followed up with what many consider the greatest event of all, the 1893 Columbian Exposition in Chicago. The United States would take the French knack for the grandiose and spectacular and take it to a new

3.10: Left;
The Administration Building of the 1893 World's Columbian Exposition in Chicago.
This exposition had a great impact on American society. The event influenced and shaped American culture and architecture well into the twentieth century and is still fondly thought of by Americans today.
The building itself occupied a prominent position on the exhibition grounds and acted as an important focal point for administrators and visitors alike. Its dome was 36 m in diameter and 67 m in height. (D Breen's collection)

3.11: Right The 1904 St Louis Exposition.
St Louis was twice the size of Chicago's 1893 event, containing an amazing 1,576 structures, exhibits that would fill 12,000 railroad wagons and 20 million plants. The Palace of Agriculture by itself covered an area of 21 acres and included a working diary, two bakeries and a meat processing plant. The Palace of Education and Social Economy displayed the latest teaching methods from around the world. Classes from kindergarten to university level were held under the watchful eyes of thousands of visitors. (D Breen's Collection)

3.12:
An illustrated bird's-eye view of The 1893 World's Columbian Exposition 686-acre site in Chicago. (Daniel Breen's collection)

level of ostentation (3.10, 3.12). The 1904 Louisiana Purchase International Exposition, for example, on a mind-boggling 1,200-acre site containing 1,576 structures, was sixty times larger than the Crystal Palace (3.11). American organizers exploited expositions to help heal the wounds of a bloody Civil War that had torn the country apart during the 1860s. Each of their major World's Fairs commemorated an important event from American history that helped to foster a sense of national unity and common celebration.[63] Through the architecture, language and exhibits on display, Americans were shown what it meant to be part of the United States. Exhibitions allowed the fledgling United States to define and represent itself on a dramatic scale. It also allowed individual cities to do the same. The Panama-Pacific International Exposition held in San Francisco in 1915, for example, was envisaged as an urgent international advertisement to show the world that the city had recovered from the great earthquake and fire of 1906.

France continued to take exhibition planning to monumental levels during the 1878, 1889 and 1900 expositions, turning Paris and its chief exposition symbol, the Eiffel Tower, into a beacon of modernity and progress. Britain's most successful events after 1851 did not occur until the first decade of the twentieth century. The Glasgow Exhibition of 1901 and the 1908 Franco-British Exhibition brought UK exhibitions more in line with international trends, as they included many entertainments not previously associated with British shows. Between 1851 and 1915, exhibitions were held in many diverse locations, such as Dunedin, New Zealand (1865), Vienna (1873), Calcutta (1883), Melbourne (1888–89) and Omaha (1898). Overall, 283 national and international expositions were held during this period, an average of four a year.[64] The last two decades of the 1800s were the golden age of expositions, and Cork's 1902 example came at the tail end of this period. It is obvious that Cork's exhibitions could never compete in size or scope with their more flamboyant 'cousins' from across the globe, but nevertheless they did share common causes, hopes and aspirations.

Reasons for Hosting International Exhibitions

Expositions are the timekeepers of progress. They record the world's advancement. They stimulate the energy, enterprise, and intellect of the people and quicken human genius. They go into the home. They broaden and brighten the daily life of the people. They open mighty storehouses of information to the student. Every exposition, great or small, has helped this onward step.[65]
– US President McKinley at the 1901 Pan-American Exposition, Buffalo, New York

Let the exposition be a display, not merely of material products, but of the teachings of science and experience as regards their value, importance and use. The exposition should not be merely a show, a fair or a colossal shop, but also and pre-eminently an exposition of the principles which underlie our national and individual welfare, of our material, intellectual and moral status; of the elements of our weakness and our strength, of the progress we have made, the plane on which we live and the ways in which we shall rise higher…
– Wilbur O. Atwater of the US Agriculture Department at the 1893 Chicago World's Fair

Despite the grand sentiments expressed above, at their simplest, expositions were conceived as money-making enterprises inspired by a certain formula: the bigger the crowds, the bigger the profits. However, they were much more than that. For example, they were grandiose interpretations of a new world order where industrial and urban-centric markets displaced the 'outdated' agriculture-based economies as the new dominant sources of wealth and commerce. They were supported and endorsed by businessmen and industrialists as a means to expand trading and economic horizons. Free Trade capitalism, spawned in the UK by the repeal of the Corn Laws in 1846, became the new way to do business, and expositions were the temples where this new economic religion was practised and preached. Exhibitions brought the newest products, inventions and innovations to world markets and inspired the growth in consumer-driven economic growth so commonplace in our own society today.

Free Trade was not supported by everyone, though. The organizers of the 1851 Exhibition, for example, had to underplay the free trade aspects of the their enterprise so as not to alienate support from sections of English society who clung to the ethos of protectionism and regarded the prospect of importing foreign goods and services as deeply alarming.[66] Though trade and profit were at the heart of all expositions, organizers tended to play down the vulgar fiscal inspiration and instead focus on more idealized motives. As historian Paul Greenhalgh notes 'Whatever the real reasons behind any particular show, the professed reasons had to be laudable and profoundly ideal.'[67] This 'exhibition rhetoric' promoted far nobler goals like the spread of technical education, peaceful international relations and the onward progression of humankind, thus giving justification to the expenditure of the gargantuan sums of money which often made them possible. Though Cork's exhibitions could never match the international examples, exhibition supporters, as we shall see in Chapter 5, were still keen to spend sizeable amounts of money to achieve their aims. One Cork reporter underlined the reality of the relatively small financial outlay of the 1902 project when compared to foreign expositions. He noted that big industrial firms from Britain and America sometimes 'spend more in advertising a single ware in one month than the Cork Exhibition will cost altogether', deeming the expense of running the Cork Exhibition worth the risk.[68] Cork organizers were also equally intent on promoting the more beneficial aspects of exhibitions outside of trade and commercial considerations.

Educating the Masses: Nineteenth-Century Ireland and Technical Education

The most useful kind of knowledge we could have is to know the extent of our knowledge, or to put it otherwise, to know the extent of our ignorance.[69]
– William K. Sullivan, President of Queen's College Cork, writing about the 1883 Cork Exhibition

During preparations for Cork's 1902 Exhibition, the over-riding message was about education and how it could help improve Irish trade and industry. It was a message voiced loudly by all the Exhibition's supporters, and echoed across all sections of society. According to James Long, Vice-Chairman of Cork County Council, this exhibition had one purpose. It was to 'revive, if possible, Irish trade and industry, and to prove to the world, if proof was necessary, that they were capable of manufacturing within the four corners of their own little Isle anything and everything that can be manufactured abroad'.[70] For the Earl of Cadogan, the Lord Lieutenant of Ireland from 1895 to 1902, the Exhibition 'must at all times be useful in drawing attention to the various local industries', while there was a strong opinion that the Exhibition 'should leave a permanent mark on the character and pursuits of the population'.[71] Nationalist opinion supported the project provided that it would 'succeed in driving British goods from Irish markets' as well as give the Irish public the chance to judge how they can 'combine economy and patronage by giving their support to the manufactures of their own country'.[72] There was an oft-repeated opinion amongst nationalists during the nineteenth century that the adoption of Free Trade, the proximity to Great Britain and the lack of self-determination had severely hindered and damaged Irish manufacturing and industrial growth. One commentator, Edward A. Wright, in a lecture to the Cork Literary and Scientific Society in 1882, lamented the lack of tariffs or some form of protectionism as Irish shops and warehouses 'teemed with English and foreign goods, instead of the products of this country'.[73] To people like Wright, Irish prosperity could only come about with 'national hope' where 'free institutions, and personal liberty and responsibility, act as tonics and strengtheners on the body politic'.[74] The emergence of Home Rule as a viable option for self-governance gave nationalists like Wright great heart and belief for the future ability to protect Irish industry.[75]

Horace Plunkett (3.13), pioneer of the Irish co-operative movement and leader of the Irish Department of Agriculture and Technical Instruction (DATI)

3689-5

SIR HORACE PLUNKETT

did not support protectionism or Wright's belief in the economic promise of Home Rule. The 'Irish Question', for Plunkett, should be approached with sound economic reasoning and not be biased by historic political and religious prejudices (both of which he encountered setting up the Co-op movement). Plunkett believed Irish social and economic problems were rooted in rural Ireland. It did not matter whether Ireland was governed from London or Dublin, the same economic and social problems would remain unless the plight of the Irish farmer was improved. He proposed that a strong collaborative effort by both the British Government and the Irish people themselves would get economic recovery underway. According to Plunkett, the Irish politicians and Catholic clergy who controlled the will and energy of the vast majority of the people needed to forge a new path away from anti-English sentiment and towards one of friendship and openness. Though he sympathized with those who sought Home Rule and berated England for implementing historically disastrous policies in Ireland, he felt nationalists needed to move on and unionists needed to do more. Anglo-Irish history, wrote Plunkett, 'should be remembered by the English and forgotten by the Irish'.[76] Both Plunkett and, before him, Wright welcomed Cork's participation in the exhibition tradition but both saw different socio-political messages in it. While opinion on how best to grow the economy varied, Lord Mayor Fitzgerald was adamant that in relation to Cork's 1902 Exhibition, his organizers had erected a platform on which all were welcome and where 'there was no room for division'.[77] Besides the hoped-for economic and industrial benefits, the belief that they improved educational standards was a more potent factor in why so many exhibitions were organized. At the heart of this belief was the notion that devolution of some colonial power (e.g. via DATI) would better direct the course of Irish educational and industrial policies.

In promoting the 1902 project as an 'educational institute', Fitzgerald was echoing his predecessors in stressing the need for life-long learning and technical instruction to be the cornerstones and legacy of any exhibition. Supporters of Cork's nineteenth-century exhibitions were heavily influenced by the wider global desire to make education at all levels accessible to everyone. When Cork held its second Exhibition in 1883 for example, there was an increased emphasis on technical education, to help instruct 'farmers, artisans and working classes' and boost manufacture across all sectors of society.[78] Indeed it had also been intended to use any money made from the 1883 Exhibition to

3.13:
Facing page,
Sir Horace Plunkett
(1854–1932).
As head of the Department of Agriculture and Technical Instruction, Plunkett played a very important part in Cork's 1902 exhibition. Despite his willingness to work with all political classes regardless of his own views, his strong opinions on Ireland's rural problems brought him into conflict with nationalists. (© CPM)

3.14:
Technical Education
in Cork, *c*.1900.
During the nineteenth
century, there was a greater
demand for scientific
and technical training
to improve educational
standards and make Ireland
competitive globally. Men
like Brother Burke (in his
laboratory, above) pioneered
the practical application of
science and technology in
Irish schools. (© Christian
Brothers, North Monastery)

help fund a Technical School in Cork City or at least fund travel scholarships for local artisans to be trained in technical centres in Ireland and abroad.[79] The nineteenth century saw an ever-increasing demand for adequate facilities to help raise the standards of education in Ireland. Though hampered by religious interference and control, many progressive reforms were introduced to the Irish educational sector, from primary to third level. For example, in 1833, two years after the introduction of the National School system, there were 789 National Schools in Ireland; by 1900 there were 8,000.[80] The 1892 Education Act (Ireland) made attendance at school compulsory for children between six and fourteen years old. When the new county councils were formed under the 1898 Local Government Act, they became responsible for enforcing the Education Act in rural areas. As a result of these and other initiatives, illiteracy levels fell from fifty-three per cent in 1841 to fourteen per cent in 1900. However, secondary level education received little state support until the late 1870s and remained largely in the control of the Catholic and

Protestant church authorities. The 1878 Intermediate Education Act provided for an examination system that brought structure and standardization to the curriculum.[81] By the mid-nineteenth century, there was a demand for third-level instruction by those who had completed secondary-level education. It had once been the domain of elite male students, but the founding of state-funded Queen's Colleges in Belfast, Cork and Galway in 1845 set in motion a plan to broaden the student base to include all classes and women. There was however a protracted political struggle between church and state over how university education should be provided for the Catholic laity, and this was not resolved until the 1908 Universities Act.[82]

Alongside this drive for traditional academic subjects was an increased demand for specialized instruction to incorporate the latest technological advances into Irish industrial and agricultural practice. Prior to the formation of the DATI in 1900, provision of resources to aid technical and scientific training was inconsistent and poorly organized. The Royal Dublin Society (founded in 1731) did its best to fulfil this demand, while institutions like the Farming Society of Ireland (1800) and Irish Agricultural Improvement Society (1833) continued the trend into the nineteenth century. Under the National Education system set up in 1831, the government encouraged the inclusion of agriculture in national school curriculums where students were 'assured of a balance between basic literacy and numeracy in the ordinary school and instruction in the theory of farming'.[83] However, teacher training colleges and model agricultural schools set up in Ireland during the 1800s were allowed to close during the 1870s, when state support dried up. Two important educational hubs did survive: St Albert's in Glasnevin and the Munster Institute in Cork (Model Farm Road).[84] The lack of state involvement in the latter decades of the nineteenth century meant the burden of responsibility for improving Irish agriculture fell on these two venerable institutions.[85] Industrially, there was also an inconsistency in state intervention. In the early decades of the century, the Mechanics' Institutes were established across Great Britain and Ireland, and took on the task of improving the standards of technical education in manufacturing and engineering. They were generally seen as middle-class establishments that did little to stimulate industrialization or improve employment opportunities for the working classes. [86]

It took until the 1850s before the London government began to set about improving technical education across the British Isles. In 1853 the Department of Science and Art was established in South Kensington, London, partly funded from the profits of the Great Exhibition. Its first superintendent was Henry Cole, the motivator who had helped make the Crystal Palace a reality.[87] The Department was responsible for British national and colonial policy on art, science, technology and design.[88] Pioneering attempts had also been implemented by Irishmen like Brother James Dominic Burke and Catholic educationalists like the Christian and de la Salle Brothers, who believed that less emphasis on the classical and theory-based learning would better benefit working-class children (3.14, 3.15). Brother Burke had introduced science, experimentation and practical methods to the North Monastery National School in Cork City and involved his students in two of Cork's industrial exhibitions.[89] However, the lack of coherent government action in addressing Ireland's obvious industrial weaknesses made the formation of the DATI all the more necessary. Though commentators like Edward Wright and Horace Plunkett had different political views, they both shared the common wish for Ireland to be able to exercise more control of its own technical and educational needs.

The Department of Agriculture and Technical Instruction

The formation of the DATI in 1900 changed the face of technical and agricultural education in Ireland. It was the first time that a government department with responsibility for important elements of policy would be run from Dublin and not London. Though the budget was channelled through South Kensington, the final decision on where the money should be allocated rested with the various committees of the DATI. Previous legislation was flawed, as it had attempted to find a universal solution to the economic problems of Great Britain and Ireland that could be implemented across the entire British Isles. This failed to recognize the variation in needs between the different territories. Horace Plunkett, Unionist MP for South Dublin (1892–1900), identified this flaw in British policy, and in 1895 set up a 'Recess Committee' of Irish MPs dedicated to rectifying the situation in Ireland. This Irish-driven, bi-partisan initiative was carried through parliament, and resulted in the 1899 Technical Instruction Act that ultimately created the Department. The legislation provided for the Chief Secretary of Ireland to be president *ex officio* of the DATI, and Plunkett was installed as vice-president. Plunkett explained the role of the DATI as entering 'the business affairs of the country in a way unknown to the British Constitution [and] it makes a departure from the *laissez faire* system'.[90] The early years of the Department were marked by his encouragement of cross-denominational collaboration. He had previously advocated this in his co-operative movement, having established the first agricultural co-op and creamery at Doneraile, Co. Cork, in 1889. As the co-operative ideal took hold in Ireland, Plunkett established the Irish Agricultural Organization Society (IAOS) in 1894 to help run the ever expanding operation. Plunkett envisioned the DATI and the IAOS working closely together solving economic stagnation in rural Ireland. In 1904, Plunkett wrote *Ireland in the New Century*, in which he emphasized economic rather than 'national' development, but his critical remarks on the detrimental influence of the Catholic clergy drew fire from his political enemies. For many nationalists, like John Redmond, leader of the Irish Parliamentary Party, Home Rule was the only answer to Ireland's problems, and came to see the DATI as just another example of the old Tory policy of 'killing Home Rule with kindness'. Plunkett would eventually resign from the DATI in 1907 amid further nationalist pressure in the House of Commons, and his grand design for the economic revival of rural Ireland was never fully realized before the formation of the Free State.

3.15:
Technical Education in Cork, *c.*1900.
Young girls working looms in the Convent School in Queenstown (Cobh) in about 1900.
(© CPM)

The DATI came into existence with clear legal guidelines and a well-defined vision. Plunkett hoped it would have 'a wide reference and a free hand' in aiding, improving and developing all branches of agriculture and forestry, the inland and deep-sea fishing industry, access to markets and of course technical education.[91] The DATI would be part state-funded with the strict stipulation that the DATI could only allocate money to a project or scheme if a similar financial commitment was made by the local authority or other local sources.[92] The provisions of the 1898 Local Government Act and the 1899 Technical Education Act came as a joint package and were intended to show how targeted government funding and expert local knowledge might improve Irish prospects. This, for Plunkett, signalled a new and positive era in Irish–British relations which should be used as the template for future economic co-operation on both islands. Under his influence, technical education became an integral part of local and national policy. Cork was the second city after Belfast to form a Technical Instruction Committee and begin to raise funds for the committee through a small local authority rate. The base of operations for Cork's committee was the existing Municipal Schools of Science and Art (now Crawford Art Gallery) that had been bequeathed to the city by William Crawford in 1884. The DATI would help support the School of Music and the Crawford Municipal Schools of Science and Art and other affiliated technical schools and it also took the Munster Institute under its control.

Cork's 1902 Exhibition was the first major national and international showcase for the DATI to highlight and emphasize the importance of technical education to Irish industrial and agricultural improvement. This was a challenge as many in Ireland viewed technical education as 'a means towards relieving unemployment rather than meeting a direct and existing educational need'.[93] At the time of the exhibition, the DATI enjoyed wide nationalist support. The message of economic prosperity through political consensus and the genuine belief that the DATI was a stepping stone to full Home Rule placated ardent nationalists but the DATI, and especially Plunkett, would eventually struggle to keep politics out of what began as an apolitical crusade. The DATI was the first big organization to get behind the 1902 event, immediately subscribing £5,000 to the cause, which signified a very serious and concerted effort to make their exhibitions and demonstrations a success.[94] We will see in Chapter 7 how well they achieved their aims.

The nineteenth century had seen major developments in Cork City's educational system. Learned bodies and societies like the Royal Cork Institution (1803), the Cork Society of Arts (1815), the Cork Mechanics Institute (1825), the Cork Horticultural Society (1834), the Munster Institute (1853) and the School of Music (1878) had been founded by influential and enlightened citizens to bring education to a wider audience, especially the working classes. However, many of these organizations were more successful as 'middle-class establishments, not centres for working-class instruction'.[95] Some amateur societies like the Cork Literary and Scientific Society (1820) and the Cork Historical and Archaeological Society (1891) attempted to enlighten all classes by holding public talks, lectures and field trips.

Cork became a university city with the opening of Queen's College Cork in 1849 (designed by Thomas Deane). Edward Wright remarked that 'Invention and improvement follow one another with rapidity; if you do not keep yourself *en rapport* with the knowledge of the day, you will be left behind, or stranded high and dry like the barque, when the waters are gone!'[96] Later, an 1885 House of Commons Select Committee Report in which the lack of education was cited as one reason Irish industry was failing supported this opinion.[97] Andy Bielenberg of UCC notes that despite the national trend, low levels of literacy in Munster, especially in West Cork, would have hindered any economic or industrial growth during the later nineteenth century.[98] Thus, it was intended that exhibitions would act as large public classrooms in which workers, manufacturers and business owners were encouraged to 'up-skill' and be shown how to adapt and make use of the latest technological and scientific advances.

In his closing remarks on the 1883 Exhibition in Cork, President Sullivan of UCC reminded his readers that if the Exhibition impressed upon people the need for practical education, especially technical instruction, then the 'labour and expense attending it will not have been in vain'.[99] However, up to this point, the strides made in Irish education and the proliferation of national cultural institutions were only made possible through imperial support and initiative.[100] Educational and cultural reform in nineteenth- and early-twentieth-century Ireland suffered from an identity crisis. Institutions like the National History Museum (1857), the National Gallery of Ireland (1864) and the National Museum of Science and Art (1890) brought cultural civility to Ireland and increased public access to knowledge and learning, yet they were heavily modelled on British examples and were, according to Fintan Cullen 'to all intents and purposes agents of a colonial structure'.[101] In the next chapter, we will explore how issues of identity and nationhood formed an integral part of the exhibition tradition. Through participation in expositions, Ireland was able to assume a greater responsibility for showing itself and could attempt to answer the broader and more complex questions about its union with Britain.

Conclusion

In every way, politically, economically, ideologically and technologically – the fairs were creatures of the modern age, and could not have happened in any other.[102]
– Paul Greenhalgh, Exhibition Historian and current Director of the Sainsbury Centre of Visual Art at the University of East Anglia

Throughout the period in question, Cork was a moderate-sized and modestly significant city within a vast empire. It was emerging as a modern city with the infrastructure, landscape and utilities necessary to help navigate the choppy waters of an increasingly industrialized, technologically savvy and economically competitive world. The Mitchell and Kenyon footage we discussed in Chapter 2, bears witness to a bustling commercial city centre equipped with an important transport system and public utilities to allow the city to face the twentieth century with self-assurance. Historically, the city and its harbour served as a vibrant trading post and base for imperial operations. The exhibition movement that sprang from Hyde Park afforded Cork the ability to communicate to the world, not via London or Dublin, but on its own terms and by its own hands. All of Cork's exposition projects were advertisements; the nature of the message did of course change over time. The 1852 National Exhibition was a rescue mission designed to help revive an economy severely stunted by the Famine. Its fundamental aim was to 'inspire confidence, remove doubt, banish prejudice and awaken interest' in Ireland's recovery and future stability. Thirty years later, there was a greater confidence amongst the city's leaders to nurture and expand on what had been achieved in 1852. By 1902, all aspects of Cork life had evolved so dramatically that public conviction was such that there should be 'no reason why Cork should not distinguish itself in the race for fame'.[103] In the fifty years since its first exposition, Cork's attention was no longer just limited in focus to local or regional agendas but was striving to push the city further and establish an international reputation.

When Fitzgerald and his colleagues began the arduous task of defining the exact scope and style of their exhibition, they were not only influenced by the city's previous undertakings, but also by the latest international trends, high public expectation and diverse political opinion. They were keenly aware of just how important receiving a favourable reception from both native and foreign audiences would be to guarantee commercial and socio-political success. We have seen in this chapter how educational and industrial improvement became the foundation stones for the whole Exhibition. Opening day had announced loudly and with great confidence that the city was moving in the right direction. The 1902 and 1903 Exhibitions would serve as 'timekeepers of progress', charting the city's physical and social development over the previous century while acting as yardsticks by which to measure its future potential to modernize and improve. Hosting exhibitions brought Cork prestige, an enhanced national reputation and a foothold in an international movement dedicated above all else to the progression of humankind and the promotion of civilized modern living. Though the city had enjoyed modest success with earlier exhibitions, there was an almost immediate attraction amongst organizers and the general public that the 1902 venture needed to be larger and more ambitious. Indeed one reporter suggested that damage would be done to our international reputation if we did not fully grasp the opportunity afforded by Lord Mayor Fitzgerald's proposal: 'we would be simply confessing to the world that we were a poor-spirited race, with not "grit" enough to go through with an Exhibition project, and not confidence enough in our own work to show it in public for all corners to see and examine'.[104]

Notes

1   John Francis Maguire (1815–72) was a politician, author, businessman who was heavily involved in Cork's nineteenth-century history. He was MP for Cork from 1865 to 1872, Mayor of Cork in 1853 and 1862–64 and founded the *Cork Examiner* newspaper in 1841.

2   *Cork Examiner*, 16 February 1901.

3   Quoted from an advertisement pamphlet printed by the Executive Committee to encourage subscriptions to the Industrial Exhibition. An example of this pamphlet is kept in Cork Public Museum, forming part of the Fitzgerald Papers donated to the museum in the 1970s.

4   *Cork Examiner*, 8 March 1901.

5   J.F. Maguire, *The Industrial Movement in*

Ireland as illustrated by the National Exhibition of 1852 (Cork: John O'Brien, 1853), p.7.

6   In theory, Catholics had been given the franchise with the Catholic Relief Act of 1793 but in practice, obstacles remained that prevented Catholics total freedom from the penal laws. Catholics were still barred from sitting in parliament, from the offices of Lord Lieutenant, Chief Secretary, Chancellor of the Exchequer, and from other senior political positions. They could not be King's Counsel, judges or governors, sheriffs or sub-sheriffs, and could not hold higher military rank than colonel.

7   Most historians agree that Cork's population hovered in and around 80,000 during the nineteenth century, and any loss in population due to the effects of the Famine were offset by migration into the city from rural areas. See the following articles for more information: J. O' Brien, 'Population, Politics and Society in Cork, 1780–1900', in P. O'Flanagan and C. Buttimer (ed.), *Cork: History and Society, Interdisciplinary Essays on the History of an Irish County* (Dublin: Geography Publications, 1993) and M. Murphy, 'The Economic and Social Structure of Nineteenth Century Cork', in D. Harkness and M. O'Dowd (eds), *The Town in Ireland: Historical Studies XIII* (Belfast: Appletree Press, 1981).

8   M. Murphy, 'Cork Commercial Society 1850–1899: Politics and Problems', in P. Butel and L.M. Cullen (eds), *Cities and Merchants: French and Irish perspectives on urban development. 1500–1900: proceeding of the fourth Franco-Irish Seminar of Social and Economic Historians* (Dublin: Trinity College, 1986), p.235; J. O'Brien, 'Merchants in Cork before the Famine', in Butel and Cullen (eds), *Cities and Merchants*, pp.223–6.

9   See J. O' Brien, 'Population, Politics and Society in Cork, 1780–1900', p.710.

10 See Murphy, 'Cork Commercial Society 1850–1899', pp.241–3.

11 J. O'Donovan, 'Class, conflict and the United Irish League in Cork, 1900–1903', *Saothar: Journal of the Irish History Society*, 37, (2012), pp.19–30.

12 Ibid., p.23.

13 The Irish Parliamentary Party and the United Irish League were the two major political vehicles for Irish nationalism at the beginning of the twentieth century. The Irish Parliamentary Party was led by John Redmond, a lifelong supporter of Parnell, and they eventually amalgamated the United Irish League into its organizational structure by 1903, forcing its founder William O'Brien into political isolation. He later returned with the All-For-Ireland League in 1908 that contested many local and national elections with the IPP for the next decade.

14 J. Borgonovo, *The Dynamics of War and Revolution: Cork City, 1916–1918* (Cork: Cork University Press, 2013), pp.26–40. See J. Murphy, *Abject Loyalty, Nationalism and Monarchy in Ireland During the reign of Queen Victoria* (Cork: Cork University Press, 2001), p. xviii. Murphy details the four prominent and distinct types of nationalism in Ireland throughout the Victorian period. These included those who wanted reform within the UK, those who wanted an 'Irish mode' of government and society within the UK, those who favoured some form of autonomy together with a continued connection to Britain (Home Rule) and those who wanted a completely separate and independent republic.

15 J. O'Donovan, 'Class, conflict and the United Irish League in Cork, 1900–1903', p.23.

16 Ibid., pp.26–7.

17 See Borgonovo, *The Dynamics of War and Revolution: Cork City, 1916–1918*, p.26.

18 See O'Brien, 'Merchants in Cork before the

Famine', in Butel and Cullen (eds), *Cities and Merchants*, p.222

19 See Maguire, *The Industrial Movement in Ireland*, p.13.

20 A. Bielenberg, *Cork's Industrial Revolution 1780–1880: Development or Decline?* (Cork: Cork University Press, 1991), p.116; M. Murphy, 'The Working Classes of Nineteenth Century Cork', *JCHAS*, IXXX (1980), p.29.

21 See Bielenberg, *Cork's Industrial Revolution 1780–1880*.

22 See Maguire, *The Industrial Movement in Ireland*, p.9.

23 Ibid., p.8–11. Maguire also believed that the jealousies of English manufacturing and commercial interests affected Irish industry as they 'confined it to a narrow channel, or compelled it to flow in quite an opposite direction'.

24 Ibid., p.7.

25 See Bielenberg, *Cork's Industrial Revolution 1780-1880*, pp.121–2; T. Farmar, *Privileged Lives – A social history of middle-class Ireland 1882–1989* (Dublin: A. & A. Farmar Ltd, 2010), p.36.

26 A. Fahy, 'Residence, Workplace and Patterns of Change: Cork 1787–1863', in T. Barry (ed.), *History of Settlement in Ireland* (Oxford: Taylor & Francis, 2000), p.43.

27 *Anon, Guy's City and County Almanac and Directory 1891* (Cork: Guys, 1891), pp.263–4

28 See Murphy, 'Cork Commercial Society 1850-1899: Politics and Problems', pp.233–4.

29 See Bielenberg, Andy, *Cork's Industrial Revolution 1780–1880*, p.126.

30 St Patrick Street and the Grand Parade were two of the city's main thoroughfares turned from quays into usable streets in the late eighteenth century.

31 The Harbour Commissioners took steps to enlarge and improve the facilities of the city's waterways from its harbour to its quays, building a new Custom House and bonded warehouses. Architect, Abraham Hargrave, who designed this new harbour complex, also supervised the building of Victoria Barracks (1801–06). Two of Cork's modern-day bridges were also built in this century, Parliament Bridge (1806) and St Patrick's Bridge (1861).

32 The Glanmire Road station at Albert Quay, just east of the Municipal Buildings; The Cork and Macroom Direct Railway station at Summerhill South (now the Capwell Bus Depot); the Cork, Blackrock and Passage Railway station at Victoria Road and the Cork and Muskerry Light Railway station on the Western Road (now the site of River View Hotel). A sixth station, situated at Summerhill (North) near the back of St Patrick's Church served Youghal and Queenstown (Cobh) until 1893 when both services were moved to the newly opened Glanmire Road station. Cork could also boast a world-class harbour and along with Queenstown (Cobh) enjoyed trading and passenger connections with Europe and the United States. New road networks were also built, linking the city to important regional towns like Mallow and Youghal.

33 L. Harrington, *An Introduction to the Architectural Heritage of Cork City* (Dublin: NIAH Publications, 2012), p.38. This book is a great summary of Cork's extensive building programme during the 1800s.

34 A Sligo native, Benson's work at the 1852 Exhibition was widely praised, earning him the commission for the 1853 Dublin Exhibition building. He would later be knighted for designing the 'Irish Crystal Palace'. For a full biography, please visit the website of the Directory of Irish Architects.

35 Walker's numerous commissions include Parnell Bridge, the old Opera House and

many other warehouses, offices and an electricity station in Cobh. He also received many commissions for a variety of Methodist churches throughout Co. Cork. For a full biography, please visit the website of the Directory of Irish Architects.

36 The electric tram system linked the city centre with the suburbs of Blackpool, St Luke's Cross, Tivoli, Blackrock, Douglas and Sunday's Well.

37 St Patrick Street, for example, was awash with grocers, jewellers, chemists, tailors and dressmakers, while similar patterns are found on the other main thoroughfares.

38 Greater George Street (now Washington Street), built as part of the 1822 Wide Street Commission, is Cork's greatest planned street and is testimony to the pioneering attempt to move Cork closer in layout to the larger boulevards of other European cities. The South Mall also underwent a makeover during the nineteenth century, when the Commercial Buildings (now the Imperial Hotel), the Cork City Club (the former Bank of Scotland building), the Cork Savings Bank (ex-Permanent TSB) and the Assembly Rooms were added to its evolving landscape.

39 See Farmar, *Privileged Lives – A social history of middle-class Ireland 1882–1989*. This book gives an excellent account of the Irish middle class and how they came to influence various aspects of modern urban living including fashion, food, shopping and housing. Generally, worldwide, the nineteenth century was the era of the middle class, and their rise helped shape the commercial- and commodity-driven culture we take for granted today.

40 K. Hourihan, 'The Evolution and Influence of Town Planning', in P. O'Flanagan and C. Buttimer (ed.), *Cork: History and Society, Interdisciplinary Essays on the History of an Irish County* (Dublin: Geography Publications, 1993), p.955; See Murphy, *The Working Classes*

of the 19th Century Cork, p.29.

41 C. O'Mahony, *In the Shadows – Life in Cork 1750–1930* (Cork: Tower Books, 1997). This is an excellent book that paints a vivid picture of what life was like for ordinary Cork people. Nineteenth-century Cork was a city in constant social flux. Regardless of how much the city moved forward, it continued to struggle to escape its many lingering social problems.

42 Ibid., pp.58–69

43 T. Spalding, *Cork City, A Field Guide to its Street Furniture* (Cork: Finchfortune, 2009), p.47.

44 See O'Mahony, *In the Shadows*, p.66.

45 Ibid., pp.75–8. Interestingly, at the time of writing (early 2013), water wastage rates in Cork City are about the same.

46 See Hourihan, 'The Evolution and Influence of Town Planning', p.954.

47 In 1896, local building contractor John Sisk was so appalled by the living conditions of his workers in the area around Barrack Street that he built four streets of eighty terraced houses (St Kevin's, St Finbarr's, St Nessan's and St Brigid streets). See E. Cullinan, *Building a Business – 150 Years of the Sisk Group* (Dublin: Associated Editions Ltd, 2009), p.13. John Sisk founded his contractor business in 1859 and it is still operational today. He experienced first-hand the precarious social conditions in Cork City when he was orphaned, aged 11, in 1848, when his parents died in one of the city's many cholera epidemics.

48 M.A. Dwyer, 'Housing conditions of the working classes in Cork City in the early 20th Century', *JCHAS*, 117 (2012), p.91. Dwyer estimates that there were seven hundred less houses in the city in 1901 than there had been in 1891. This indicates how house-building rates were falling behind the 'slum' clearances that occurred at this time.

49 See Hourihan, *The Evolution and Influence of*

Town Planning, p.955.

50 See Dwyer, 'Housing conditions of the working classes in Cork City', p.93. Dwyer highlights a 1925 report entitled, *Cork: A Civic Survey* which found that one ninth of the 80,000 population still lived in tenements or small houses.

51 See Spalding, *Cork City, A Field Guide to its Street Furniture*, p.47.

52 Public Works Committee, *City Engineer Report on the Comparative Cost and Efficiency of the Public Lighting* (1905). This report is currently kept in the Cork City and County Archives.

53 The *Cork Gas Consumer's Company* and the *Cork Electric Tramways and Lighting Company Limited* were responsible for the city's electrical needs.

54 R.T. Cooke *The Mardyke – Cork City's Country Walk in History* (Cork: Seamus Curtin Publishing, 1990), p.116. This chapter contains the personal account of Mr John Cummins, who worked as a Gas-Lamplighter for Cork Corporation until 1936.

55 See Fahy, 'Residence, Workplace and Patterns of Change', p.42.

56 It was designed by Joseph Paxton, the head gardener for the Duke of Devonshire and a self-taught architect. It measured 1,851ft (564m) in length and 408ft (124m) in width. Its highest point was 108ft (33m) and it covered an area of roughly 20 acres. It required 4,500 tonnes of iron, 293,655 panes of glass and 24 miles of guttering to construct. Though there were over 100,000 exhibits and nearly 14,000 exhibitors housed within, the building itself became the centre of attention. Never before in human existence had it been possible to create such a massive and awe-inspiring building without the use of traditional materials like brick and cement. What makes it even more remarkable is the fact that it only took nine months to complete.

57 J.R. Davis, 'London 1851', in J.E. Findling and K.D. Pelle (eds), *Encyclopaedia of World's Fairs and Expositions* (Jefferson VA: McFarland & Company, 2008), p.14.

58 P. Beaver, *The Crystal Palace* (Chichester: Phillimore, 1993), p.12; P. Greenhalgh, *Fair World, A History of World's Fairs and Expositions from London to Shanghai 1851–2010* (Winterbourne: Papadakis, 2011), pp.22–5.

59 R.W. Rydell, J.E. Findling and K.D. Pelle (eds), *Fair America: World's Fairs in the United States* (Washington DC: Smithsonian Institute, 2000), p.1.

60 See Greenhalgh, *Fair World*, p.73.

61 Ibid.

62 Great Britain would hold a series of annual International Exhibitions between 1871–74. These were deemed a failure due to an over-reliance on educational and technical display.

63 The 1876 Exposition in Philadelphia commemorated the 100th anniversary of American Independence. The 1893 Chicago marked the 400th anniversary (a year late), of Columbus' discovery of America and St Louis 1904 celebrated the 100th anniversary of the Louisiana Purchase (again a year late), which doubled American territory at the start of the nineteenth century.

64 See Findling and Pelle (eds), *Encyclopaedia of World's Fairs and Expositions* (2008).

65 Shortly after giving this speech, McKinley was shot by anarchist Leon Czolgosz as he meet well-wishers in the exposition's concert hall, known as the Temple of Music. McKinley initially seemed to survive the attack but died a week later from gangrene.

66 See Greenhalgh, *Fair World*, pp.22–3; J.A. Auerbach, *The Great Exhibition of 1851: A Nation on Display* (New Haven CT: Yale University Press, 1999), pp.55–88.

67 See Greenhalgh, *Fair World*, p.32.

68 *Cork Herald*, 18 March 1901.

69 W.K. Sullivan, J. Brenan, and R. Day, *Cork Industrial Exhibition 1883, Report of Executive Committee, Awards of Jurors and Statement of Accounts* (Cork: Purcell & Co., 1886) p.23.

70 *Cork Examiner,* 8 March 1901.

71 *Cork Examiner,* 10 May; 16 May 1901.

72 *Freeman's Journal,* 27 April 1901.

73 E.A. Wright, *Irish Industries, their promotion and development – A lecture* (Cork: Guys, 1883), p.5.

74 Ibid., p.11.

75 The call by many nineteenth century nationalists for tariffs on imported goods into Ireland delibertly overlooked how impossible this would be, given Ireland's position within Great Britain. London could never have allowed Ireland to practice a policy of protectionism within its own empire especially if it damaged British exports. This train of thought was however, something very similar to the policies adopted by the Fianna Fail under De Valera during the 1930s through to the 1960s. From a modern perspective, it is an economic policy widely seen as a failure, severely hindering Ireland's development into a modern state.

76 H. Plunkett, *Ireland in the New Century* (London: J. Murray, 1904), p.26.

77 *Cork Constitution,* 27 April 1902.

78 H.C. Hartnell, *Illustrated Guide to the Cork International Exhibition* (Cork: Guys, 1883), p.56.

79 Though the profits from the 1883 Exhibition were insufficient to establish a technical school, a scholarship was set up to send a pupil, John Lenihan, to South Kensington to be trained as a wood carving teacher. He would later apply his training at the Cork School of Art where he started teaching in February 1886.

80 S.M. Parkes, *A Guide to Sources for the History of Irish Education 1780–1922* (Dublin: Four Courts Press, 2010), pp.39–42.

81 Ibid., pp.60–5.

82 Ibid., pp.81–6.

83 Ibid., pp.59–60.

84 A. O'Sullivan and R.A. Jarell, 'Agricultural Education in Ireland', in N. McMillan (ed.), *Prometheus's Fire – A History of Scientific and Technological Education in Ireland* (Cork: Tyndall Publications, 2000), p.383. The Munster Institute only survived extinction because a group of local farmers and businessmen formed a committee and raised £526 to ensure the school remained open without state aid.

85 Ibid., pp.385–6.

86 R.A. Jarrell, 'Technical Education and Colonialism in Ireland in the Nineteenth Century', in N. McMillan (ed.), *Prometheus's Fire – A History of Scientific and Technological Education in Ireland* (Cork: Tyndall Publications, 2000), p.175.

87 Henry Cole was an extraordinary man who was successful at whatever he turned his hand to. He was an accomplished painter and etcher and wrote books on history, architecture and art. He was a music critic and wrote children's books. He collaborated with Rowland Hill to introduce the Penny Post and is credited with publishing the first Christmas card.

88 By the late 1800s, South Kensington had become the home to a vast cultural complex that also included the Victoria and Albert Museum, the Science Museum and the Natural History Museum.

89 Brother Burke and his students would take part in the 1883 and the 1902/3 exhibitions in Cork and even sent exhibits to the 1904 World's Fair in St Louis World's Fair. For further information on the fascinating and pioneering life of Brother Burke, please read D. V. Kelleher, *James Dominic Burke – A Pioneer of Irish Education* (Dublin: Irish Academic Press, 1988) and J. O'Connell,

North Mon 200 (Cork: Echo Publications, 2010). In 1889, the Christian Brothers held an exhibition in Cork Corn Exchange. In collaboration with electrical contractor, Gerald Percival, Brother Burke designed and built an electric tramcar that ran around the stalls and sideshows. It proved the Exhibition's leading attraction. See W. McGrath, *Tram Tracks Through Time* (Cork: Tower Books, 1981), p.26-8.

90 *Cork Constitution* 20 June 1902.

91 See Plunkett, *Ireland in the New Century*, p.231.

92 Ibid., p.239.

93 S. Mac Cartáin, 'Technical Education in Ireland 1870–1899' in N. McMillan (ed.), *Prometheus's Fire – A History of Scientific and Technological Education in Ireland* (Cork: Tyndall Publications, 2000), p.188.

94 By the time, the 1907 Dublin International Exhibition occurred, the department was only able to give £2,000 and limit their involvement to helping small industries. This was a great deal short on the time and effort invested in the Cork's 1902 event.

95 See Jarrell, 'Technical Education and Colonialism', p.175.

96 See Wright, *Irish Industries – A lecture*, p.40.

97 See Farmar, *Privileged Lives*, p.35.

98 See Bielenberg, *Cork's Industrial Revolution*, p.126.

99 See O'Sullivan, Report of Executive Committee – 1883, p.270.

100 F. Cullen, *Ireland on Show – Art, Union, Nationhood* (Surrey: Ashgate Publishing Ltd, 2012).

101 Ibid., p.3.

102 See Greenhalgh, *Fair World*, p.51.

103 *Irish News (Belfast)*, 11 May 1901.

104 *Cork Daily Herald,* 16 March 1901.

4
Making an Exhibition of Ourselves
Defining Ireland at International Exhibitions 1851–1908

Daniel Breen and Tom Spalding

Ireland was simultaneously a bulwark of the Empire, and a mine within its walls. Irish people were simultaneously major participants in Empire, [and a] significant source of subversion.[1]
– Alvin Jackson, *Ireland, the Union, and the Empire* (2010)

To any impartial observer it is a miracle how the hall-mark of our race has not been obliterated, how the sharp handwriting of Providence has not been blurred or smeared or erased, and how we to-day remain as ineffaceably Irish as when Caesar turned back from our shores.
– Young Irelander and prominent businessman Denny Lane, 1893[2]

4.1a Previous Page. Celebrations During the Visit of the Lord Lieutenant for the Opening of Cork's 1852 Exhibition. This image contrasts the enthusiastic public reception in Bandon (p.85) with the solemn atmosphere as the Lord Lieutenant presided over the opening ceremony in the exhibition art gallery. (© Cork City Library, from the *Illustrated London News*)

From the outset, international expositions were important stages from which participating nations displayed and defined themselves. They were also expressions of global co-operation and harmony. For example, Prince Albert, one of the pioneers behind the 1851 Exhibition, believed that such an ambitious undertaking could only serve to bring nations together in industrial and commercial harmony. This promotion of 'pacifist internationalism' became the central theme of the 1851 Exhibition, and it was a message continually repeated during the following decades by other exposition hosts. It was hoped that exhibitions would celebrate at once the material progress of humankind and serve to encourage peaceful relations among nations, replacing the usual battlefields with what Auerbach has described as a 'new arena in which nations could compete with each other … by encouraging commercial, linguistic and scientific ties among them'.[3] When you examine the course of world history during the lifetime of the exhibition movement, it is hard to find evidence of this 'peace-loving' agenda. In every year of Queen Victoria's sixty-three-year reign (1837–1901), British soldiers were engaged in some military conflict enlarging or maintaining the Empire. Napoleon III at the height of France's participation in the Crimean War welcomed spectators to the 'Temple of Peace' at the 1855 Paris Exposition. Weapon manufacturers like Colt and Krupp became household names by displaying their wares at expositions. The arms race and the rise of nationalism which characterized the later decades of the nineteenth century, and which would eventually contribute to the outbreak of the First World War ended the illusion of international fraternity through industrial display. Britain, France and America eagerly exploited exhibitions as an ideal opportunity to show off their imperial possessions and position themselves at the centre of the world's industrial, manufacturing and cultural orbit.

The contradiction between good intentions and competitive reality has lead Paul Greenhalgh to state that the '*raison d'être* of many World's Fairs was not the love of peace, but competition and envy'.[4] For example, the organizers of the 1876 Centennial Exhibition in Philadelphia briefly toyed with the idea of not inviting any country with a monarchy, given that their event commemorated American Independence, and all European royal families refused to attend the 1889 Paris Exposition as the event marked the centenary of the birth of the French Republic. There were also numerous occasions where representatives from the major nations grumbled about inadequate exhibition space or complained about the lack of awards. The vision shared by Prince Albert of all nations peacefully displayed side by side under one roof became untenable by the 1870s, as nations began to demand their own pavilions and refused to be over-shadowed by their rivals.

Colony or Nation: Constructing Ireland at Exhibitions

Behind the evolving political and social climate we explored in the previous chapter was an uneasy and often contentious debate about Irish identity and the country's status in the world. The nineteenth century saw greater integration between Ireland and Great Britain as well as intensive political (and revolutionary) efforts to lessen these bonds. The British system of government was simultaneously blamed for the death and emigration of millions of Irish people and exploited by socially mobile Irishmen to garner great wealth and patronage. Surprisingly, Queen Victoria and her family continued to enjoy the goodwill of the majority of the Catholic and nationalist population, despite the growth of distrust amongst the same social groups towards her government's institutions and policy makers. Thousands of Irish nationalists were arrested, imprisoned, deported or executed trying to achieve Irish Independence, while thousands more nationalists gave their lives in service in the British armed and police forces. Recent scholarly attention has been brought to bear on Ireland's multifaceted and contradictory relationship with Britain and her Empire throughout the nineteenth century.[5] The purpose of this chapter however, is not to explore fully this complex subject matter; instead we will focus our examination on how exhibitions fitted into the overall Irish imperial experience. Irish exhibitions could be dismissed as minor events in what was otherwise a turbulent century, but we would be doing Ireland's exposition involvement a great disservice if we push it to the periphery. From the many national endeavours held in Cork and Dublin from 1852 on, or the 'Irish Villages' constructed at foreign expositions, Irish participation in the exhibition movement offers a unique historical perspective on the nature of Irish nationalism and ideals of nationhood. The following sections will aim to show how Ireland was perceived abroad, and indeed represented itself, in a variety of ways that reflected its ambiguous status within the British Empire.[6]

In contemporary literature relating to the Crystal Palace for example, 'Ireland' was referred to as part of the Empire, a 'province', and a 'sister isle', 'land' or 'kingdom', and sometimes given the titles of 'Sister of Erin', 'emerald isle' or 'Green Isle'.[7] Though it was occasionally identified as a nation, Ireland's political status at the Great Exhibition remained 'unresolved and contested'.[8] A country's importance was measured by its industrial strength, and at this first International Exhibition Ireland came up short. Despite being Britain's closest geographical neighbour, of the 13,000 exhibitors present in the Crystal Palace, only 300 were Irish.[9] Ireland was predominantly viewed as impoverished and industrially backward and this was expressed in how its exhibits were displayed. Unlike India, Canada and many other colonies, Irish exhibits did not warrant their own section and were subsumed into the British area. Also, differences between the Irish and British products on show were emphasized, and Ireland was subjected to what Louise Purbrick has termed 'contradictory processes; it was both assimilated and distanced'.[10] Ireland was seen as 'developing', slowly beginning to mechanize and modernize its linen and lace industries, but not to the extent that it be considered fully civilized.[11]

Irish workers were simultaneously commended for their industrious work ethic and stereotyped as 'the lazy Irish subject'.[12] Though religious and geographical bias would have influenced these opinions, the Great Exhibition seemed to support the long-held belief within the British government and beyond that Irish economic and industrial policy should remain under colonial influence and guidance for the foreseeable future. Turning our attention to Ireland's early domestic exhibitions until the 1880s, there was little on display to challenge this perception.

The celebrations to open the 1852 Cork Exhibition were supervised by the Lord Lieutenant of Ireland, Queen Victoria's Viceroy, the Earl of Eglinton and Winton (4.1a). It marked the beginning of what many felt could be a new epoch in Irish history, where reform and conciliation would heal the wounds caused by both the Famine and decades of political agitation. The opening ceremony placed the British monarchy at the heart of any future reform in Irish industrial

4.1b
The enthusiastic public reception in Bandon during the Visit of the Lord Lieutenant for the Opening of Cork's 1852 Exhibition. Note the banners 'God Save The Queen' and 'Erin Go Bragh' that hung over the processional route, highlighting the complex nature of allegiances in nineteenth-century Ireland and how this was displayed at national exhibitions. (© Cork City Library, from the *Illustrated London News*)

and agricultural affairs. The Catholic Mayor of Cork and Chairman of the Executive Committee, William Hackett, praised the example of 'our beloved Queen' in 'sustaining our humble efforts to rouse the drooping energies and to stimulate into greater activity the exertions of the Irish people'.[13] The hope was expressed for the continued 'munificent patronage' of Queen Victoria for Irish manufacture that would encourage similar patronage from other like-minded individuals.[14] Moreover, Prince Albert readily subscribed £100 to the endeavour, and Mayor Hackett was also knighted after the opening ceremony, underlining the interest the monarchy had in Ireland's first national industrial show. In a speech given at the celebratory banquet held in the evening of the opening day, the Lord Lieutenant describes how the 1851 Crystal Palace Exhibition was originally feared by many in Britain as a 'monster Bazaar, the novelty of which would wear off in a single fortnight'.[15] However, under the guidance of Queen Victoria (and Prince Albert, whom the Lord Lieutenant failed to credit) the first industrial exhibition became a 'triumph of peaceful art and civilisation'.[16]

Being the first country after the events at the Crystal Palace to take up the industrial exhibition concept, Ireland was displaying a willingness to leave its troubled past behind. Ireland's Viceroy and others within the British administration saw the cross-denominational and non-partisan effort behind the 1852 project as evidence of a progressive Ireland, where 'you will see happy faces, full haggards [*an enclosure beside a farmhouse in which crops are stored*], and empty barracks – that you will see our harbours filled, British capital flowing in, and railway enterprise carried through every corner of the country'.[17] Organizers of Dublin's Exhibitions in 1853, 1865 and 1872 continued to seek the patronage of the royal family. Queen Victoria and Prince Albert visited the 1853 Exhibition and their sons, the Prince of Wales (who later became King Edward VII) and Prince Alfred, Duke of Edinburgh, performed the official openings of the 1865 and 1872 events, respectively. Queen Victoria visited the 1853 Exhibition four times during her stay in Dublin and was particularly impressed by its instigator and financial backer, William Dargan. Victoria and Albert even paid a personal visit at Dargan's home, Mount Anville, an honour rarely bestowed on a commoner.[18] The Exhibition's royal visit helped to solidify in the public consciousness Britain's role in Ireland's exhibitions and its importance to the country's future economic and industrial recovery.

The early Irish exhibitions received substantial coverage in the British press and were praised as examples of how Ireland could be an invaluable colonial asset. The success of the 1853 Exhibition and the friendly and warm reception received by Queen Victoria was evidence of 'great change' in Ireland and that the 'old notions of famine, fighting, fustian, and rebellion' could no longer apply.[19] *The Times* lamented that English people 'have been taught to consider the Irish as a race thoroughly disloyal and adverse to all constituted authorities', but that these opinions were now outdated and unhelpful in Ireland's quest for prosperity. There is a strong sense of solidarity evident in the British reportage towards Ireland's earliest industrial exhibitions that underlined a genuine desire by some in English society for a better understanding of Ireland and its ailments. The fact that Cork and Dublin were the first cities to imitate what Britain had achieved in 1851 was proof for many British commentators that Ireland no longer needed to be pitied. It was time, according to the *Daily News*, that English people should discard 'the poor-relation view of Ireland' and remove their 'inability to suppose that she can feel cheerful, bold, independent, hearty, and hopeful, like England'.[20] All the reports also went to great effort to emphasize the 'broad distinction between the Irish agitators and the Irish people'.[21]

It is clear that the British media championed an ideal of an Ireland with a loyalist majority who strived to put Ireland on a path away from rebellion and the political upheaval that usually dominated Anglo-Irish discourse. There was a sense of optimism in the press during the 1850s that a progressive and peaceful Ireland could be created 'free from sectarianism and nationalism'.[22] Ireland's industrial expositions were predominately praised not for their exhibits or displays, but for the positive image they created of Ireland and its role within the Empire. It was hoped that the Cork and Dublin events of the 1850s and 1860s would inspire Ireland to put her shoulder to the wheel and force 'England to acknowledge her superiority in the various manufactures and agricultural products peculiarly adapted to her soil'. In doing so, *The Times* believed 'she will realise the often repeated boast that she is not a province of England, but a country in herself, and will thus compel her richer sister to court her co-operation, and to consider her as a valuable and integral portion of the British islands'.[23] The image of a self-reliant Ireland and a mutually beneficial relationship with Britain appealed not just to the English media but also to Ireland's Exhibition organizers.

In the period from the Great Exhibition in 1851 to the Chicago Exposition in 1893, Irish exhibitors had little choice but to remain under the banner of Great Britain at foreign shows, as they were neither an independent country nor an autonomous state. For International Exhibition organizers, Ireland was not a colony but an accepted component of the British industrial and colonizing machine. This was clearly illustrated at the 1886 Colonial and Indian Exhibition in London, where Britain's imperial possessions were paraded and celebrated – yet Ireland was nowhere to be seen. Territories like Australia, India and Canada were afforded the largest representation at the specially commissioned buildings in South Kensington, while even the smaller territories, like Hong Kong, Ceylon, Malta and the Falkland Islands, took their place alongside their larger siblings in this portrait of the British colonial family.[24] This exhibition, more than any other, underlines the complex and constantly shifting nature of Ireland's exhibition status within the Empire. Ireland was part of Great Britain and it was intrinsically linked and intertwined with British imperial policy. Irishmen filled the ranks of the army that guarded and expanded borders and eagerly staffed the mammoth civil service that ran the ever-expansive enterprise. In the thirty years after Cork's first exhibition, the primary message emanating from Ireland's domestic exhibitions favoured maintaining the political and industrial status quo between both countries.

As we have already seen in the previous chapter, Irish participation in nineteenth-century exhibitions was to a large extent motivated by the desire to improve the state of Ireland's meagre industrial and agricultural economies. All political classes agreed that Irish economic development was a 'good thing', without agreeing on the exact context in which such development should take place. This 'illusion of consensus' was commonplace throughout Ireland's exhibition history. Notwithstanding this, there was a growing debate amongst promoters of Irish exhibitions, as to how 'national' these exhibitions should be and how beneficial the presence of international exhibitors was to the development and nurturing of native industry and trade. J.F. Maguire, in the preface to his history of the 1852 Cork Exhibition and the condition of Irish industry, stressed the existence of a bias towards English goods amongst Irish consumers and manufacturers that 'disdained everything Irish, and purchased everything English'.[25] The role of Cork's 1852 Exhibition and subsequent domestic events was to challenge this prejudice and promote Irish manufacturers as economically viable, of high quality and distinct from British-made items.

4.2: Left.

Commemorative medal for the 1852 Cork Exhibition

This medal features a downcast embodiment of Éireann as a harper being cheered by a goddess (perhaps Flora) who points to the new dawn. The 'darkest hour' is presumably the recent Famine. These motifs were to be repeated endlessly during the Celtic Revival. Courtesy N. Murray

4.3: Below. The Opening of the 1883 Cork Exhibition is the Subject of Political comment.

'Pat' chooses the well-paved path towards 'Work for All' and shuns Parnell, Michael Davitt and the Land League perched on the rocky road to ruin. Once again Flora, with her cornucopia and a distaff of flax, is a companion. Courtesy N. Murray

Irish identity and its position within the British Empire and the wider modern world. However, just as had been the case with the Young Ireland, not everyone involved with this Cultural Revival shared the same vision of Ireland's political future. Although these organizations strived to remain apolitical, they cannot be thought of as non-political. Despite the fact that they would come to be synonymous with Irish nationalism, they initially enjoyed the patronage and support of the Protestant and elements of the Unionist community. Unionist MP Horace Plunkett, for example, viewed the Gaelic Revival as an important intellectual force that would strengthen Irish character.[46] It generated for Plunkett a 'sense of healthy self-respect which comes from the consciousness of high national ancestry and traditions'[47] – and yet Plunkett opposed Home Rule until at least 1908. W.B. Yeats was also an early supporter but would later become a harsh critic of the revival based on its political and cultural philosophies.[48] Over the rest of this section we hope to explain how the displaying of Irish culture at industrial exhibitions highlighted the challenge of finding a way to display Ireland's national and colonial status that would cater for all shades of political opinion.

This display of 'Gaelic Ireland' at International Exhibitions began, as much else in exposition tradition, at the Crystal Palace. In her work on how Ireland was portrayed in Hyde Park, Louise Purbrick highlights how there were two divergent ideas of 'Irish Nationhood' on display.[49] On the one hand, there were exhibits that promoted the ethos that Irish industry should develop along the same lines as the British model of industrial economy. On the other hand, the examples of exquisite handcrafted furniture, by Dublin maker Arthur Jones, heavily decorated with imagery from Gaelic heritage, myth and legend, harked back to a historic past when Ireland flourished under self-rule.[50] It could be said that the chief characteristic of the nineteenth-century Celtic Revival was its recollection (or re-invention?) of a time when Ireland prospered, a time when she was free to govern herself. It is little wonder then that the idea of hosting their own exhibitions appealed to Irishmen of the business, political and intellectual elite, who saw opportunities in not just tackling Irish economic and industrial issues but also in promoting a healthier international perception of Ireland's culture, history and ultimately, its ability to manage its own affairs. Ironically, but very much in keeping with the spirit of the times, exhibition organizers delved into Ireland's past in order to help support its future claims for self-determination.

To this end, a key feature of Cork's 1852 Exhibition and all subsequent similar Irish events was the display of archaeological and historical artefacts. Aside from their value as items of curiosity, exhibiting Irish antiquities served a far greater and nobler purpose. In the opinion of J.F. Maguire, such collections 'offered a ready answer to the flippant cavalier, and the self-sufficient opacity of the Utilitarian, who can discover no evidence of either civilisation or progress in Ancient Ireland until she had been schooled by her stern Saxon teachers'.[51] The public were to be educated about ancient Irish civilization through the display and explanation of ogham stones, ring-money, torcs, weaponry, illuminated manuscripts and other examples of early Christian metallurgy such as St Patrick's Bell, the Cross of Cong and the Tara Brooch (found two years before in County Meath). The Tara Brooch in particular was praised as proof that the ancient Irish had 'attained the highest cultivated skill' in the arts of metalworking.[52] Similarly, according to Maguire, the display of finely made medieval trumpets and Irish Harps helped evoke a time when Irish music had attained such perfection its peoples could not be regarded as 'savage', instead they must have 'advanced far in civilisation'.[53] In what was otherwise a modern, forward-thinking industrial exhibition, the organizers had placed equal importance on the demonstration of ancient industrial, religious and cultural treasures. For men like Maguire, such displays were just as valid as the modern goods, and he hoped their high standard of workmanship would serve to encourage and inspire contemporary Irish manufacturers. Ireland, he reported, had once attained 'a high position in arts and manufactures' and it was hoped a similar level would be reached in the future.

The links drawn between ancient Irish achievements and modern industrial aspirations fitted well with the popular argument amongst contemporary nationalists that Ireland had suffered long enough under inadequate and unfair British policies designed to retard any potential industrial growth or political development. Some Irish manufacturers attempted to incorporate into their products elements of ancient craftsmanship. One French visitor to the 1853 Dublin Exhibition wrote about such a product: a medium-sized bell manufactured in the capital.[54] The bell was decorated with images of Ireland's historic past, such as the harp, wolfhound, round tower and ruined castle. Four phrases were also engraved on the bell: 'Erin, I call thee from slumber'; 'Let Erin remember the days of old'; 'The harp that once resounded through Tara's hall'; and 'Erin go bragh'. For this French visitor, the bell represented

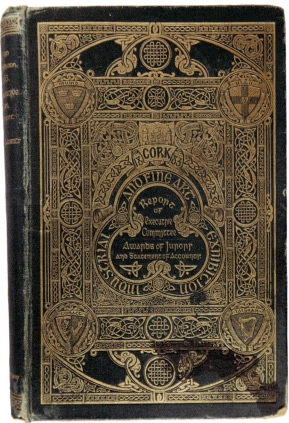

the 'regrets, the tears, the aspirations, the hopes of Ireland – her whole history is there written, very significantly it must be owned, upon a bell'.[55] Imbuing an object with such symbolic power underlines how, when used in tandem, the Cultural Revival and the exhibition movement could be used for political purposes. This was clearly seen at the exhibitions held in Cork and Dublin during the 1880s, when Celtic lettering and design motifs were used in exhibition publications became associated with the Home Rule movement and its objectives (4.4a–d).[56] The 1883 Cork Exhibition was proclaimed as an index of the 'material advancement of Ireland in the paths of progress and civilisation, and affording a new starting point from which the Nation will direct the exertions through the time that is yet to come'.[57] The subsequent decade saw a new development in the exhibition tradition that was to promote Gaelic Ireland at a higher level and to a much larger audience.

4.4a - d:
National Exhibitions and Gaelic Ireland
Organizers of Dublin's 1882 and Cork's 1883 Exhibition incorporated Gaelic lettering and imagery in the production of many items relating to the events. These items from 1883 exhibition comprise (from top): the published *Report of The Executive Committee*, an exhibition ticket and an example of one of the medals (obverse and reverse) awarded by jurors to winning exhibitors. (© CPM)

Irish Villages: Advertising Home Rule

We have our faults and our vices. Who has not? But still in our heart of hearts there appears a fire as inextinguishable as that which the holy nuns of old maintained before the shrine of St Brigid, shining on through the ages to mark the purity of Irish women, and to shed its lustre on the gallantry of Irish men. Whence has the spirit come that has maintained this sacred flame? I believe, mainly from the cottage homes of Ireland.

– Denny Lane's Review of the Irish Village at 1893 Chicago Exposition[58]

Before focusing on the phenomenon of the 'Irish Village', it is important to briefly examine the history of 'human showcases' that became a very prominent part of French and American exhibitions during our period of research. These took the forms of native villages, exotic streetscapes and anthropological shows. From a modern perspective, they appear vulgar and racist but at the time they were seen as educational and functioned as effective propaganda tools. These living exhibits introduced millions of exhibition visitors to strange and mysterious peoples and cultures, bringing the far-flung corners of globe to one spot for all to see. They proudly emphasized the superiority of the host nation in conquering these 'uncivilized' people from Africa, Asia and other territories (4.5). According to Paul Greenhalgh, they legitimized their colonial actions and 'justified European (and American) expansion without troubling the minds of the spectators with economic or military factors'.[59] The perceived educational values of these human showcases can be noted by the fact that no lesser body than the Smithsonian Institute was charged with handling all government anthropological displays at American World's Fairs.[60] International Exhibitions helped structure 'global inequality along lines of colour as well as cultural difference', and helped cement in popular consciousness views about non-European, non-Christian and non-industrialized peoples.[61] These 'savages' were portrayed as fortunate for having been brought into the modern and civilized world by their colonial masters. This xenophobic attitude was particularly visible at American

4.5:
Exhibiting People and Culture at Chicago, 1893. Anthropological displays were an integral part of the exhibition tradition. Peoples and cultures from far-flung locations were gathered together, allowing millions of visitors to marvel at the exotic, the strange and the wonderful, for the price of an admission ticket. (D Breen's Collection).

World's Fairs, where the history, culture and views of African Americans and Native Americans were ignored and downplayed in favour of a white Christian worldview. Despite their less than admirable qualities however, these ethnographic exhibits were both extremely popular and profitable and would form part of the exposition tradition until the Second World War. Even the 1907 International Exhibition in Dublin had a Somali village complete with several 'Somalian' families.[62] It proved the most popular and profitable attraction at the event.

Beginning with the 1893 Columbian Exposition in Chicago, Irish exhibition organizers began to assert Ireland as a unique entity, as its products began to be displayed at the larger international events. This new direction came in the form of 'Irish Villages' specifically designed and planned to function as both semi-official pavilions and 'calling cards' for Irish culture, heritage, industry and architecture. No longer would Ireland only be included within the vast British sections; promoters behind the Irish Village could now represent Ireland and its attributes as they saw fit. It must be stressed that these villages were not overtly anti-British in tone, but they did illustrate the ideas of those who saw another path for Irish economic and industrial progress. Similar to other national movements at the time, like the Gothic Revival in Britain and the Colonial Revival in the United States, the Celtic Revival searched for 'an idealised past that could define, connect, and anchor the present'.[63] Though these other movements were reactions against modernity and industrialization in both Britain and the United States, Ireland's Celtic Revival was rallying against the perceived modernization brought by British imperialism. Central to these nineteenth-century idealizations of the 'Irish Village' was the concept of the traditional stone-built thatched cottage. In the present-day, the 'Irish cottage' is synonymous with Irish tourist initiatives designed to sell an image of the Emerald Isle to foreign audiences. However, for nineteenth-century nationalists and exhibition organizers, the Irish Village and cottage represented far nobler aspirations.

Two prominent philanthropic organizations run by a pair of formidable and enterprising women were primarily responsible for championing Irish Villages. Alice Hart, a member of London's suburban middle class, was inspired to found the Donegal Industrial Fund (DIF) in 1883 after witnessing the misery suffered in the poorest areas of Ireland on a trip to the country with her husband. Lady Aberdeen (born Ishbel Maria Gordon, 4.6) was the wife

4.6:
Lady Aberdeen (1857-1939)
This image shows the formidable Lady Aberdeen making her way across the grounds of the 1902 exhibition grounds. Walking beside her is Mr McCartney-Filgate, the most important representative of the DATI at the exposition who often guided important visitors through their exhibits and demonstrations.
(© CPM)

of Lord Aberdeen; two-time Lord Lieutenant of Ireland (1886 and 1905–15) and seventh Governor General of Canada (1893–98). She would take it on herself to tackle many social issues both in Canada and in Ireland including healthcare, working women's rights and industrial reform. She founded the Irish Industries Association (IIA) in 1886 and intended, like Alice Hart, to 'stimulate the production of home industries, provide information to workers, establish depots from which goods could be sold, find markets, and promote the use of all Irish manufactures'.[64] Both women began by arranging small exhibitions of Irish goods to showcase their causes such as: the Health Exhibition, London (1884); Inventions Exhibition, London (1885); the Edinburgh and Liverpool Exhibitions (1886); the Irish Show at Olympia, London (1888); and the Paris Exposition (1889).[65] The DIF and IIA received some state aid, but largely depended on the patronage and generosity of the wealthy Anglo-Irish and English classes. Hart and Aberdeen employed the imagery and symbols of the Gaelic Revival to market and sell their products. Hart intended the DIF to be an entrepreneurial organization and set up shops in London and marketed a line of 'Kells' embroidered products (based on designs from the Book of Kells). Her products won prizes at foreign exhibitions and showcased the best of Irish craftsmanship.[66] For her part, Lady Aberdeen announced her role in the revival of Irish art and cottage industries

4.7a:

The Irish Industries Association at the Chicago Exposition.

Lady Aberdeen travelled around Ireland in the months before the exhibition to personally select the staff who would work at 'her' village. Over forty Irish worked on site and were housed in the various floors of the village's Blarney Castle. Note the man sitting in the wheel chair at the entrance in the photgraph. Visitors could rent wheel chairs (and pushers) as getting around large expos could be tiring work. (© CPM)

4.7b - d: Facing page The Irish Industries Association at the Chicago Exposition.

The architecture of ancient Ireland, in this case Muckross Abbey featured heavily in the village (Facing page - centre).

with an extravagant garden party at her Dublin home in 1886 at which she wore a costume 'resplendently embroidered with Celtic motifs'.[67] Her Irish-themed parties, often held in the homes of other influential aristocrats became the trademark of the IIA and helped maintain Irish lace's position as highly fashionable and sought-after products.[68] The history of women's involvement in philanthropy and social reform in Ireland is beyond the scope of this book but it is important to remember that it was already over a century old by the time of Alice Hart's and Lady Aberdeen's diligent efforts.[69] Despite some early collaboration between Hart and Aberdeen, class, political and operational differences would come between them which culminated in two separate Irish Villages being constructed at the Chicago World's Fair in 1893 (4.7a – d, 4.8).

These villages would come to influence and dictate the style and layout of future examples employed at other foreign and domestic expositions.[70] Under the supervision of Hart and Aberdeen, the villages were located on Chicago's official amusement section, known as the 'Midway' (4.9a & b). The villages were dedicated to promoting various indigenous industries including jewellery-making, lace-making, knitting, embroidery, wood and marble carving and dairy production. Both sought to encourage domestic confidence, a sense of Irish pride and industrial independence. The Gaelic artistic and cultural revival was extremely important in shaping the message exhibited at Chicago. Reminiscent of the beautiful hand-worked furniture on display in 1851 at the Crystal Palace, these villages showed the art and civilization of 'those far-away days', when the Irish people were 'full of skill, delicate refinement, and artistic taste'.[71] From the splendid reproductions of Blarney castle, Cormac's Chapel, the concerts of Irish music and the sale of miniature replicas of Irish antiques, Lady Aberdeen and Mrs Hart were selling an idealized vision of the 'mother country' where rural ingenuity and an abidance to pre-colonial principles could help Ireland overcome its economic problems.

However, for many nationalists, the concept of the 'Irish Village', and more specifically the Irish cottage, went beyond promoting home industries and enhancing the lives of the impoverished working classes. As expressed by the opening quote at the beginning of this section, Denny Lane (and no doubt many others) believed the Irish cottage represented an ideal, a spiritual connection Irish men and women shared that spanned the centuries and the globe.[72] Whether resident in Ireland, an

IRISH VILLAGE—Donegal Castle.
Midway Plaisance.

FROM FERRIS WHEEL LOOKING DIRECTLY EAST.

4.8: Above left.

Donegal Industries Irish Village at the Chicago Exposition.
Mrs Hart's village was located close to Lady Aberdeen's (see 4.9b). Even though both villages contained similar buildings and promoted the same industries, Hart did not receive the same media attention as her rival. Finding photographic evidence of Hart's endeavour is a challenge (© CPM).

4.9a: Above right.

View of Chicago's 'Midway Plaisance' From the Ferris Wheel. The Midway was the first specially constructed amusement area at an international exhibition. It made over $4 million (1893 figure) and helped make it a most memorable part of the Chicago exposition. In the years after the Exposition closed, the term Midway came to be used commonly in the United States to signify the area for amusements. (D Breen's Collection)

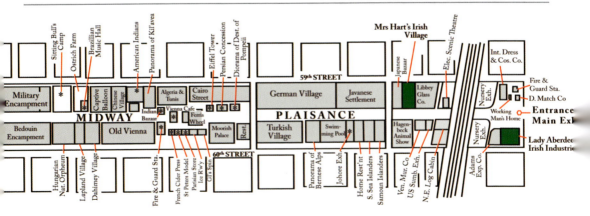

4.9b: Above **Map of the Midway.** The areas shaded in green represent the two Irish villages at the Fair. Lady Aberdeen's village had a very prominent position on Midway to the left of the main entrance ensuring a steady stream of visitors. The replica of Blarney Castle would have been hard to miss. (© Tom Spalding)

emigrant, or a soldier on a foreign battlefield, nineteenth-century Irish people were guided by what Lane called an 'ideal truth that has resisted every effort to pollute or exhaust it'.[73] Lane envisioned idealized villages acting as nurseries 'of hardy men and pure women', who despite their poverty were 'strong, stalwart, and laborious'; words that were to be echoed by Éamon de Valera decades later.[74] Influenced by the dire state of Ireland's agricultural economy in the decades following the Famine, Lane described the reality of nineteenth-century rural homesteads as 'sepulchres rather than villages, melancholy evidence of catastrophe' haunted by the memories of emigrated kin people and the 'ghosts' of those who lost their lives 'slain by famine or fever'.[75] Lane and fellow supporters of Chicago's Irish Villages believed the re-emergence of the cottage home in rural Ireland would help re-establish and sustain the country's ancient moral, social and spiritual heritage for future generations. This romanticized view was particularly influenced by Catholic dogma which placed great credence on the family unit as the basis for the restoration of the imagined rural class that was morally pure, diligent and patriotic. This is encapsulated by Lane's final paragraph when he describes a farmer returning home to his cottage after a hard day toiling on the land:

> But in the evening when he returns and finds his wife and daughter spinning, as Eve spun, and the children climb their daddie's knee, and clamour to kiss his nut-brown face, then he is rewarded for his day of toil. Heart opens to heart, and in that sacred family union he finds a pleasure often denied to the great.[76]

The construction of these villages overseas served practical and symbolic purposes but their use as potent and powerful visualizations of what it meant to be Irish helped cement in the minds of contemporary audiences a bond between the post-1800 search for greater political freedom in Ireland and Ireland's ancient legacy.

Supporters of Lady Aberdeen's village came from all sides of the political divide and included William Gladstone, Horace Plunkett and William Redmond as well as nationalist activists Justin McCarthy and Michael Davitt. The project was funded by generous donations of $5,000 from prominent businessmen from both sides of the Atlantic (Sir John Arnott, James Talbot

Power, P.J. Sexton and Mr A. Shuman) as well as Horace Plunkett. Lord Aberdeen gave $7,500 to his wife's endeavour.[77] The exact socio-political message projected from Lady Aberdeen's village was interpreted very differently depending on one's allegiance.[78] One incident that captures the contradictory and complex nature of the Irish Villages and its supporters occurred on the evening of Saturday 23 October 1893. A small group of boisterous Irishmen twice attempted to pull down the Union Jack flag at the top of Blarney Castle which had been hoisted to mark the visit of Lord Aberdeen to the village. The incident turned violent when, on the arrest of the ring-leaders, a large group of supporters gathered around and clashed with the exhibition guards and the Chicago police. This 'ebullition of Irish patriotism' was widely reported and was taken as a personal insult by Lady Aberdeen and her husband.[79] Both Lady Aberdeen and Alice Hart supported Home Rule and believed its introduction would alleviate many of Ireland's economic issues. Paradoxically, many of those who supported the DIF and IIA would have not, and as a result both organizations attempted to steer an apolitical course. However, this was not always possible. Though both these villages placed Home Rule at the centre of Ireland's future prosperity, their association with representatives of the British government was a source of discomfort for many nationalists, especially more radicalized Irish-Americans.

As well as attempting to alter the international perception of Ireland's capabilities, Lady Aberdeen and Mrs Hart were also keen to attract (or exploit) the Irish diaspora newly settled in America. Recent scholarship has shown how the Irish Villages in America were part of a wider propaganda discourse about the role of the Irish in America's developing democracy.[80] In an Ode specifically composed by the Irish poet Catherine Tynan for the opening of Lady Aberdeen's village, Irish emigrants were compared to Christopher Columbus in setting sail in search of 'El Dorado' in the new world, free from 'Old World chains and Old World hunger'.[81] America was portrayed as a glorious and flourishing new nation that had severed its colonial bonds. It was spiritually linked with Ireland and its kin people by history and culture. For organizers of the Irish Village, America and its Irish-American citizens held the potential for Ireland's economic and industrial recovery. It was hoped that Ireland would someday soon stand alongside the United States, economically strong and politically free. Tynan's Ode contained the following:

We, too, the sunset's children, and your kin,

With but the seas between,
Seeing we have built your cities with our hands
And delved your fruitful lands,
And with your wounds have bled,
And sown your battle-fields with Irish dead.
We, too, have part in this your jubilation
And great commemoration,
Marching in rank with the world's army vast,
Endlessly marching past,
Army of peace and love and brave endeavor,
Great as a new world ever

When it came to the 1902 Cork Exhibition, an advertisement in the Boston-based *Donahoe's Magazine*, encouraged American readers to come to Cork in 1902 so as to 'be present at this great national home-coming to renew your strength and faith by contact with the mother earth and with representatives of your widely dispersed kindred to continue the struggle for national existence'.[82]

This promotion of Ireland abroad reached new levels of flamboyance by the time of the 1904 St Louis World's Fair. Under the patronage of the British Government via the DATI and wealthy Irish-American entrepreneur, Thomas F. Hanley, the Irish Village in St Louis included not only perennial favourites Blarney Castle and Cormac's Chapel, but also reproductions of St Lawrence's gate in Drogheda, Dublin's Parliament House, an Industrial Hall and a theatre. To further underline the links between Ireland and America, there was a replica of the ancestral home of the former American President McKinley.[83] The Irish enterprise at St Louis would prove the largest undertaking of its kind and was supported not only by the DATI, but also by other institutions like the Royal British Commission (formed to organize the 1851 Great Exhibition), the Agricultural Board, the Congested Districts Board, the Arts and Crafts Society of Ireland as well as influential Irish-Americans who put together an exhibit that illustrated Ireland as a country 'advancing in industrial spirit and offering good guarantees for the investment of capital'.[84] There was also an impressive exhibition of Irish antiquities and other historical items covering ancient and more recent periods. Cork's Lord Mayor Augustine Roche generously loaned his extensive Irish silver collection to the St Louis exhibition (as he did in the

Cork Exhibition) while Cork antiquarian Robert Day supplied a large amount of eighteenth-century Volunteer memorabilia.[85] There was also a display of relics belonging to famous and internationally renowned Irishmen like Father Mathew, Daniel O'Connell, Charles Parnell, Edmund Burke, and the writers Dean Swift and Oliver Goldsmith. A further exhibition of specifically chosen artefacts belonging to important Irish-Americans who had 'distinguished themselves in the history of the United States from the Colonial period downward' helped re-enforce the close bonds between Ireland, her immigrants and the 'New World'. [86]

The 'Ballymaclinton Village' at the 1908 Franco-British Exhibition in Sheppard's Bush, London was a very different operation (4.10a & b). Though it followed the same format pioneered in Chicago and St Louis, Ballymaclinton was motivated by commercial and charitable concerns. It was primarily constructed as an 'advertisement device' to market the product 'McClinton's soap' made in Co. Tyrone but as well as that, all proceeds generated from the project went to the Irish Tuberculosis Fund.[87] This fund was organized by the Women's National health Association that was led by ubiquitous Lady Aberdeen. Ballymaclinton was the largest and most successful Irish Village ever staged, attracting two million visitors. It was one of only two 'native' villages exhibited in 1908, (the other being from Senegal) and contained an Irish Cross, a round tower, a priest's house, a doctor's house and a range of traditional cottages to take the visitor 'at a step from the whirl of London to

4.10a
'Ballymaclinton'
Irish Village.
This village at the 1908
Franco-British Exhibition
saw the commercialism of
peasant Ireland reach new
heights. (© CPM).

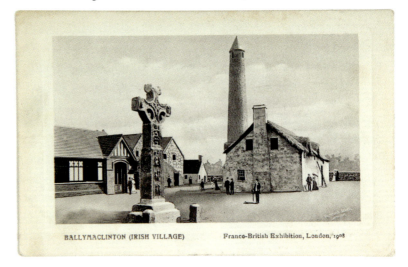

BALLYMACLINTON (IRISH VILLAGE)   Franco-British Exhibition, London, 1908

the heart of Ireland'.[88] Though a full study of this village is beyond the scope of our book, it is important to recognize Ballymaclinton's place as the last great 'Irish Villages' before the outbreak of the First World War.[89]

Despite the serious intent behind these villages and the time and effort invested by individuals and organizations involved, they were open to the accusations, then and now, that they re-affirmed Ireland's need for colonial supervision.[90] Historian Neil Harris reminds us that all other European 'villages' at the 1893 Columbian Exposition, for example, were representations of by-gone times, but the Irish examples were intended to represent contemporary Ireland with little or no hope of an industrial revolution on the scale witnessed in other countries.[91] Though they were successful in attracting high attendances and in bringing Irish products to the attention of American and British audiences, they did little to improve or propel Irish industry forward.[92] Any economic benefits would have only had a limited effect in areas where cottage industries were practiced and not necessarily on an industrial scale. The hoped-for regenerative effect of the Irish Village was plagued by two inherent weaknesses. Firstly, many supporters of Irish Villages and the Gaelic Revival tended to disregard the difference between luxury craft items and mass-produced consumer goods. After all, how many antique reproductions or traditional handmade garments would it have taken to be made and sold in order to bring real economic comfort to Ireland's impoverished masses? Secondly and even more crucially, the disparity between the poverty of those

Ballymaclinton Colleens

4.10b:
'Ballymaclinton' Irish village was staffed by 150 women in traditional costume who were referred to as 'colleens' in publicity and literature associated with the village. Their ostensible purpose was to demonstrate cottage crafts and welcome visitors (© CPM).

who made the products and the affluence of those who bought and wore Irish lace or jewellery brings into focus the weakness of the idea that Irish Villages could be instruments of national industrial improvement.

These villages also helped cement Irish stereotypes in the public conscience, especially to American audiences. Visitors at Chicago 'with Irish sympathies' were encouraged to take away a native blackthorn as 'a memento of this bit of "Ould Ireland" in the New World!'[93] It must also be remembered that these 'fake' villages were located in the amusement sections of the expositions, far removed from the 'official' areas. Like the other ethnographic human showcases from Africa and Asia, Ireland was there to be viewed, not perhaps as entirely primitive, but certainly as less than civilized. Many Irishmen found the Irish Villages to be mawkish and unrealistic. W.B. Yeats, for example, refused to have his plays performed in St Louis as he felt it was neither the place nor audience for his work.[94] John McCormack, the famous Irish tenor, who gave his first American performance in St Louis, left after only a few weeks. Legend has it that he strongly objected to the presence of one *uilleann* piper, Patsy Touhey, whose stage act included playing the drunken Irishman. McCormack was enraged by this stereotyped performance and refused to fulfil the remainder of his contract. It can be argued therefore that these Irish Villages helped to promote an image of Ireland and its people still contested today. For example, at the 2010 Shanghai Exhibition, one of the exhibits housed

4.11:

Irish Village at the 1933 'A Century of Progress' Exposition, Chicago. It is striking, from an Irish perspective, that there were two different Irish exhibitions at this show commemorating Chicago's centennial. One was an exhibition of business, science and arts that was sponsored by Irish Free State while the other was a commercial venture in the form of an Irish village, squeezed between the Midget Village and Merrie England! Recent scholarship has highlighted that the event only served to bring to the surface tensions that existed between Free State Ireland and Irish America. It would seem 'official' Ireland no longer wanted to use the Irish village to represent a modern country (© CPM).

in the 2,500m² Irish Pavilion was the interior of an Irish cottage, complete with turf fire and traditional furniture. The aim of the exhibit was to show how the Irish had progressed from 'rural cabin to suburban sprawl and urban high-rise', much in the same way that China is currently developing. [95] The images of Ireland created in the minds of Americans in the summer of 1893 have stood the test of time. In the summer of 2011, a group of eight American travel journalists were invited to tour around Ireland as part of a Fáilte Ireland initiative. Despite all that modern Ireland had to offer, the journalists seemed predominantly interested in castles, and as if back in Chicago or St Louis over a hundred years earlier, kissing the Blarney Stone was, to them, a central holiday activity (4.7a). [96]

The 1902 Irish Village

In an early illustration of the Cork exhibition grounds, there is a wonderful representation of the Irish Village intended to feature in 1902 (6.24). It is a scene that immediately draws comparison with the Irish Villages seen at foreign expositions. The construction of the village in fact never came to pass, but the genesis of it is instructive. It seems the original suggestion for a Village came from the Executive Committee, possibly from Henry Tivy, but it was widely supported. [97] In a meeting with the Executive Committee in December 1901, a deputation led by the President of the Cork Branch of the Gaelic League, the Very Revd Austin O. O'Quigley, and Mr Michael Murphy implored the committee members to make space in the exhibition programme 'for the great movement that was spreading throughout the country for the cultivation of the Irish language, art, literature, music and pastimes'. [98] The Gaelic League had been founded in 1893, with the aim of promoting the speaking of Irish, and the development of study into old Irish literature and folklore, and the production of new works in Irish. It grew quickly, the first Cork branch was founded in 1894, and by 1904 there were approximately 50,000 members nationwide. [99] By 1907, there were seven branches in Cork city, with perhaps 1,000 members. It had been intended that the League (referred to today as *Conradh na Gaelige*) would organize an 'Irish Village' similar to those seen at Chicago. It would differ somewhat from these exhibits as it would have more of a didactic focus, presenting Irish as a living language, rather than primarily promoting Irish hand-crafts.

The Gaelic League hoped that the village would be small, representative of Irish cottage industries and Irish-speaking (initial plans did not include a round tower or replicas of other historic buildings). To Cork members of the Gaelic League the Irish industrial movement, evident in exhibits of the Industrial and Machinery Halls, was 'bound up' with the Irish language movement, and whatever was done to help one would indirectly help the other. In this they were in advance of Gaelic League national policy.[100] Both the Executive Committee and the League were well aware of the potential for such an undertaking to attract British and American visitors, who were keen to see the 'real' Ireland. On the other hand, they were acutely conscious that an 'Irish Village' in Ireland could be seen as a mere 'shamrockery'. The imprimatur of the Gaelic League was encouraged by the organizers so that the exhibit would be 'genuinely Irish and not a caricature as such villages often are'.[101] They perhaps had in mind the 'villages' in Chicago. According to *Donahoe's Magazine*, 'the miniature … [village would] contain many of the characteristic features of Irish life as are considered worth portraying and the aim will be to show the peasant in the best light'.[102]

The Executive Committee gave the proposal their blessing and plans were put in place to start work on the Irish Village, known as 'Innis Fáil'.[103] Innis Fáil was to have a large, 300-capacity hall for entertainments, concerts and plays, and also exhibit examples of products made in Gaelic-speaking communities nationwide. It would also include a museum of archaeological and historical objects as well as a summer school, and organize excursions to Irish-speaking districts. The Executive Committee also promised to waive the site fee plus £500 to aid in bringing the village to fruition. Revd O'Quigley and the officers of the Cork Branch sought the approval of Patrick Pearse and the national executive of the League at a meeting in Dublin in early January 1902.[104] The response was lukewarm, and Pearse and his team resolved at the following executive meeting that:

> Whilst we do not consider we have any right to interfere with the free action of the Cork Branches in regard to the Exhibition, at the same time we cannot see our way to do anything that would make, or appear to make, the League at large responsible for the proposed Irish Language and Industries Section at the Exhibition.[105]

Support for the project was not unanimous in Cork either: a dissident League member protested against the very idea of an Irish Village, and asked his fellow Corkonians if they could 'invent anything more original than to make an exhibition of themselves and a side-show of their fellow-countrymen?'[106] The idea became further politicized when it was tentatively suggested that King Edward VII may open the Exhibition (4.12, 4.13): the Revd O'Quigley, emphasized that the village would be 'a strong and practical protest both to the presence of the King and the action of those who might encourage him to visit Cork'.[107]

Despite the brush-off from headquarters, a League member from Fermoy, Patrick McSweeney, wrote an article laying out the arguments for supporting the Irish Village, it would, he said be a shame if they did not get involved as it was a prime opportunity to teach foreign visitors about Irish culture: 'The people or Ireland will come to the Exhibition, the English, the Scots and many others will be looking at it. The lovers of Irish (*gaedhilgeóiridh* (sic)) will be outside and there won't be anything inside to show the travellers that the Irish have language, music, manners and customs of their own.' There also appeared to be a fear amongst some that Irish companies would be swamped by foreign competitors, whose governments had not had to spend a penny setting up the show.[108] Yet another point of view could be found in *The National Hibernian* newspaper, which believed that many of the exhibition organizers were 'partly

4.12:
The Prince of Wales (future King Edward VII) Arriving at Custom House Quay, Cork 1885.
In the corresponding article in the *Illustrated London News*, their Royal Highnesses were said to have been 'heartily welcomed by all the respectable inhabitants of Cork, and that the attempt at a counter demonstration, on their crossing "Parnell Bridge," proved an utter failure. The voices of the malcontents were drowned by the cheers of the loyal spectators, and those who took part in these discreditable scenes were, speaking generally, of the lowest class.' (Ó Cork City Library, from the *Illustrated London News*)

English', and if the Irish section had not been consented to then the entire exposition enterprise would 'not have been any more Irish than if it had been held in Timbuktu'.[109] This would hint at the tension behind the scenes between the various shades of nationalist politics witnessed at Chicago and later, at St Louis.

By the end of March 1902, the plans to build Innis Fáil had been abandoned. The Gaelic League blamed the Executive Committee for reneging on the £500 grant (they had 'rather pitifully shuffled out of (*their*) undertaking' according to *An Claidheamh Soluis,* perhaps forgetting the equivocal attitude of the League's executives)[110] while the exhibition organizers insisted that the Gaelic

League were not happy with the suggestion that Innis Fáil be re-located to the western field, and wanted instead to situate their venture closer to the main buildings to the east of the grounds.[111] The organizers arguably wanted to avoid duplication, as many of the displays and demonstrations intended for the Irish Village were already being organized by the DATI and within other sections of the exhibition. Another underlying reason was perhaps the ambitious nature of the project given the time and resources of the Gaelic League. In the event, the Exhibition was rarely mentioned from this time forward in the League's organ, *An Claidheamh Soluis*, apart from a piece recommending the potato exhibit (!)[112]

An 'Irish Cottage' was eventually constructed on an acre of ground at the western end of the exhibition site, and this will be explored in Chapter 6. Whatever the reasons behind its non-appearance, the Irish Village popularized at American World's Fairs would never feature in Irish exhibitions and existed solely for foreign consumption.

Conclusion: What was the Socio-Political Message of the 1902/3 Cork International Exhibitions?

Nationalism is a vague ideology, not least because it draws upon a broad range of different and even rival political vocabularies.
– David Dwan, *The Great Community: Culture and Nationalism in Ireland* [113]

Ireland's exhibition experience highlights the ambiguous processes involved in the search for Irish nationhood and identity. Exhibitions were eagerly exploited by many influential people and groups to represent Ireland as they saw it. The evolution of this representation was susceptible to outside influences and contemporary events. Depending on what a person's social, religious or political persuasion was, the message one took from Ireland's exhibitions varied. For unionists and imperialists, exhibitions were occasions to sell Ireland as a country with the right attributes to remain a valuable contributor to the British Empire. Conversely, nationalists viewed Irish participation in exhibitions as an opportunity to justify patriotic claims for greater political, industrial and economic freedom. However, the multi-faceted nature of Irish nationalism meant the extent of this freedom was always a matter of debate. Nonetheless, leaving aside the obvious political divisions, Irish participation in domestic and foreign expositions was an arena where public

4.14a – c:
Exhibitors and Politics. Even simple innocuous items like the hand-made boot by John O'Brien of 32 Lower George St (now Lower Oliver Plunkett St) could be politicized. On the sole of the boot were depictions of leading nationalist figures, O'Connell and Parnell. (© CPM)

discourse on a range of problems was not delineated by the frequent unionist/nationalist divide. These included issues such as the economy (Free Trade versus Protectionism), industry ('cottage' versus factory), culture (national versus international) or modern living (urban versus pastoral). Expositions continually threw up important questions about what it meant to be Irish in Victorian and Edwardian times. It is also important to remember that regardless of their opinions or allegiances, the majority of those involved in Ireland's exhibition history considered themselves Irish, and all sought to do what they believed was best for their country.

With this in mind, it should come as no surprise to learn that the organizers of Cork's 1902/3 Exhibitions had to tread what was often a precarious tightrope between satisfying national interests and colonial obligations while also attempting to project a good image of the city and country (4.14a – c). As we have seen in Chapter 2, there was a genuine hope that the Exhibition could act as a blueprint for future cross-denominational co-operation, but such inclusiveness was rare in Irish politics and was destined to be rendered ineffective by subsequent decades of political upheaval in Ireland.

So what was the socio-political message of the 1902 and 1903 projects? For Fitzgerald, and the majority of the venture's supporters, Cork's Edwardian expositions were important vehicles for endorsing Home Rule in Ireland. They were to embody the philosophy of political cooperation and stand as a symbol for what Fitzgerald termed the 'practical side of Home Rule'.[114] However as we have witnessed in this chapter displaying 'Home-Rule' was never easy at exhibitions involving Ireland. Cork would prove no exception. The question of who should be given the role of opening the 1902 Exhibition, for example created 'animated discussion' amongst members of the Executive Committee in the weeks prior to 1 May.[115] As had been the case in 1883, the Earl of Bandon was chosen as a compromise option. Nationalist feeling in Ireland had evolved to such an extent in 1902 that there would be no repeat of the overtly royalist display of 1852. There were no references to King Edward VII or Ireland's colonial status in any of the opening day's speeches. Bergin's opening day 'Ode to the Exhibition' and the aspects of the Celtic Revival evident in the architecture of some of the exhibition structures symbolized the new-found place for Irish language and heritage in the public consciousness. Yet, despite the lack of a royalist tone at the opening day's events, the 1902 and 1903 Exhibitions would be supported and visited by numerous members of the royal family and other British representatives, including King Edward himself (see Chapter 9). The role of the Irish National Foresters on the opening day also symbolizes the paradoxical nature of Ireland's imperial experience and identity. Despite being the heralds of Irish nationalism and celebrants of rebellion, the Foresters readily acted as protectors of the Earl of Bandon as he paraded through the city, even if he was a symbol of British rule and the political status quo.

The opening day celebrations for the 1903 Exhibition, on the other hand, could not have been any more dissimilar to its predecessor. Gone were the marching trade unionists, representatives of other local authorities, the 'neutral' Earl of Bandon, and the especially composed Gaelic poetry. In their place were a hundred soldiers of the King's Royal Rifles, fifty members of the Royal Irish Constabulary, various military bands, the Lord Lieutenant of Ireland, the Earl of Dudley and several royal artillery salutes from the nearby Gillabbey Rock.[116] The political factions that had motivated and formed events of 1902's opening day were now surprisingly absent, and the celebrations were more reminiscent of the inaugural events held at Irish Exhibitions between 1852 and 1865.[117] Just as the 1882 Dublin Exhibition had marked a low point in Anglo-Irish relations, the 1903 event appeared to symbolize a far more positive and comfortable atmosphere. No doubt this mood was greatly helped by the constructive steps recently made in land reform in the form of the 1903 Wyndham Land Act and the London-endorsed, but Dublin-led, educational initiatives under the DATI. The land question especially had been a thorn in the side of Anglo-Irish politicians, but as 1903 arrived there was a real sense that progress could be made to improve Irish political and economic prospects. It was hoped by Irish and British leaders that Ireland could now function as a peaceful and contributing part of the Union, no longer held back by rebellion and destitution. The official announcement made during the opening day dinner by the Earl of Dudley that King Edward VII would visit the Exhibition sometime in 1903 would have only re-affirmed this belief.

In many ways, the 1902 and 1903 opening days are two sides of the same coin and represent an issue that was at the heart of all the city's exhibitions: was the planned undertaking to be 'national' or 'imperial' in character? As we hope to show in following chapters, it turned out to be a little of both. Where the 1902 and 1903 expositions differ from their predecessors however, is in how international in nature, technologically innovative and popular they

36 Ibid., p.17.

37 *Cork Examiner,* 8 August 1853.

38 See Jackson, *Ireland, the Union, and the Empire, 1800–1960,* pp.135–7.

39 Ibid.

40 Sheehy, Jeanne *The Rediscovery of Ireland's Past – The Celtic Revival 1830–1930* (London: Thames and Hudson, 1980), p.15.

41 Young Ireland was a political, cultural and social movement that changed forever the face of Irish Nationalism. They led an abortive rebellion in 1848. After the group disbanded, many of its members went on to form important movements like the US-based Irish Fenian Brotherhood and the Irish Republican Brotherhood.

42 See Dwan, *The Great Community,* pp.31–2.

43 Ibid.

44 Ibid.

45 Ibid., p.8. Meagher feared that democracy would place equality over other political freedoms such as 'security of property and of persons'.

46 H. Plunkett, *Ireland in the New Century* (London: J. Murray, 1904), p.148.

47 Ibid., p.152.

48 See Dwan, *The Great Community.* Dwan traces the ambiguous nature of Yeats's initial love, gradual mistrust and eventual abandonment of Irish nationalism and its cultural ideals.

49 See Purbrick, 'Defining Nation: Ireland at the Great Exhibition of 1851', pp.47–75.

50 Ibid., p.75.

51 See Maguire, *The Industrial Movement in Ireland,* p.349.

52 Ibid., p.354.

53 Ibid., p.363.

54 *Cork Examiner,* 8 August 1853. Writing under the nom de plume 'Savote', the French visitor published a letter about his experiences in Ireland at the 1853 exhibition in the Parisian newspaper *Siecle.* The letter was subsequently re-printed in numerous nationalist Irish newspapers. In the letter, Savote displays an obvious anti-British bias and readily blames England for Ireland's poverty and suffering.

55 Ibid.

56 See Rains, *Commodity Culture and Social Class in Dublin,* pp.102–3.

57 H.C. Hartnell, *Illustrated Guide to the Cork International Exhibition* (Cork: Guys, 1883), p.7.

58 See Lane, 'The Irish Industries Association', p.240.

59 See Greenhalgh, *Fair World,* p.125.

60 See R.W. Rydell, J.E. Findling and K.D. Pelle (eds), *Fair America: World's Fairs in the United States* (Washington DC: Smithsonian Institute, 2000); A. Böger *Envisioning the Nation: The Early American World's Fairs and the Formation of Culture* (Frankfurt: Campus Verlag, 2010); R. Rydell, *All the World's a Fair* (Chicago IL: Chicago University Press, 1984); J.P. Burris, *Exhibiting Religion: Colonialism and Spectacle at International Expositions 1851–1893* (Charlottesville: University Press of Virginia, 2001).

61 P. Young, 'Mission Impossible: Globalisation and the Great Exhibition', in J.A. Auerbach and P.H. Hoffenberg (eds), *Britain, the Empire and the World at the Great Exhibition of 1851,* p.6.

62 B. Siggins, *The Great White Fair – The Herbert Park Exhibition of 1907* (Dublin: Nonsuch Publishing, 2007) pp.61–4. Siggins notes how the *Irish Times* described the Africans as 'good-natured, dark, but not unthreatening'. Also see Rains, *Commodity Culture and Social Class,* pp.163–6, where she argues that the villagers may not have been Somali after all.

63 S.E. Cahill, *Crafting Culture, Fabricating Identity: Gender and Textiles in Limerick Lace, Clare Embroidery and the Deerfield Society of*

Blue and White Needlework, Unpublished MA Thesis (Kingston: Queen's University, Ontario, 2007), p.43.

64 J. Helland, *British and Irish Home Arts and Industries, 1880–1914: Marketing Craft, Making Fashion* (Dublin: Irish Academic Press, 2007), p.77.

65 P. Larmour, 'The Donegal Industrial Fund', *Irish Arts Review Yearbook* (1990), p.131.

66 The Fund's art embroideries won a silver medal at the New Orleans International Exhibition and other products won gold at the London International Inventions Exhibition (both 1885). At the 1889 Paris Expo, the Donegal Industrial Fund won more awards than any other British exhibitor.

67 See Helland, *British and Irish Home Arts and Industries*, p.82.

68 Irish lace had been desirable as early as the 1850s and the patronage of many aristocratic women, including Queen Victoria, helped ensure its popularity, status and high pricetags.

69 See M. Luddy, 'Women and Philanthropy in Nineteenth-Century Ireland', *Voluntas: International Journal of Voluntary and Nonprofit Organisations*, 7, 4 (December 1996). This is a detailed and informative exploration of the many religious and laywomen and organizations that helped blaze the trail followed by later nineteenth-century women like Alice Hart and Lady Aberdeen.

70 There was a Donegal Village at the 1888 Irish Show in Olympia, London, but it did not compete with the size and scale of Chicago and St Louis.

71 Anon., *Irish Industrial Village Guide at 1893 Chicago Exposition*, p.14. This document is available online to view or download.

72 For a brief biography of Denny Lane, please consult *Cork: A Biographical Dictionary*, pp.161–2.

73 See Lane, *The Irish Industries Association*, p.240.

74 Ibid.

75 Ibid., p.241.

76 Ibid., p.241.

77 Irish Industries Association, *Guide to the Irish Industrial Village and Blarney Castle, the Exhibit of the Irish Industries Association at the World Colombian Exposition, Chicago*, (Chicago IL: Irish Village Bookstore, 1893), p.27.

78 Hart's 'Donegal Village' enjoyed similar support as Lady Aberdeen's. Though deemed more nationalistic in outlook, Hart's village did contain a 3m bronze statue of British Prime Minister William Gladstone, presumably in recognition of his pro-Home Rule stance.

79 *Aberdeen Evening Express,* 27 October 1893; *The Evening Telegraph and Star*, 23 October 1893.

80 Cullen, Fintan *Ireland on Show – Art, Union, Nationhood* (Farnham: Ashgate Publishing Ltd, 2012), pp.125–52.

81 The Chicago World's Fair was commemorating the 400th anniversary of Columbus's discovery of America.

82 *Donahoe's Magazine*, December 1901

83 The complex nature of Irish allegiances is once again underlined by the sudden death of President McKinley and the attempt to pass a resolution in Cork Corporation in 1901. As recorded in the *Edinburgh Evening News* (14 September 1901), Alderman Sir John Scott proposed a resolution of sympathy for the American people after McKinley's assassination. Labour and nationalist councillors attacked the proposal claiming McKinley was not a friend of Ireland and 'Rebel Cork' should not pass a vote for a man 'who did all he could against freedom at home, and in every country he could besides'.

84 Published letter from the DATI to Irish manufacturers about exhibiting at St Louis.

See *Cork Examiner*, 26 January 1904.

85 Department of Agriculture and Technical Instruction, *Irish Industrial Exhibition, World's Fair, St Louis, 1904: Handbook & Catalogue of Exhibits* (St Louis MO: DATI, 1904), pp.33– 51.

86 Ibid., p.11.

87 The owners of the McClinton's brand, Brown & Son, of Donaghmore, Co.Tyrone, exhibited at Cork in 1902. They emphasized their 'old-fashioned' process, which was to tie in well with the 'traditional' exhibition stands they used in Dublin (1907) and London (1908 & 1911).

88 *The Times*, 14 May 1908.

89 See S. Rains, 'Colleens, Cottages and Kraals: the Politics of "Native" Village Exhibitions', *History Ireland*, 19, 2 (March/April 2011); 'The Ideal Home (Rule) Exhibition: Ballymaclinton and the 1908 Franco-British Exhibition', *Field Day Review*, 7 (2011). In her research on Ballymaclinton, Stephanie Rains has shown that the village was much more than a colonial display of 'either Irish "primitivism" or Irish contentedness' and more than just a marketing campaign for Home Rule. It should also, according to Rains, be read as an example of the enthusiasm in Britain at the time for 'home, community and unspoilt rural life'. Inspired by the wider Arts and Crafts movement, the popularization of Tudor-style architecture and publications like *Country Life* (first published in 1897), Ballymaclinton was part of a wider, turn-of-the-twentieth-century reaction against the urbanized industrialization of British society and the increased uncertainty of domestic and imperial peace caused by fermenting tensions across Europe. Ballymaclinton served therefore as a living monument, a nostalgic re-imagining of simpler times that resonated with British visitors who were already acutely aware of the 'near-extinction' of their own traditional rural heritage. This interpretation of Ballymaclinton by the British public was also shaped by the 'Ideal Home' movement that became popular across Britain at the time.

90 See Rains, *The Ideal Home (Rule) Exhibition*, p.7.

91 See Harris, 'Selling National Culture: Ireland at the World's Columbian Exposition', p.99.

92 On a practical level, Lady Aberdeen was able to set up a permanent Irish depot in Chicago from where Irish products could be sold to the American markets. Her village was visited by 20,000 people on opening day, and ranked in the top three most profitable exhibits at the World's Fair after the Ferris Wheel and the Cairo Street. It made an operating profit of in or around £50,000 and estimates put the total number of visitors at over half a million people.

93 Irish Industries Association, *Guide to the Irish Industrial Village at 1893 Chicago Exposition*, p.15.

94 See Potterton, 'Letters from St Louis', pp.247–8.

95 The theme of the Irish Pavilion was 'Better City, Better Life', and was designed to show the 'creativity of the Irish, their ancient history vibrant modern culture, educational traditions and technical innovation'. It is interesting to see how little Ireland's exhibiting strategy has changed since becoming an independent country and how obsessed we remain in displaying how progressive we are.

96 *The Irish Times*, 1 July 2011, 'Ireland: land of sheep, music and castles, castles, castles'.

97 'Cork Exhibition – Gaelic League Section Suggested', *Freeman's Journal*, 6 December 1902, p10.

98 *Cork Examiner*, 5 December 1901. O'Quigley was Prior of the Dominican community on

Pope's Quay, Cork, Murphy a local lawyer.

99 P. Ó Dalaigh, 'Connradh na Gaedhilge', *Celtic Review* (1904), pp.185–7.

100 The League's first Industrial Committee was set up on 12 July 1902, and included Arthur Griffith, Count Plunkett and George Russell (AE) of the IAOS. *An Claidheamh Soluis*, 19 July 1902.

101 *Saturday Herald (Dublin)*, 21 December 1901. This is part of an interview conducted by the newspaper with Herbert Honahan, Assistant Hon. Secretary of the exhibition.

102 *Donahoe's Magazine*, October 1901, cited in *Catholic Union Times*, 27 May 1902, after the project was abandoned.

103 This is a mythological name for Ireland, after a coronation stone, the Fál at Tara.

104 'The Gaelic League – Executive Committee', *Freeman's Journal*, 10 January 1902, p.4. O'Quigley was at pains to point out no money was being sought, just permission to make it an official League event.

105 'Gaelic League', *Freeman's Journal*, 25 January 1902

106 *Evening Echo*, 30 December 1901.

107 *Evening Echo*, 25 January 1902.

108 'Taisbeánadh Mór Chorcaighe', *An Claidheamh Soluis*, 22 March 1902.

109 *National Hibernian*, 15 March 1902.

110 Notes on Cork, *An Claidheamh Soluis*, 12 April 1902. Local members were instructed to devote their energies instead to the Munster Feis in August.

111 *Freeman's Journal*, 27 March 1902 for the Gaelic League opinion; *The Independent*, 29 March for an opposing view.

112 'Notes', *An Claidheamh Soluis*, 20 September 1902.

113 See Dwan, *The Great Community*, p.3.

114 *Glasgow Examiner*, 3 May 1902.

115 *The Daily Mail*, 19 March 1902. It had been initially hoped that King Edward VII would visit Ireland in April 1902 and include the opening of the exhibition as part of his touring schedule. It was also suggested that the Lord Lieutenant, the Earl of Cadogan, who was the patron of the entire enterprise, should perform the honour. Both these suggestions drew criticism from many nationalists, leaving the Earl of Bandon as the only feasible option

116 *Cork Constitution,* 29 May 1903.

117 The United Irish League, who had been the loudest critic of royal patronage of the Exhibition, were very much pre-occupied with their own internal struggles in 1903, as their leader William O'Brien resigned from the party following unresolved differences with Michael Davitt. The cause of the dispute was the 1903 Land Act, which Davitt saw as too conciliatory. O'Brien, isolated within his own party, resigned as MP and closed his paper, *The Irish People*. This threw the league into disarray from which they never truly recovered, highlighting once more that Irish politics was often more divided along nationalist lines than any other. The popularity and success of the first exhibition meant any protest with an anti-monarchist or ultra-nationalist agenda was never going to derail the 1903 project.

118 *Cork Examiner,* 16 May 1901.

123

5

'Not Grit Enough'?

Committees, Funding, Location and Style

Daniel Breen

Funding the Exhibition

Hosting an International Exhibition was a mammoth task that required sure-footed logistical preparation across many disciplines, including finance, planning, architecture, construction, exhibit building and publicity. As they developed, International Expositions owed their extravagant character in part to creative financial thinking, which drew on private and public sources for fundraising.[1] Exhibitions were costly, especially for smaller cities like Cork, but the larger capital cities spent fantastic amounts of money to realize their ambitions. The Crystal Palace consumed £335,742 (about £40 million) in funding, while the St Louis World's Fair, held fifty-three years later, cost over $50 million (about $1.3 billion). In the decades after 1851, exposition expenditure increased dramatically as a consequence of the physical expansion of these fairs. The budgets invested in nineteenth-century World's Fairs clearly highlight the gulf in funding capabilities between major metropolises (London, Paris and Chicago) and the smaller cities (Cork, Wolverhampton and Dublin). The organizers of French and American expositions employed a variety of schemes to raise money. Private companies were formed or lotteries were organized, and shares and stocks sold in order to cover their gargantuan costs. Ensuring popular support for an exhibition was essential, as its popularity directly influenced the level of financial support. Other factors relating to funding were: the wealth, size and location of the host city, how involved the national or colonial government would be in the exhibition and what form or style the exhibition would take. The direct correlation between

5.1: Previous Page
Exhibition Workers
This image captures the large number of workers, mainly carpenters and painters, who constructed the many buildings for the exhibition under the direction of the main contractor, William O'Connell of Hanover Street. In the background is the wooden skeleton of the Industrial Hall. (The method of construction is very similar to the 1883 exhibition, see 5.9b). Note the very young apprentices sitting at the front of the group.
(© UCC Special Collections)

the growth in acreage of exhibition sites and their rising costs eventually encouraged organizers to incorporate popular attractions and amusements in order to help subsidize the more laudable aspects of the exhibition. Financial success was never guaranteed when hosting an exhibition, but that never seemed to deter cities and countries from trying.

Unlike Cork's previous exposition's organizers, the 1902 and 1903 Executive Committees failed to publish any official report after the exhibitions had closed. In our case, there is a deficiency of organizational documentation from the exhibition aside from some surviving guides, catalogues, brochures and letters. In the absence of the individual committee accounts, staff employment records and construction contracts, we are heavily reliant on the extensive coverage given to the weekly Executive Committee meetings in the local papers. This dearth of first-hand financial evidence becomes all the more lamentable when you compare it with the abundance of archives available to historians of the 1907 Dublin Exhibition.[2] It is debatable whether this weakness in Cork's exhibition record can be described as negligent or unlucky, but the lack of a permanent city hall in Cork until 1906, and the burning of that building by the Black and Tans in 1920, no doubt contributed to the loss of many records. In light of this we should emphasize that the financial information used in this chapter are rough figures drawn from limited fiscal statements and passing references made in relation to the budget in contemporary sources.[3] Fortunately, the available records allows us a broad

5.2:
Apprentice's Indenture
One young lad, Jonas Mansfield Wagner was 16 when he began his apprenticeship on 1 May 1902 with P. Daly of 7, Market Ave, Cork. His first job was to paint signage at the exhibition. These included the 'Cead Mile Failte', 'Ladies Rest Room' and 'Gentlemen's Rest Room', which had to be re-painted daily.
(© Jack Lyons)

substantial aid and to spend their resources in the furtherance of this project, how much larger and more imperative on every section of the community must be the obligation to strenuously assist in this work?'[10] It is safe to assume that without the assistance of the DATI, the technical and educational elements of Cork's 1902 exhibition would not have been addressed in such a thorough and comprehensive manner.

Lord Mayor Fitzgerald estimated that an amount 'close upon' £100,000 (£10 million) was spent during the 1902 season.[11] The bulk of this figure is made up of £56,000 paid out by the Executive Committee and £25,000 expended by the DATI. The rest of his estimate probably includes the £10,000 used in the building and stocking of the Canadian Pavilion and other miscellaneous expenses. About two-thirds of the £56,000 spent by the Executive Committee went towards erecting the site's structures, installing electricity and gas, and landscaping the exhibition grounds. One fifth of the total was used for: providing the musical entertainments for the season (c.£5,000); paying the wages and salaries of exhibition staff (c.£4,000); and on advertising (c.£3,000). The rest of the expenditure covered a variety of costs including printing, insurance, fuel and gas and other miscellaneous items (for exact figures, see Appendix 3). What becomes abundantly clear is that the £16,000 received in private donations would have been nowhere near adequate for the total expense. Cork Corporation made an impressive £26,000 (£2.6 million) from admissions and season tickets and £9,000 (£900,000) from renting exhibit space for the 1902 season.[12] Combined with the initial subscriptions received, these three revenue streams accounted for over ninety per cent of all expenditure and helped make the 1902 season cost-effective. The remaining ten per cent of expenses were more than adequately covered by revenue generated from the rides, sideshows and other entertainments located throughout the exhibition grounds. In total, the Executive Committee could declare a working profit of about £6,500 (£650,000), which they re-invested on behalf of the city into running the 1903 season and the purchase of the land that would eventually become Fitzgerald Park (see Chapter 10).

Politics and the Exhibition

As has been previously mentioned, in the months following the announcement of the 1902 exhibition, deputations visited Dublin, Belfast and other towns and cities to drum up support and gather subscriptions. The Lord Mayor of Dublin called the proposed 1902 Exhibition 'a project which is of much importance to the industrial development of the country at large'.[13] The northern newspapers reported on the visit to Belfast as evidence of 'more friendly intercourse for the prosperity of the country', adding that it was 'unnecessary to waste time on frivolous and political matters which were not of the least profit'.[14] These deputations were well received and were promised the full support of both cities to ensure the success of the project. Things did not however go as smoothly in Limerick. Having sent a cordial letter to Mayor John Daly seeking his help in organizing a subscription committee in Limerick, Fitzgerald received a somewhat dismissive and blunt reply:

Dear Lord Mayor,

Your kind favour of 14th inst. to hand, and I regret I cannot avail myself of the honour you would confer upon me. As Mayor of Limerick, I am with the citizens, without distinction, in everything, which concerns their interest, their honour, and even their pleasure – as I much [*most*] undoubtedly would be with the citizens of Cork, or any other city in Ireland, with the same object in view. But there I must draw the line.

You, my Lord Mayor, and the Patrons of your Exhibition represent England's King and England's authority in this country. Surely, my Lord Mayor, you, with your knowledge of Ireland, could not expect the present Mayor of Limerick to be identified in any way with you or your English patrons. Should your lordship require any further reason for my declining your kind favour, I will be most happy to furnish it, and as I am forwarding a copy of your lordship's letter with this to the press, I feel sure it will be the best introduction I can give you and your lordship's friends, to such of the citizens of Limerick as may be of your way of thinking, and disposed to help your lordship. I am, your lordship's most obedient servant,

John Daly,
Mayor of Limerick

John Daly, a prominent and popular nationalist and former Fenian, was a colourful figure who had already denounced the exhibition as a 'West Britain foundation'.[15] He received little support from the mainstream media across Ireland and Britain for his course of action against Lord Mayor Fitzgerald and the exhibition.[16] The *Birmingham Gazette* remarked that 'the Cork International Exhibition, we trust and believe will do much to stimulate Irish trade, but being to some extent under Saxon patronage, it is denounced by the man [Daly] whose sole idea of saving his country is to throw bombshells on the table of the British House of Commons'.[17] The *Munster News* believed the citizens of Limerick would 'take an early opportunity of repudiating the ignorant and gratuitous insult to the promoters of the Exhibition'.[18] Other newspapers responded to Mayor Daly's letter by pointing out that, whatever his political views, the Cork International Exhibition was, first and foremost, a vehicle to promote Irish industry and agriculture, and those who were working to that end should provide it with their full support. Daly's attitude to the Exhibition, though of the minority, did symbolize an undercurrent of nationalist belief at odds with the majority Home Rule movement. For example, the Mayor of Clonmel, Alderman T.J. Condon MP, said he would not assist the subscription committee if the Lord Lieutenant of Ireland opened the Exhibition.[19] Similar feelings were voiced in Cork about who should officiate at the event. In a bitterly contested Cork municipal election held in January 1902, Fitzgerald found himself at odds with some of his fellow nationalists for his nomination as Alderman in one of the city's wards. Led by former Mayor of Cork and United Irish League (UIL) member Eugene Crean MP, Fitzgerald was accused of wanting to 'degrade and destroy the power of the League' in inviting King Edward to visit the Exhibition during the 1902 season.[20] Crean and his fellow UIL members believed Fitzgerald's actions only made the Exhibition 'anti-national', and would leave a 'trail of misery behind it'.[21] They proposed Augustine Roche to stand against Fitzgerald on the election ticket.[22] In the end however, Fitzgerald won the election, comfortably ensuring his tenure as Lord Mayor for another year; more importantly, he had also received a strong mandate from the people of Cork to stay the course and complete his exhibition project.

Despite this endorsement from the local electorate, Fitzgerald still had to contend with other hard-line nationalist opinion in the press. One nationalist newspaper, *The Irish People* (published by William O'Brien MP, founder of the

United Irish League) asked the Exhibition organizers to 'have some toleration' for Irish nationalists 'who do not think it is the principal business of a National Exhibition to unnecessarily exhibit Lord Lieutenants and other appurtenances of foreign rule for popular adoration'.[23] The same newspaper opposed any proposed visit by King Edward VII to open the Exhibition, as this would hurt 'Cork's unsmirched reputation as a centre of uncompromising opposition to British Rule', and if the King officiated the opening day the paper and its readers would make it 'extremely unpleasant for all the parties involved'.[24] United Irish League members of Cork Corporation were generally supportive of the exhibition as a whole but they remained the most likely to oppose any action that brought the project too close to its colonial overseers, especially the King, the Lord Lieutenant of Ireland and the Chief Secretary for Ireland. As we shall see in Chapter 8, although the subsequent visit by the King in 1903 did not produce the negative reaction hinted at in the above *Irish People* article, it did suggest potential trouble for the Exhibition organizers if they did not respect the views of as wide a constituency as possible. Mayor Daly would later be over-ruled by Limerick Corporation, and a Fitzgerald-led deputation was invited to attend a meeting in Limerick Town Hall in September 1901. The project received the support and encouragement of all those in attendance, and the substantial sum of £500 was subscripted. A similar reversal was later seen in Clonmel. Although rivalries and animosities often appeared during debates on the progress of the Exhibition, the murky world of Irish turn-of-the-century politics failed to derail the project. This would not be the case five years later, when the 1907 Dublin International Exhibition was plagued by criticisms and boycotts from Sinn Féin and the Gaelic League, and a general lack of support from many in the nationalist community.[25]

The Organizing Personnel
The patron for each year of the Exhibition was the serving Lord Lieutenant of Ireland: the Earl of Cadogan in 1902 and the Earl of Dudley in 1903 (5.3, 5.4). Early on in the process, the Earl of Bandon, Lord Lieutenant of Cork, agreed to be President of the Executive Committee (5.5).[26] Twelve vice-presidents were appointed, and these were men whose interest in or knowledge of commercial and business matters made their expertise invaluable.[27] Some were aristocrats like Dermot Robert Wyndham Bourke, the seventh Earl of Mayo, who held a deep and abiding interest in the social and industrial well-

being of Ireland. He founded the County Kildare Archaeological Association in 1891 and the Arts and Crafts Society in 1894.[28] Under his stewardship, the Arts and Crafts Society, held two successful expositions in 1895 and 1899. Other vice-presidents were local politicians like Alderman Augustine Roche (a late appointment). He was nominated by Fitzgerald in an effort to heal political wounds caused during the municipal election campaign mentioned above. In 1852, the main committee had been made up of 47 members while the 1883 general committee contained 193.[29] The 1902 organizing group consisted of a general committee of over 230 men, from which the 72-strong Executive Committee was formed, with Lord Mayor Fitzgerald as its Chairman. Ten sub-committees were created, covering a wide range of functions from finance to machinery.[30] The finance committee had, for example, four bank managers and several businessmen, and it was their responsibility to oversee the collection of subscriptions, make payments to contractors and ultimately balance the books. Similarly, the Fine Arts and Archaeological Committee's remit was the preparation of suitable exhibits and donations to be displayed in the art gallery, as we will see in Chapter 8.[31] All committees were called upon to deliberate on costs and feasibility and propose ideas to the Executive as to what shape the Exhibition should take. The Executive, who usually met once a week, took all the final

From top:

5.3: George Henry Cadogan, 5th Earl Cadogan (1840–1915). He was a Conservative politician, philanthropist and served as Lord Lieutenant of Ireland from 1895 to 1902. He was also the first Mayor of Chelsea in 1900. (© CPM)

5.4: William Humble Ward, the 2nd Earl of Dudley (1867–1932). He was a Conservative politician who served as Lord Lieutenant of Ireland from 1902 – 1905. He was subsequently appointed the fourth Governor-General of Australia from 1908-1911. (© CPM)

5.5: James Francis Bernard, the 4th Earl of Bandon, (1850–1924). The Earl is an important figure in Cork's exhibition history, acting as President of the 1883 and 1902/1903 events. He was one of the few representatives of the British crown intimately involved in the 1902/1903 enterprises deemed acceptable by both nationalists and unionists. (© CPM)

decisions (5.6). For the first time in Cork's exhibition history, there was a significant women's committee (162-strong) with a fifty-five-person Executive Committee, who directed the exhibits in the Women's Section for both years of the Exhibition.[32] The American expositions at Philadelphia in 1876 and Chicago in 1893 had pioneered the inclusion of women in directing and designing their own exhibition buildings. Whilst women still lacked universal suffrage across most of the world, their relatively early involvement in the exhibition tradition pointed to a gradual change in social attitudes towards them. Though there were some changes in the sizes of the committee for the 1903 Greater Cork Exhibition, their composition changed little over both seasons.[33]

Cork Exhibitions had traditionally been organized by prominent peers, MPs, local political representatives, officers of social and trade societies as well as 'professional men, manufacturers, merchants, traders'.[34] These were the men who had shaped and moulded Cork during the nineteenth century. Prominent architects Sir Thomas Deane and Sir John Benson, for example, as

5.6:
The Chief Organizers Pictured Prior to the Opening.
The Executive Committee during a site visit outside the unfinished Industrial Hall. Lord Mayor Fitzgerald and the Earl of Bandon are sitting in the centre of the front row. (© CPM)

well as designing and building many of the city's contemporary buildings, were also respectively vice-chairman and chief architect of the 1852 Exhibition. Cork's 'Merchant Prince' families, including the Beamishs, Crawfords, Dalys, Jennings, Roches and Murphys, readily gave their time, knowledge and money to ensure the Exhibitions became realities. Famous Corkonian Denny Lane was heavily involved in the 1852 and 1883 Exhibitions, as was Thomas Lyons, first president of the Cork Incorporated Chamber of Commerce and Shipping and Cork's first Catholic mayor. Newspaper men J.F. Maguire and Thomas Crosbie of the *Cork Examiner* and H.L. Tivy of the *Cork Constitution* strongly supported the exhibition movement, and along with the other daily newspaper in Cork, the *Cork Daily Herald*, urged their readers to 'SUBSCRIBE! SUBSCRIBE! SUBSCRIBE!'[35] There was therefore a tradition of eminent Cork men getting behind the city's Exhibitions, and the 1902–3 events would prove no different – men such as Lt Col Sir John Alex Arnott, who was involved in numerous organizations, including Cash & Co., City of Cork Steamship Company, Cork & Macroom Direct Railway and the Passage Docks Shipbuilding Company.[36] His son, Captain Loftus Arnott, would also serve as a vice-president while his wife, Emily Lady Arnott, would hold the same position in the women's section. In fact it was a common trend for the wives, daughters and sisters of the prominent men on the Exhibition committees to fulfil similar roles on the female committee. Another prominent figure was Alderman Henry Dale, who served as director on the boards of several local businesses, and enjoyed a successful political career. In his lifetime, he was president of the Flour and Bread Trade Association, the Cork Butter Exporters Association and the Cork Literary and Scientific Society. He also established the Cork Anglers Club in 1870. Other successful Cork businessmen and politicians included Henry O'Shea[37], Henry Shanahan[38] and Alderman Augustine Roche[39]. The men on the Executive were at the heart of the city's existence and key to any future growth and improvement.

Edward Fitzgerald: Master of Ceremonies

At the heart of the 1902 and 1903 projects was Lord Mayor Edward Fitzgerald. He brought much of himself to the preparations, often at the expense of his own building and contracting business.[40] From the very start of the exhibition enterprise, Fitzgerald proved himself to be a steadying influence, willing to work with men and women of all political persuasions while travelling the length and breadth of the country to promote the undertaking. Fitzgerald was held in the highest respect by all, and there was a genuine belief that 'his brilliant personality was a rallying point for all well-directed efforts'.[41] The experience he brought as a successful businessman and his understanding of local politics gave his leadership an authority and deference few others on the Corporation would have been able to achieve. He chaired the Executive Committee meetings with a firm hand, encouraging debate while at the same time censuring any local animosities spilling over into Exhibition business. He also showed his wisdom in 'mending fences' by co-opting his political rival Augustine Roche, which prevented any lingering bitterness disrupting progress. He would remain Chairman of the Executive Committee until September 1904, devoting nearly four years of his life to the Exhibition and its legacy.

However, his greatest asset seems to have been his personality. Despite the dour and serious impression one gets from contemporary photographs of the man (3.1), Fitzgerald was a jovial character who rarely stood on ceremony. This is clearly reflected in reports from the British press regarding him hosting members of the British royal family. In one report in *The Evening Telegraph*, headlined 'How Cork's Mayor Amused the King', we learn anecdotally how Fitzgerald's colloquial style helped endear him to the royal visitors:

> When Prince Henry of Prussia visited the Cork Exhibition last year, Mayor Fitzgerald wrung his hand at parting, and said – 'Look here, don't forget to send your brother [*Emperor Wilheim II of Germany*] over here, and the Cork boys will give him the time of his life.' While the Duke of Connaught and the Duchess were visiting the Exhibition in state, the Duchess and the Countess of Bandon hesitated about stepping into a carriage, the horses being restive. Fitzgerald unceremoniously bounded in from behind, saying, 'Hurry up girls, the lunch will be cold.' On taking leave of King Edward on another day, Fitzgerald consolingly said, 'I'll see you before long again, as I'm going to London in October.' Both the King and the Queen were delighted with Fitzgerald.[42]

Another popular story from the King's visit relates to how Fitzgerald earned the nickname 'Ate the Meat'. According to family legend, during the luncheon in Shrubbery House, Fitzgerald observed Queen Alexandra 'picking' at her food and gently admonished her to 'at least eat the meat, Ma'am, eat the meat!'[43] In an age when social etiquette was rigourously enforced, Fitzgerald's ability to communicate with both royalty and commoner in such a down-to-earth manner helped instil an air of positivity about the 1902/3 Exhibitions, both in Cork and further afield.

Fitzgerald was born in 1846, the son of Daniel Fitzgerald, of Gurtsmaurane, Treleary, Co. Cork. He began his working career as a carpenter before establishing a successful building business in Cork City. Municipal contracts formed the bulk of his construction business, earning him another nickname 'Up with the Shaft'.[44] He married Johannah Anne O'Donoghue in 1872 and they would have eight children together. After entering public life in the 1870s he held the positions of Alderman and Justice of the Peace before being elected Lord Mayor for three successive years from 1901 to 1903; Fitzgerald took the anti-Parnell side in the Irish Parliamentary Party's split.[45] The highlight of his public service was the 1902/3 Exhibition project, turning him from a relatively unknown politician from the edge of the British Empire into, for a while at least, a figure frequently featured in the British and international press. Of course, there was a political dividend for him due to his involvement in Cork's third and fourth Exhibitions: he had the city's largest public park named in his honour; he was awarded a Baronetcy from King Edward in recognition of his work; and also the Diploma and Insignia of a Commoner of the Order of Sacred Treasure was conferred on him by the Emperor of Japan for hosting a visit from the Japanese Navy to Cork in August 1902 (8.9). One English newspaper called him the 'Carpenter-Baronet', while another reported that he may have 'burned his boats' with many nationalists on accepting this honour, but the reporter felt his popularity in the city should ensure his political survival and even make him a future leader of the nationalists in Cork City.[46]

However, in the decade after the Exhibition, local and national politics came to be dominated by John Redmond's Irish Party, leaving Fitzgerald as an outsider, forced to continually defend his baronetcy. A Cork Corporation meeting held in March 1906 to decide the make-up of several local committees descended into a melee between various nationalist factions. Fitzgerald accused some of his fellow members of 'allying themselves with the Unionists'.[47] He continued by stating that 'he himself never had looked for a title' but that it

had come along in the 'ordinary way', and any status and privilege
it gave him in the city or county, 'his influence would always be
at the disposal of anyone of the people'.[48] By 1910, his perceived
closeness to the British establishment may have hindered his
political ambitions and he failed to win a seat as an Independent
Nationalist in that year's General Election. He would continue to
serve the people of Cork City well into the 1920s, sitting on various
boards and committees. He passed away in relative obscurity at his
home in Ovens, Co. Cork, on 22 June 1927, aged 81.

Fitzgerald was aided in the organization of the Exhibition by
people as enthusiastic and willing as him to give so much of their
personal time to the project. These included the hardworking
Henry Cutler, the Exhibition's chief architect and designer, as
well as Richard A. Atkins, its Honorary Secretary (5.7a, 5.7b).
Apart from Fitzgerald, Atkins had one of the hardest positions to
fill. An executive and ten sub-committees generated a mountain
of paperwork that all went through Atkins's office. All foreign
and national correspondence dealing with exhibits, buildings,
advertising and press relations were also handled by Atkins and
his staff. Like all good Victorian bureaucratic operations, the 1902
Exhibition was a triumph of exacting standards and can-do attitude.
Atkins would only fulfil this role in 1902 and stepped down before

Mr. Arthur Hill.

the beginning of the new season, no doubt exhausted by his exertions. M.D. Daly, JP, and W.B. Harrington acted as the Exhibition's honorary treasurers, while Mr Maurice Healy was Exhibition solicitor. It must also be remembered that all the Exhibition's important position holders worked pro bono.

Location, Location, Location

Once the committees and funding structure were put in place, the next issues to concern the organizers were location and layout. Initially it was proposed that the Exhibition would take place on the site of the Cornmarket on Anglesea Street, located behind the municipal buildings. This had served as the site for the previous Exhibitions in the city (5.9a & b). However, by May 1901, the local newspapers had begun to debate the issue. In an editorial entitled 'Exhibition – Second Thoughts', the *Cork Daily Herald* expressed concern that the 'infant project has so outgrown itself that the cradle prepared for its reception is no longer capable of accommodating its dimensions, and that its appetite has so

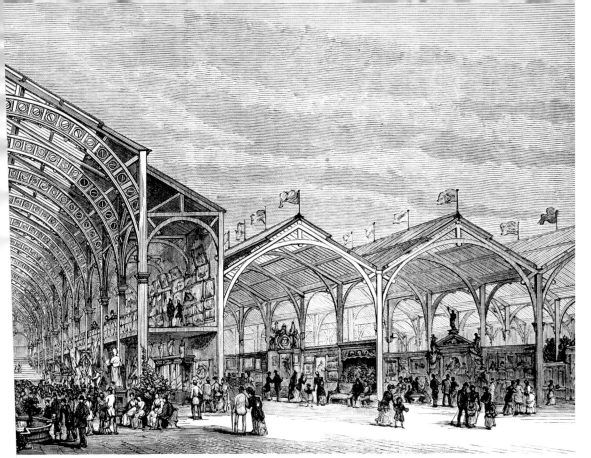

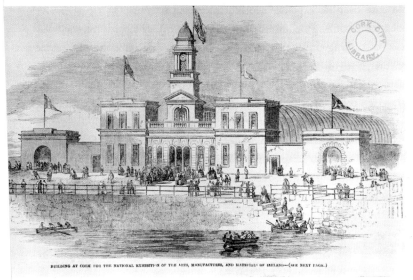

BUILDING AT CORK FOR THE NATIONAL EXHIBITION OF THE ARTS, MANUFACTURES, AND MATERIALS OF IRELAND—(SEE NEXT PAGE.)

5.9a & b:
The Cornmarket on Albert (now MacSwiney) Quay.
This was the site chosen for Cork's 1852 and 1883 Exhibitions. It was ideal for the modest events as it required little in the way of construction work to turn it into a useable space. By 1902, the site could not accommodate the outdoor amusements and entertainments that were planned for the city's third exhibition. The cutaway image (top) shows the 1883 exhibition halls with the Corn Exchange building removed. (© CPM)

MARDYKE WALK.CORK ___.W

5.10:

The Mardyke at the Beginning of the Twentieth Century, looking East.

The Mardyke proved a picturesque location for the 1902/3 Exhibitions. The creation of Fitzgerald Park after the exhibitions helped to cement it as a popular leisure location for the people of Cork, a destination it had held since the early eighteenth century. (© CPM)

Echo, he outlined why the Mardyke fulfilled the four main criteria for a successful location: sufficient and suitable space, accessibility, agreeable surroundings and convenient approaches.[59] It would seem that no sooner had the Mardyke been identified as a potential location than it was unanimously supported. It was finally endorsed as the site of the 1902 Cork International Exhibition at the meeting of the Executive Committee on 27 June 1901, just ten months before the proposed opening.

With hindsight, it is hard to see an alternative to the Mardyke. It covered an area from the present-day Cricket Club through to the end of the Western Road, where the UCC Mardyke Arena is now situated, stretching about three-quarters of a mile (1.2km) from east to west, and covering approximately forty-four acres. The land in this area was privately owned but landlords readily consented to lease their land to the Executive Committee. These owners were: the Cork County Cricket Club; the Sunday's Well Boating and Tennis Club; Mr Cornelius Desmond, who owned Shubbery House and adjacent land (now Cork Public Museum and Fitzgerald Park); and Captain Jennings, who owned the area that presently makes up the Mardyke Arena. The picturesque nature of the Mardyke was one that was keenly commented on by observers and rightly emphasized in the official Exhibition guide: 'Nature seemed to lavish in her endowment of the site which admirably adapted itself for the purpose of an Exhibition, and which for beauty, variety, and natural loveliness would be difficult to equal and impossible to excel.'[60]

When you contrast the Mardyke with the cramped urban setting of the Cornmarket (now the site of the City Hall Annex), one can immediately sense that the 1902 Exhibition was going to be a different kind of event to Cork's previous expositions. The Cornmarket area in 1901 also included a hay market, a disinfecting chamber and the city morgue. These were not the impressions (or smells) that visitors to the Exhibition and the city should be greeted with. It had became apparent to all involved that the Exhibition project had outgrown the constraints of 1852 and 1883 but in allowing it to do so, the committees had placed themselves under an enormous amount of pressure to fill the suburban site with the right mix of industrial, educational and technical exhibits along with amusements, entertainments and other popular amenities.

The 1903 Season: 'A Daring Departure from Precedent'

We extend a hearty welcome to all visitors to our Greater Cork International Exhibition, and crave their earnest attention for a few moments while we refer to the cause which led up to our daring departure from precedent by promoting a huge exposition two years in succession in the same city.
– Opening sentence of the *1903 Official Guide*

The pressure behind the 1902 preparations had dissipated by the time Fitzgerald made the announcement, several weeks before the scheduled end of the season, that the Exhibition would re-open in 1903.[61] There was an

5.11: left: George Noble Plunkett (1851–1948), Honorary Secretary in 1903.
Plunkett was created a Papal Count in 1884 by Leo XIII. He became curator of the National Museum from 1907 until 1916. His son, Joseph was a senior figure in the IRB and signatory of the Proclamation of Independence, and was subsequently executed for his part in the 1916 Rising. His own politics became far more radical after his son's death. Count Plunkett would become an ardent nationalist and republican, holding positions in the First Dáil and taking the anti-treaty side during the civil war. He was also a distant relative of Sir Horace Plunkett. (© CPM)

5.12: right: William Herlihy (1877–1932), Assistant Secretary in 1903.
Herlihy was a Limerick native and aged just 27 years of age. He was a journalist by trade and was a junior member on the staff of the 1902 exhibition. He went on to become Chief Reporter of the *Cork Examiner*, until his death. (© CPM)

was placed in the national press. The Executive Committe sought a person 'who shall devote his entire time to the business management of this Exhibition', justifying the fee of £1,000.[71] It was a testimony to the amount of documentation handled by Atkins, that his position was filled by two men: Count George Plunkett and an assistant, William N. Herlihy (5.11, 5.12).[72] New 'Bee-Keeping' and 'Poultry' committees were added to the organizational structure, bringing the total number of sub-committees involved to twelve. The Women's Section marginally increased its organizing membership from 270 to 294 in line with its increased allocation of exhibition space during 1903. The decision to rename the second season the *Greater Cork International Exhibition* indicates the self-belief the promoters possessed and what the *Cork Constitution* identified as the 'riper experience' they would bring to its administration. The paper went on to say:[73]

> This is our fourth Exhibition, and the merest glance at its amazing extent will be sufficient to convince the most casual visitor

that the prefixing of the word 'Greater' to its title is no mere flourish of phraseology.[74]

Conclusion

Before the Exhibition opened its gates to the public on 1 May 1902, it was already clear to those involved that the city had achieved something special. The 1852 and 1883 Exhibitions had been heavily influenced by the dour and predominately technical remit of the 1851 Great Exhibition, but the present Cork Expositions broke new ground in Ireland as a whole. These were the first Irish exhibitions to bring modern influences from America and France, outgrowing the constraints of the 'one-building' model favoured by former Irish organisers. Over the coming chapters we will see how commercial exhibits and technical demonstrations housed in multiple halls and pavilions were situated alongside the latest amusements and contemporary entertainments. Artistic, musical, sporting and other cultural displays existed harmoniously next to manufacturing and industrial products and machines. The men and women who spearheaded improvements in Cork's nineteenth-century education, industry, infrastructure and economy were also pivotal to making the exhibitions a reality.

Notes

1   For a great overview of financing International Exhibitions and the different funding methods employed by British, French and American organizers, see P. Greenhalgh, *Fair World – A History of World's Fairs and Expositions*(Winterbourne: Papadakis, 2011), pp.51–73.

2   See K. Finley, *The Biggest Show in Town* (Dublin: NonSuch, 2007). Finlay includes the complete financial accounts of the Exhibition from 1903 until 1909. He is also able to quote statements from contractors involved in the project detailing the amount of men and material they used. We would have loved to

have such secrets revealed to us during our research of the 1902/3 Exhibition.

3   The 1902 statement is found in both the *Cork Examiner* and *Constitution* on 14 November 1902. The 1903 statement was in the same newspapers published on 1 July 1904.

4   See Greenhalgh, *Fair World*, p.55.

5   H.C. Hartnell, *Illustrated Guide to the Cork International Exhibition 1883* (Cork: Guys, 1883), p.59. It must be noted however that for the 1852 Exhibition in Cork, prominent local citizens, Sir Thomas Deane, renowned architect and patron of the arts, and Colonel William Beamish, brewer, both promised to cover any costs incurred during the event.

Luckily, Ireland's first national exhibition only lost twelve pounds (€800).

6   *Cork Constitution,* 2 November 1903.

7   *Cork Examiner,* 14 August 1901.

8   W.K. Sullivan, J. Brenan, and R. Day, *Cork Industrial Exhibition 1883, Report of Executive Committee, Awards of Jurors and Statement of Accounts* (Cork: Purcell & Co., 1886), p.446.

9   The contemporary newspapers put the approximate figure of £5,000 on the DATI donation but a report published after the Exhibition puts this figure at £4,000. According to the report the DATI contributed £2,500 to the general exhibition fund itself while also paying £1,500 for renting 30,000ft² in the Industrial Hall. Whatever the actual amount, the DATI's contribution far exceeded any other single donation by an individual or company.

10   *Cork Examiner,* 11 May 1901.

11   This is the figure that Lord Mayor Fitzgerald gave in a speech at a public meeting on 5 November 1902 in City Hall. This meeting was called to garner support and ideas for the upcoming 1903 season. See *Cork Examiner,* 5 November 1902.

12   Though the Executive Committee would recoup their money at the end of the Exhibition, it remains unclear where the balance of the upfront money for construction came from.

13   *Cork Daily Herald,* 20 April 1901.

14   *Belfast Newsletter,* 4 June 1901.

15   *Saturday Herald (Dublin),* 29 June 1901. During the Fenian rising of 1867 he led the raid on Kilmallock Barracks. Having spent time in America, where he was active in the Fenian cause, he returned during the land war and was involved in the conspiracy to blow up prominent buildings in England. He was arrested at Birkenhead in 1884 for having in his possession a number of highly sophisticated, American-made grenades. E.G. Jenkinson, a British Home Office official, who through his network of agents and double agents knew what was about to be attempted, wrote:

The bombs are of first rate workmanship … Daly intended to go up to London and throw one of these bombs into a nest of cabinet Ministers … from the gallery of the House of Commons. He was quite prepared to sacrifice his own life …

John Daly was sentenced to life imprisonment, but was released from gaol in 1896. He was very popular and was Mayor of Limerick from 1899 to 1901. He died, perhaps appropriately, in 1916. His nephew Edward Daly was the youngest man executed for his part in the 1916 Rising. Edward's sister Kathleen married Thomas Clarke, signatory of the 1916 Republican Proclamation. He was also executed after the rising.

16   *The London Times, The Daily Telegraph, The Munster News, The Daily Express, The Birmingham Gazette,* and *Cork Examiner* all carried reports or editorials condemning Daly's letter and his attitude towards the Exhibition. All these newspaper reports date from between the 17–19 September 1901.

17   *The Birmingham Gazette,* 18 September 1901.

18   *The Munster News,* 19 September 1901.

19   *Cork Examiner,* 8 March 1902.

20   *The Sheffield Daily Telegraph,* 11 January 1902.

21   Ibid.

22   During the course of electioneering, many derogatory remarks were made, insinuating Fitzgerald only proposed the Exhibition to further his own political career. The tragic deaths of two workers and the injuring of two others on the exhibition grounds in December 1901 were also unfairly used as political fodder to attack Fitzgerald. Both he and the

Exhibitions' builder, William O'Connell, were forced to answer the false accusations from Augustine Roche and the UIL that they had left the families uncompensated over Christmas. This caused a backlash against Roche and the UIL, forcing them to row back on their apparent anti-exhibition and anti-Fitzgerald stance.

23 Editorial, *The Irish People*, 23 May 1901.

24 Ibid., 1 June 1901.

25 See Finlay, *The Biggest Show in Town*, pp.11–20.

26 The Fourth Earl of Bandon, James Francis Bernard, died in May 1924. He became a target of the IRA in West Cork because of his position as Lieutenant of the County and City of Cork. In June 1921 during the War of Independence, his residence, Castle Bernard near Bandon, was burned to the ground and he and three others who were justices of the peace in the area were kidnapped and held hostage. It was made known to the British authorities that all four would be killed if any IRA prisoners were hanged or shot. To quote Tom Barry, commander of the Third (West) Cork Brigade Flying Column, 'They were held until the peace talks had made it obvious that a truce was imminent when Sealy King, Fitzpatrick and Gillman were released but Lord Bandon was held our prisoner until after the Truce became operative.' The War of Independence ended in July 1921. His cousin Percy, who served with distinction as acting Air Vice-Marshall in South East Asia and Burma during World War II, succeeded as the Fifth Earl of Bandon.

27 Five of these men would re-fill their positions in 1903 but only nine vice-presidents were appointed for the second season. A full list of all organizing committees and vice-presidents can be found in Appendix 2.

28 He would also be one of the four landlord representatives during the 1903 Land Conference and would later serve in the Seanad from 1922–27.

29 See Hartnell, *Illustrated Guide to the Cork International Exhibition 1883*, p.26 for 1852 committee details and p.57 for 1883 details.

30 Anon., *Official Catalogue, Cork International Exhibition 1902* (Cork: Guys, 1902), pp.21–4; Anon., *The Official Catalogue and Guide, Greater Cork International Exhibition 1903* (Cork: Guys, 1903), pp.1–5. A full list of sub-committees and their members can be found in Appendix 2. There were twelve sub-committees formed in 1903, including the extra Poultry and Bee committees.

31 This committee contained John Paul Dalton, who would later become curator of Cork's first museum.

32 See Anon., *Official Catalogue, Cork International Exhibition 1902*, pp.21–7. There was a 24-woman committee involved in needlework exhibits at the 1883 Cork Exhibition.

33 See Anon., *Official Catalogue and Guide, Greater Cork International Exhibition 1903*, pp.1–5. The Women's Section would assume a larger role in the 1903 Greater Cork Exhibition, resulting in their general and Executive committee increasing to 225 and 79 respectively. The men's Executive committee would shrink slightly (about 20 per cent).

34 See Hartnell, *Illustrated Guide to the Cork International Exhibition 1883*, p.57.

35 *Cork Daily Herald,* 16 March 1901.

36 Arnott was elected Mayor of Cork three times from 1859–61 and MP for Kinsale from 1859–63. He was awarded his baronetcy in 1896. Surprisingly, neither his Dublin department store nor his breweries exhibited at the 1902/3 Exhibitions.

37 Henry O'Shea was a member of the Irish Parliamentary Party and Lord Mayor of Cork

on five occasions (briefly in 1911, 1912–15). He was a master baker and owned premises on South Main Street and Patrick's Street.

38 Henry Shanahan followed his father into the butter industry, and both men established a butter factory that introduced a new system of butter making and packing into Ireland. He was the Managing Director of the Irish Creameries and Exporters Association, a Trustee of the Cork Savings Bank and a member and chairman of the Cork Harbour Board.

39 Augustine Roche was a member of the IPP and MP for Cork from 1905 until 1910, and 1911 until his death in 1915. He was a wine merchant with premises on King Street (now MacCurtain Street), was Mayor of Cork in 1893 and 1894 and would succeed Edward Fitzgerald as Lord Mayor in 1904.

40 *All-Ireland Review*, 2, 42 (21 Dec 1901), p.349.

41 See Anon., *Official Catalogue and Guide, Greater Cork International Exhibition 1903*, p.7.

42 *The Evening Telegraph,* 24 August 1903.

43 P. Poland, *For Whom the Bells Tolled*, (Stroud: History Press Ltd, 2010), p.333.

44 Ibid., 'Up with the shaft' refers to the practice of paying the final instalment of any public contract once the chimney stack was erected.

45 Ibid.

46 *The Evening Telegraph*, 12 and 24 August 1902.

47 *The Aberdeen Daily Journal,* 7 March 1906.

48 Ibid.

49 *Cork Daily Herald*, 27 May 1901.

50 Ibid.

51 *Belfast Evening Telegraph*, 31 May 1901.

52 *Cork Daily Herald*, 25 May 1901.

53 Ibid., 10 May 1901.

54 Ibid., 25 May 1901.

55 Ibid., 29 May 1901.

56 *Cork Examiner*, 28–9 May 1901.

57 The Town Hall issue re-surfaced after the closing of the 1903 season when the Executive Committee offered to give the roof of the Concert Hall to Cork Corporation to use in building any new Town Hall, but this offer, though accepted, failed to come to fruition. See *Cork Examiner*, 18 April 1904.

58 Ibid., 25 June 1901.

59 *Evening Echo*, 25 June 1901.

60 Anon., *Official Guide, Cork International Exhibition 1902* (Cork: Guys, 1902), p.8.

61 *Cork Constitution*, 17 October 1902.

62 Canadian National Archives, *Report of the Minister of Agriculture for the Dominion of Canada for the Year Ended October 1902, Sessional Paper No. 15*, p.261. Fitzgerald mentions this two-month delay in a speech given in support of re-staging the Exhibition in 1903, quoted in *Cork Constitution,* 5 November 1902.

63 *Cork Constitution,* 17 October 1902.

64 Quoted from a circular that was distributed to 1902 exhibitors encouraging them to come onboard for the new season. See *Cork Examiner,* 12 December 1902.

65 *Freeman's Journal,* 1 December 1902.

66 See J.E. Findling and K.D. Pelle (eds), *Encyclopaedia of World's Fairs and Expositions* (North Carolina: McFarland & Company, 2008). Between 1851 and 1904, there were twenty cities that held concurrent exhibitions, both international and national. These included: Melbourne (1866–67, 1880–81, 1888–89), Sydney (1879–80), Louisville (1883–84), Calcutta (1883–84), New Orleans (1884–85), Dunedin (1889–90), Hobart (1894–95), Charleston (1901–02) and Hanoi (1902–03). European cities are infrequently represented but do include Edinburgh (1861–62), Marseille (1883–84), Nice (1883–84) and London (1871–74).

67 Appendix 3 shows a rough breakdown of

expenditure and income for both years of the Exhibition. In fact the biggest expense in terms of preparing the site for 1903 was the purchase of Shrubbery House and adjacent land.

68 See Anon., *Official Catalogue and Guide, Greater Cork International Exhibition 1903,* p.7.

69 Ibid., p.27.

70 In a speech following the successful conclusion of the 1903 season, Fitzgerald would refer to some nameless members of the 1902 Exhibition that had 'run away' from the 1903 project. In many ways, he and his supporters felt vindicated for taking a risk on another year. See *Cork Examiner*, 23 July 1904.

71 *Cork Constitution,* 19 December 1902.

72 By August 1903, Plunkett assumed the title of 'Honorary Secretary' after deciding to complete his contractual duties free of charge.

73 See Editorial, *Cork Constitution*, 5 November 1902.

74 See Anon., *Official Catalogue and Guide, Greater Cork International Exhibition 1903,* p.10.

The Cork International Exhibition

6

The Architecture of the Cork International Exhibition

Tom Spalding

As will be clear by now, many features of the Cork Exposition owed a great deal to the practice in arranging exhibitions abroad and throughout the then-United Kingdom, and the design of the buildings is no exception. The influence of the earlier exhibitions in Chicago (1893) and Glasgow (1901) is particularly strong. The greatest novelty in examining the Cork buildings and structures is in how international influences were modified and adapted for local needs. However, before we begin an in-depth exploration of the buildings and site, it is worth pausing to discuss the issue of attribution.

In almost every press clipping and official publication relating to the event, the title of 'Honorary Architect' to the Exhibition is applied to Henry Cutler (5.7a), although there were other architects involved, namely Arthur Hill (5.8), J.F. McMullen and R.P. Gill. Henry Cutler was London-born, and was 41 at the time of the Cork show. A single man, he had moved from England in 1896 to take the job of Cork's City Engineer.[1] The competence of the previous engineer had been brought into question when the new city hall which he was supervising began to subside during construction. To ensure a highly skilled replacement, Cork Corporation set up a programme of competitive written examinations and interviews. The process was sufficiently novel to be followed weekly in the national trade press and the appointment of Cutler was generally welcomed. He was seen as an efficient and practical engineer and supervisor. He was not an architect but a civil engineer, and describes himself as such in his census return in 1901. However, engineers are not precluded in undertaking work that some would consider to be the realm of architects. Indeed, Cork's greatest City Engineer, Sir John Benson, was also one of its finest public architects. He designed churches, the halls for the Dublin Exhibition (1853)

6.1
Main Entrance Gates from the Mardyke.
The main gates stood approximately where the entrance to Fitzgerald Park is today. Two RIC men stand guard, a reminder of the strong police presence in Ireland at the time. The Cead Mile Failte banner (note the lack of fadas) was white on red. (© NLI)

and an extension to Fota House, as well as many more prosaic buildings.

In comparison with Benson, Cutler's architectural output in Cork is relatively small. Aside from his role in the Exhibition, he is associated with a development of three-storey 'Cottage' apartments, now called 'Corporation Buildings', in Dalton's Avenue (1901) and a Carnegie Library built in 1907 and burnt by British Forces in 1920. His strength seems to lie in his organizational capabilities, which were considerable. After the Exhibition closed at the end of its first season, his health broke down, but he returned the following year to supervise modifications and innovations in the second season. His efforts attracted the eye of the Belfast Corporation, who had seen his work first-hand at the opening in 1902, and he left Cork for Belfast at the end of 1903, remaining there for the rest of his life. His partner in the design of the Exhibition, Arthur Hill, was his elder, and unlike Cutler, had a distinguished architectural career in Munster.

Hill was a scion of Cork's longest-running architectural dynasty. The family were involved in the building industry in Cork from the late eighteenth century, until the death of Arthur's son, Henry, in 1951. Arthur Hill studied civil engineering in University College Cork, later training as an architect in London. He, like Cutler, was a member of the Institution of Civil Engineers, but saw himself primarily as an architect.[2] By the time of the Exhibition, the 55-year-old Hill had built many buildings with which Corkonians will be familiar today, including the Metropole Hotel, the Crawford Art Gallery (then the School of Art) and the Hibernian Buildings worker's housing scheme. In addition he was a Lecturer in Architecture at University College Cork.

As we will see in Chapter 9, Hill's primary acknowledgement in the Exhibition literature is as organizer of the Art Exhibit, but he was also credited with the design of the President's and Lord Mayor's Pavilion (the only permanent structure on the site), the Central Bandstand and the Canadian Pavilion. Given their close working relationship, Henry Cutler's relative lack of architectural expertise and the nature of the designed buildings, the suspicion that Hill, in fact, was the main influence on the design is hard to avoid. Cutler appears to have been rigorous in spreading the message that he was the primary architect, and this no doubt helped his move to Belfast, a larger and more prosperous place. However, he did not build any such exuberant buildings after he left Cork.[3]

It is perhaps in the layout of the site and the organization of the various 'services' (gas, electricity, telephone, water and fire safety) that we can best detect Cutler's handiwork. The location was felicitous, and in reports of the Exhibition, it often takes precedence over descriptions of the buildings themselves.[4] Landscaped grounds were a typical feature of international expositions at this time and organizers would go to great lengths to set their buildings in naturalistic landscapes. In Chicago, miles of artificial waterways were dug, under the direction of Frederick L. Olmsted, the designer of New York's Central Park. Cork was fortunate in that it did not have to go to much effort to enhance the situation of the buildings. As we saw in the last chapter, several reports drew attention to the happy juxtaposition of the 'long white buildings, with their red turrets, open porticos, and roofs of shimmering green glass, set in the midst of abundant foliage'[5] whilst another scribe wrote of the 'pleasant contrast' between the white buildings and 'the cool green of the surroundings'.[6] Most visitors would arrive by walking (at least some of the way) down the Mardyke Walk, which had been a popular amenity with city-dwellers for 200 years. The Walk at the time was described by some Belfast visitors as 'bordered on each side by noble elms, which interlace overhead, [*forming*] a fitting approach to the grounds … over which nature has scattered her choicest gifts with a prodigal hand' (5.10).[7]

The ground upon which the Exhibition was built was marked 'liable to flooding' on the Ordnance Survey map, surveyed in 1900, and perhaps for this reason there were only two structures on the site prior to this. One was a mid-nineteenth-century house dubbed 'The Shrubbery' and the second was a small corrugated-iron cricket pavilion.[8] However, as discussed in the previous chapter, in its favour were its proximity to the city centre, its adjacency to the Lee River and steeply rising wooded hills to the north and, critically, a direct connection with Cork's electric tram system.

The site was laid out rationally (6.2, 6.4). At the west end, furthest from the city and occupying approximately a third of the site, were the exhibits relating to agriculture. This part of the Exhibition emphasized nature, albeit of the cultivated variety, with domestic and farm buildings, exhibition plots of fruit and vegetables and gardens for schools. To the east was an area primarily devoted to sport (e.g. cricket, cycling and water sports) and entertainment (a later chapter will deal with these activities in detail). In this section, our main focus will be the central area of the grounds, laid out more formally and dedicated, in the main, to industry and modern life.[9] In this area the largest

CORK INTERNATIONAL EXHIBITION.
1902.
SITE PLAN

SUNDAY'S WELL

R I

MU

IND

FIRE STATION

LADIES LAVATORY

BLAST FURNACE CARR

TEMPERANCE RESTAURANT

TURKISH BAZAAR

CANADA

CIGARS MFG.

BAND STAND

LIGHT HOUSE

TEA HOUSE

SAUSAGES

TURKY TUFFY HOUSE

WORKING DAIRY

BARS

AQUARIUM

DEMONSTRATION PLOTS

FRUIT DRYING

BYRE

CUNDY GARDEN SHOP

HAY HOUSE

CREAMERY

SCHOOL GARDEN

ROSE GARDEN

RHUBARB

FRUIT GARDEN

GOVERNMENT AGRICULTURAL EXHIBITS

EXPERIMENT GARDEN

COW SHELTER

SHED

SWITCHBACK RAILWAY

BUNGALOW

SHOOTING GALLERY

HAY SHED

GREEN HOUSE

ART GALLERY

POULTRY

SHEEP DIPPING

BEE HIVE

SKATING RINK

TICKET OFFICE

ENTRANCE

FORESTRY PAVILION

WELLINGTON BRIDGE

GEORGE THE IV BRIDGE

CORK & MUSKERRY LIGHT RAILWAY

Scale

GUY & Co. LTD. CORK.

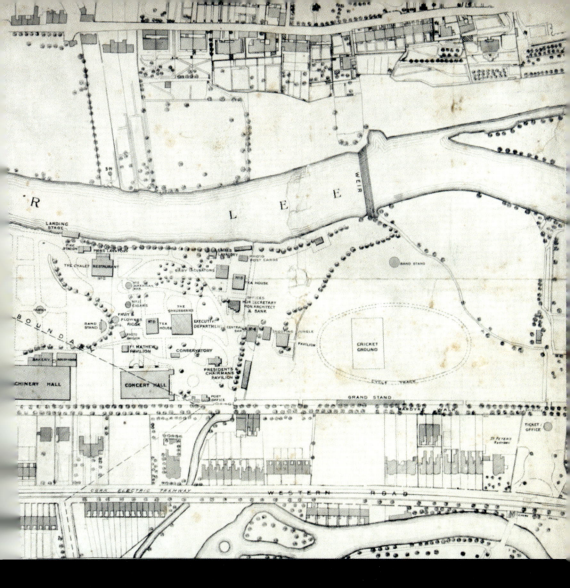

The Exhibition site covered 44 acres to the west of Cork city between the Lee and the Mardyke. As well as the exhibits, a variety of other structures for dining and drinking, sport and entertainment were built. The large, central building, the Industrial Hall covered c.150,000 ft². The Western Field to the left was the focus for the Amusements and farm demonstrations. (© CPM, Guys)

6.3
An Early Guys Impression of the Proposed Exhibition

It was intended to put the Switchback Railway (roller-coaster) on the present
Cricket pitch & and an Irish Village on the north bank, below Sunday's Well,
and connect it to the expo by a footbridge. © CPM

and most impressive buildings, containing the main exhibits, were situated. Whilst an open plaza between the main hall and the bandstand provided some focus for the central section of the exhibition grounds, the area to the west straggled over a number of acres with no obvious plan. The only access route from one end of the grounds to the other was cramped between the main hall and the Lee. All visitors wishing to go from one end to other had to pass along a couple of paths which turned rapidly into mud.[10] This design made the long vistas terminated by landmarks, or tall structures, so beloved of exhibition organizers in France and America, impossible in our case.

With this in mind, it is worth trying to put the exhibition buildings and layout in the context of other International Exhibitions. Whilst there had been many such events held across the western world since 1851, by the end of the nineteenth century something of a pattern had emerged about how one ought to arrange and design such an exhibition. Dedicated 'Halls' featuring the products and processes of industry or mechanization were a feature common to many events, and these had first been introduced at Paris in 1867. 'Pavilions' dedicated to individual nations, spheres of industry or commercial concerns were another. As far as Cork is concerned, however, the strongest immediate influence on the arrangement of the halls and exhibits was the show held in 1901 in Glasgow.

The Glasgow Exhibition had begun life three years earlier, with a competition to design the main exhibition buildings: the Grand Concert Hall, Machinery Hall and Industrial Hall (6.6). The Arts were to be catered for in the (permanent) Kelvingrove Art Gallery, the opening of which that year was a major part of the exposition.[11] The chosen site covered 100 acres to the north of the city, and was bisected by the river Kelvin. Competition entrants included Charles Rennie Mackintosh (then working at Honeyman & Keppie) but the winner was James Miller, a noted commercial and railway architect.[12] Miller's buildings were a confection of white-painted timber and plaster with red-, green- and gold-painted domes and roofs. *The Builder* described its design as 'Renaissance of a Spanish type … in one case taking the form of Italian Gothic and elsewhere the very latest German "arts and crafts" decoration.'[13] Miller's choice of style had to take into account the presence of the Kelvingrove Art Gallery, designed in 1892 in a broadly Spanish style. The main towers of this building are modelled on the great pilgrimage church of Santiago de Compostela, and this may well have influenced him. In addition,

SHOOTING RANGE

6.5 **View of the Site from Sunday's Well.**
This image was created before the exhibition was built, perhaps as part of the fundraising effort, but is substantially accurate. The bicycle velodrome is on the far left (presently Cork Cricket Club), the present Cork Public Museum building is the small house (marked 6). The Industrial & Concert Halls dominate the centre of the site, with the four domes of the Art Gallery behind. Amusements are concentrated on the right hand side of the image. (© CPM, Guys Ltd.)

the use of European Renaissance models for exhibition buildings had been a strong element in the Chicago exhibition (only the Transportation Hall, by Adler and Sullivan, broke from this style) and was widely imitated. For example, when the city of Charleston in South Carolina held their exhibition, which ran over the first six months of 1902, the overall style was that of the Spanish Baroque. In their case, the selection of this milieu was also a reflection of public enthusiasm for the United States' newly acquired Hispano-phone possessions in Cuba, Puerto Rico and the Philippines.[14]

Since its introduction at the Chicago show of 1893, the use of white for the exterior of exposition buildings had become *de rigueur* for International Exhibitions. Paris had mounted a gleaming white expo in 1900 and the use of this colour for these kinds of events continued well into the twentieth century.[15] The buildings in Charleston, for example were predominantly white,

6.6 Industrial Hall, Glasgow, 1901, James Miller. The 1901 Glasgow International Exhibition was in many ways a model for Cork's. The Industrial Hall in Glasgow was far larger, more ornate, and featured a tea-rooms in its great dome, which was surmounted by a large electrically-illuminated sculpture of 'Light'. But its general arrangement was very similar to ours. (© University of Glasgow Library)

and decorated with fibrous-plaster details. White was associated with progress, modernity, efficiency, health, moral purity and cleanliness. The generation of Modernist architects (Le Corbusier, Mies van de Rohe, Marcel Breuer et al.) were in their infancy or mere teenagers at the turn of the last century, and whilst they heartily rejected the style of buildings like these, they maintained a close belief of the relationship between the colour white and modernity, which persists to the present.

However, what interested some in the British architectural press most about the Glasgow buildings was not their style, but the materials and methods of construction. The seemingly solid walls were actually made of pre-cast plaster panels, reinforced with hemp and surrounded by wooden frames, c.5ft high x 3ft 6in wide (1.5m x 1m). Once the panels had been poured and set, they were fastened to a timber framework. It had been intended to build most of the frameworks out of steel, but insufficient supplies were available.[16] Once the pre-cast panels were in place, the gaps between them were grouted then skimmed with plaster and painted white.[17] The decorative details and flourishes (capitals, window surrounds, cornicing and so on) were made of 'Fibrous Plaster', reinforced with natural fibres and cement (this material is called 'staff' in the USA).

Members of the organizing committee of the Cork Exhibition (including Cutler) visited Scotland in June 1901, and were strongly impressed by the architecture of the Glasgow Exhibition.[18] There, they were exposed to a layout of several buildings set in the landscape, rather than the 'one big hall' concept used in previous Cork exhibitions. The team studied the exhibits and sideshows, and inspected the Irish Pavilion (6.7). This pavilion (or rather pavilions) was paid for by the British Government through the Irish Department of Agriculture and Technical Instruction (DATI), and designed by Thomas Manley Deane. The buildings were unashamedly picturesque constructions, more of an advertisement for would-be tourists than a reflection of life in rural Ireland. The exhibit consisted of a pair of large thatched bungalows, set in lawns and rose gardens, and was described as 'a very charming suggestion of an old Irish thatched country house'[19] and occupied a good location at the entrance to the section of the park which contained the various national pavilions.[20]

As we will see elsewhere in this book, the influence of the Glasgow festival upon Cork went beyond the eventual adoption of a layout based upon three

large public buildings; a Concert Hall, Machinery Hall and Industrial Hall. As we shall see in Chapter 8, the Cork committee 'borrowed' from Glasgow the idea of a 'Water Chute' and other amusements. It is clear that the Glasgow Exhibition also influenced other similar events in Great Britain. For example, the Wolverhampton Exhibition (held in 1902) also featured three main halls, a Canadian Pavilion, a water chute and other amusements suggesting that the general arrangements of exhibitions in these islands and in the United States had become almost standardized by this point. When Dublin came to hold its own international event in 1907, in what is now Herbert Park, they too followed the conventional formula of Three Halls and a Water Chute. In addition, the Dublin architects (William Kaye-Parry and George Murray Ross) adopted both the method of construction and a variant of the encrusted 'Renaissance wedding-cake' style from Chicago 1893 for their main buildings.

The Industrial Hall

The Industrial Hall (6.8, 6.9) was the largest exhibition building erected on the Cork site, and was the focus of most commemorative photographs and press comment. It was a single-storey building, 350ft (107m) wide and 418ft (127m) long, and covered an area of 147,000ft² (13,650 m²). Like the Glasgow structure of the same name, it had an internal frame of wood. However, rather than using plaster panels, the 'walls' had been made predominantly

6.7
Irish Pavilions, Glasgow, 1901, T.M. Deane. Ireland's exhibit at Glasgow was paid for by the Irish Department of Agriculture and Technical Instruction, and designed by Cork-born, TM Deane, best-known for his work on the Government Offices in Merrion Square. The 'cottages' were surrounded by lawns and roses and promoted Ireland as a rural idyll. It had a prime location at the entrance near this ornamental fountain which still stands, and the popular Russian Section. (© University of Glasgow Library)

6.8
Impression of the Industrial Hall at Night.
The façade, turrets and roofs of the Hall were covered with hundreds of incandescent light-bulbs, and the grounds lit by fairy lights with coloured celluloid globes as well as the latest in gas lighting. The idea came from Chicago via Glasgow, but the effect on visitors was mesmerising.
(© Tom Spalding)

from canvas stretched over the frame and painted white. To create the illusion of masonry, 'string courses' of stone were painted on the 'walls'. Decorative details, such as the window surrounds, were cast from fibrous plaster. It is possible that some of the plaster details in this building and others on the grounds were re-used from the Glasgow show, but it is more likely that they were made locally. It is known for certain that 'ex-Glasgow' decorations were fastened to another temporary building on the Western Road during the Exhibition.[21] This was the four-storey, 400-bed Exhibition Hotel constructed for the Glasgow hotelier, Mr Gordon, on a site to the west of the Erinville Hospital. The accommodation was 'arranged in a cubicle system' according to a local paper. This building (of which nothing remains) was 185ft x 130ft (56m x 40m), with a square tower in each corner, and topped by a 110ft (34m) dome (6.12).[22] It is also certain that even quite minor elements of the Glasgow expo, such as electrical cables, were transferred to Cork.[23] Perhaps this state of affairs was not uncommon. It was reported in 1902 that elements of Glasgow buildings were re-used at the Wolverhampton Expo.[24]

The general composition of the Industrial Hall was similar to that of the

equivalent Glasgow building (and for that matter, the one in Charleston).[25] All featured façades with central entrances beneath Classical porticos, and all had corner towers. In all three examples a dome soared above the entrance. The domes and roofs in Cork were painted red, as were many in Glasgow. The American and Scottish structures had arcades of round-headed windows running across their front elevations. This is reprised, in a simplified manner, in Cork, as a row of half-moon-shaped openings with decorative frames, and in general the decoration of the building is restrained. This may perhaps have been due to budget constraints (the quote to build it was £6,366,[26] whereas at Glasgow, the Russian Pavilions alone cost £30,000),[27] the relatively short timescale in which the project was brought to fruition (only fifteen months!), or the taste of the architects. The British architectural journal *The Builder* was certainly aware of the restrictions in place on the project, but was complimentary nonetheless.[28] The portico was open to the sky, and had Corinthian pilasters sculpted and cast by a Cork building firm, John Hegarty & Co, whom we will come across again. In other details, such as the corner towers and cupola, the building suggested Italian, or even Moorish,

6.9
Industrial Hall and Fr Mathew Fountain, from south-east, 1902, H Cutler & A Hill.
This image shows the Industrial Hall. The roofs were brick red, and a greenish glass was used for the skylights. The walls were timber and fabric, on a wooden frame. The flared roof profiles are very typical of Edwardian architecture. Exotic plants (palms, agave, cordyline & monkey puzzle) were set in the manicured lawns. (© NLI)

BREAKFAST 1/6.
Served from 7 to 10.30.

Quaker Oats and Cream.

Fried Fillets of Fish.
Findon Haddock.   Fresh Herring.

Grilled Bacon and Fried Eggs.
Scrambled Eggs on Toast.
Ham and Eggs.

Homemade Sausages.
Liver and Bacon.   Rump Steak.
Mutton Chop.

Tea.   Coffee.   Cocoa.

LUNCHEON 1/6.
3 Courses.

Consommé.   Potato Soup.
Scotch Broth.

Boiled Halibut.

Stewed Steak.   Steak Pie.
Roast Beef.
Roast Mutton.

Boiled Potatoes.   Mashed Potatoes.
Vegetables.

Rice Pudding.   Sago Pudding.
Bread and Butter Pudding.
Stewed Fruit.

Biscuits and Cheese.

6.10: Menu, Gordon's Exhibition Hotel
For 1s 6d (about £8) diners could enjoy a
substantial breakfast or three-course lunch.
Baths were 1s, cold baths. 9d.
(Courtesy Irish Distillers Limited Archive)

6.11: Cup and Saucer (below)
This delicate ware celebrates the King's
coronation (1902) are marked 'Gordon's Hotel,
Cork' and were used as part of its service.
(Courtesy S. Fenton)

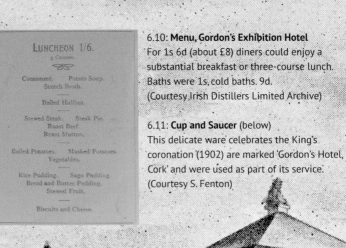

6.12: **Gordon's Exhibition Hotel, Cork,**
Neil Campbell Duff, 1902
This huge iron and wood structure included
sleeping accommodation for 800 in 400
twin rooms, each 10' x 8' (3 x 2.4m), arranged
around a series of five airshafts. The designer
had previously worked for Thomas Gordon
on the Glasgow Exhibition Hotel in 1900
and was also involved in the designing early
cinemas. The building was claimed to be the
only mechanically ventilated hotel in Ireland.
Charles McCarthy provided plumbing services
and the site.
(Courtesy Irish Distillers Limited Archive)

6.13.
Beamish & Crawford
Stables, Bishop St, 1902,
Houston & Houston.
This building, under
construction at the same
time as the Expo, may
have influenced the
overall composition of
the Industrial Hall, as well
as introducing 'bell-cast'
shaped roofs to Cork.
(© Tom Spalding)

influences. It was also clearly influenced by the design of the Canadian Pavilion in Glasgow. The flared 'bell-cast' roofs over the towers and side entrances at the end of the building, the arcade of ground-floor windows, already alluded to, and the horizontal emphasis of the 'block-work' were all *à la mode*. A recently-completed building in Cork, the stables on Bishop St for the Beamish and Crawford brewery, was probably the first to feature the 'bell-cast' roof profile in the city, and may have been an influence on Cutler and Hill (6.13). These buildings were designed by a London firm, Houston and Houston.[29]

The reaction of the British and Irish newspapers was mixed. Some held that the architecture was 'very pleasing'[30] and 'ample and ornate … in architectural style a mixture of the Orient, Switzerland and ancient Ireland.'[31] Others confined their views to expressions of utility: 'capacious, well-appointed'.[32] Others again express a certain ennui – the style was 'Twentieth Century Exhibition period,'[33] sniffed *The Engineer*, whilst the *Northern Whig's* correspondent, a veteran of the Paris and Glasgow Exhibitions, opined that; 'the buildings are after the same [i.e. the usual] design', whilst the water-chute was 'an inevitable element'.[34]

The roof of the Industrial Hall and the other main buildings were corrugated iron with greyish-green plate glass at the apex. The underside of the iron was painted Sky Blue, and the outside and domes, Tile Red.[35] It is worth noting that Sir John Benson, when he designed the exhibition hall for the 1853 Dublin event, had specified a building with a timber frame, painted blue inside.[36]

The Grand Concert Hall, Main Gates and Central Bandstand

After the Industrial Hall, the building that attracted the most interest, and was the focus for many of the public events associated with the Exposition, was the Concert Hall (6.14). It would have been the first building visitors at the main gate would have come across. The hall sat 2,000 people and was 150ft long by 87ft wide (46m x 26.5m), with a ceiling height of 50ft (15m). The design was described as 'bold and striking' by one journal, with 'four imposing towers of 60ft (18m)'. The building had a slight Italian influence, but when it is compared to its contemporary in Wolverhampton, which was

designed by Walker and Ramsay of Glasgow to look like an Indian fort, it appears restrained in the extreme.[37] Aptly, this entertainment building was built like, and decorated in the fashion of, a robust stage-set. Constructed by the same method as the Industrial Hall, the exterior of this building was also predominantly white, but much of the fabric on the upper sections of each façade was painted in imitation of marble. The Corinthian columns supporting the front porch were also likewise painted. It is in this building where the apparent permanence and solidity of the buildings comes most starkly into conflict with their temporary existence and their flimsy nature. An example of this clash occurred when concert-goers complained of being able to hear voices and noises from outside during the performance, which they would expect not to hear in a 'real' concert hall.[38]

Somewhat more concrete was the main entrance to the Exhibition from Mardyke Walk (6.1). The piers were tall and vaguely reminiscent of the minarets of Islamic Art. Similar motifs were to be found on the Central Bandstand and seem to be influenced by the decorative spires which one can see in photographs of the Chicago exhibition.[39] The gates themselves were

6.14
The Concert Hall, from inside the Main Entrance. The Concert Hall could seat 2,000 as well as large choir and orchestra and a wonderful organ. Like the Industrial Hall, the walls were fabric covered, this time with painted trompe l'œil marble to reflect the vaguely Italianate design. The opening and closing ceremonies were held here. To the left are the entrance turnstiles and one of the early pre-fabs demonstrated at the show. In 1903, the forecourt of the Hall was used to display the Gordon Bennett racing cars. (© NLI)

designed and made by Benjamin Watson and attracted favourable comment. Watson was a Yorkshireman who had trained in the Arts and Crafts tradition before settling in Cork in 1864.[40] He described himself as an 'Art Metal Worker' and predominantly worked in wrought iron, making gates, railings and church fittings. When he arrived in Cork, cast iron railings had largely displaced traditional wrought-iron work used in the city's Georgian and Regency architecture. Watson's work went a long way towards reviving the craft of blacksmithing in Cork at the turn of the last century. The exhibition gates were removed at the end of the show, but shortly afterward, the same firm erected the set which currently stand at the main entrance to the Fitzgerald Park.

As will be explained in a later chapter, music was a key element to the amusements which proved so popular in the Exhibition. There were a total of three bandstands across the grounds. Two of these were simple octagonal structures made of timber, covered by 'ogee'-shaped roofs with small pepper-pot-shaped domes at the top with simple details.[41] However, the Central Bandstand was something more unusual (6.15). Designed by Arthur Hill, the design was based on a quarter-sphere or shell, enclosing the musicians and projecting the sound. It was constructed of timber, lit electrically and painted white. It was sufficiently well-made to be retained for over a decade after the exhibition. Delicate Arab-inspired pinnacles stood to the sides of the stage, and the railings at the front of the bandstand incorporated a 'Brigit's Cross' motif, which could also be seen on the balcony of the Chalet Restaurant and on the other bandstands. This motif can also be found in decorative woodwork (such as bannister rails and screens) in contemporary high-end housing in Great Britain.[42]

The Pavilions

The idea of having separate exhibition buildings or 'pavilions' for individual countries or manufacturing companies, or to promote particular spheres of industry or points of view was first introduced in 1867 at the Paris International Exposition.[43] Whilst some late-nineteenth-century exhibitions included large numbers of different pavilions (Philadelphia is another example), many confined themselves to a few. In Cork there were pavilions dedicated to the Irish forestry industry, to Fr Mathew (the nineteenth-century temperance leader) and to Canada. In addition, a further pavilion was dedicated to the

President of the Exhibition Committee and the Lord Mayor. It was notable, as it was the only building intended from the outset to be permanent, and therefore presented the architect with an opportunity to make a lasting contribution. It cost the Exhibition Committee £350.[44]

Nothing is known about the Forestry pavilion, but the Fr Mathew pavilion attracted a fair degree of interest at the time (6.16). However, this was primarily due to the commemorative exhibits inside (the great man died in 1856). The structure was designed by a Corkman, James Finbarre McMullen, who came from a building family. He had a broad practice, primarily designing institutional buildings, but is best known today for his work on the Honan Chapel in University College Cork. This jewel-like building was built in the Hiberno–Romanesque style between 1914 and 1916. The Fr Mathew pavilion was a far simpler structure, wooden-framed and sheathed in painted canvas. Its chief interest was the ornamental neo-Classical door-case, with a strong French influence, but cast in fibrous plaster.

6.15
Main Bandstand, 1902, Arthur Hill.
A military or police band setting up on a blustery day. The shell-shaped wooden central bandstand was designed by Arthur Hill and survived for at least a decade after the exhibition. The 'minarets' add an oriental feel. It cost £150. A similar, shell-shaped, bandstand stood near the Industrial Hall at the Glasgow Expo in 1901. (© NLI)

Altogether grander was the Canadian pavilion (6.17). The 5,000ft² (460m²) structure cost £10,000 (about £1 million) to build and fit out, paid by the Canadian Department of Agriculture, supported by their Immigration Department. This was part of a dedicated programme operating since 1899 which had seen the 'Dominion' display its wares at Paris, Glasgow and London, as well as Cork and Wolverhampton and later, at Dublin (1907). The Canadians employed a full-time 'Commissioner for Exhibitions', one W.D. Scott of Ottawa, and running exhibitions had 'become almost a permanent branch of [*their*] department' of agriculture. The exhibits

From top;

6.16 Fr Mathew Pavilion, 1902, J.F. McMullen.
During the 1902 season this small building in a French Neo-Classical style housed a selection of memorabilia and relics of Fr Mathew, the Cork-based temperance and public health campaigner. In the expo's second year it was home to the 'teleautograph' an early fax-machine technology.
(© Cork City Libraries, Local Studies)

6.17 Canadian Pavilion, 1902, Arthur Hill.
No photographs of the completed Canadian Pavilion are known to exist, but it seems that this sketch is a fair reflection of it. The Canadians were one of two foreign governments to publicize their wares at Cork (left of image). In the expo's second season the delicate spires were truncated and the building was rechristened the 'Western Pavilion'. (© CPM)

6.18 Canadian Pavilion, Glasgow, 1901, R.J. Walker.
Like the Cork pavilion, the central entrance to this building was under a large arch with 'Canada' clearly displayed. Otherwise it doesn't greatly resemble 'our' Canadian exhibit, but it does seem to have influenced the roofs and other details of the Cork buildings. The architect, RJ Walker, also worked on the Wolverhampton Exhibition in 1902.
(© Glasgow University Library)

primarily served to illustrate the agricultural, mineral and sylvicultural richness of the colony, through which the Canadian government sought immigrants from Ireland to work in railway, logging and mining companies. In Cork the Canadians 'wished to show Canadian products and impress the people who are still emigrating in considerable number'.[45] Between 1900 and 1905, 130,000 people settled in Canada, and the following five years saw this increase to 280,000.[46] In Paris the North Americans' exhibits had been 'mixed up with other countries' and this was deemed unsatisfactory. Now, they decided 'a separate special Canadian pavilion [was] far more effective in drawing attention'.[47] The Canadian Exhibition Commission, represented in Cork by a Mr James Brodie,[48] supervised the project and details of the design were approved by Canadian officials.[49] The architecture was by Arthur Hill and was based on a gable-fronted hall with deep eaves, and seemed to owe a little to the Canadian Pavilion in Glasgow the previous year (6.18).[50] Four, vaguely oriental, towers pierced the roof, two at each end of the building. The main entrance on the north gable was decorated with a massive plaster arch, above which was the word 'Canada' in plain letters. The decoration on the building included giant wheat sheaves, but there are no remaining images of the entrance by which one can judge its effectiveness today.

When we examine the President's and Lord Mayor's Pavilion we are on surer ground, as the building stands to this day at the entrance to Fitzgerald's Park, and was restored in 2011 (6.19). For this building Hill looked for inspiration to English vernacular architecture. Architects working in the second half of the nineteenth century in the Arts and Crafts style, such as Philip Webb, William Letherby and Norman Shaw, had spearheaded a fresh appreciation of the architecture of the sixteenth and seventeenth centuries. In its revived form, it was characterized by the use of brick, multi-pane casement windows, asymmetrical compositions, 'pargeting' (decorative plasterwork), red tiled roofs and tall decorative chimneys. The latter had been revived in the 1890s. Hill's pavilion features all of these as well as a whimsical dove-cote to the rear. He introduced a few novel touches of his own: the Art Nouveau frieze which runs below the eaves, the use of concrete (instead of the more traditional brick) for the walls and the use of expanded metal grilles over the concrete to provide a base for the cement plaster.[51] The windows had small leaded lights and above the staircase were the city arms in stained glass. The Art Nouveau style seen in the frieze is characterized by trailing attenuated motifs, often with a vegetal

President's & Lord Mayor's
Pavilion, 1902, Arthur Hill.
The sole building left from
the exhibition has changed
substantially over time.
Originally the Art Nouveau
frieze and rendering were
unpainted. The multi-paned
windows, flowery curtains
and the little fence in the
porch have been removed.
The interior layout was also
altered. It was designed by
Arthur Hill in a picturesque
English style. During the
exposition it contained
exhibits from New Zealand
and served as a meeting
room afterwards. (© Tom
Spalding, with thanks to T.
Allen & D. Ó Riain-Raedel)

inspiration. Its source was France, and the Paris Expo of 1900 had done much to popularize it. In general however, British (and by extension, Irish) architects were suspicious of it.[52] Art Nouveau decoration is extremely rare in Cork, but its evergreen foliage and flowers (roses, lotuses and irises) are occasionally encountered in plasterwork, or more usually architectural hardware.[53]

The press response to the building was strongly positive. The pavilion was described as 'a pretty little structure in grey [*sic*] concrete with a red tiled roof and dormer windows'.[54] A visitor from a Sydney paper was enchanted by this 'little gem of a residence'.[55] It was sure to 'catch the eye of the visitor', said another journalist,[56] and it was the only building that the *Irish Builder* deigned to illustrate, using one of Hill's own photographs.[57] What particularly impressed the *Irish Builder's* correspondent was the furniture and fittings. The furniture throughout was sourced from Norman and Stacey, one of the premier suppliers in London. The furniture was 'designed in the quaint and graceful types of the "twentieth century" style' showing clearly 'the great advance made in this new phase of applique art'.[58] The walls were treated sympathetically with 'low-toned and harmonious' colours. Sadly no photographs of this interior appear to survive, nor do images of the interiors of the cafés or restaurants. Judging by contemporary images of Norman and Stacey's products, the work was likely to have been carried out in oak, and to owe a good deal to the elongated and elegant designs of C.F.A. Voysey or A.H. Mackmurdo. During the Exhibition, besides providing space for a private dining room, the Pavilion

was home to an exhibit from New Zealand, featuring samples of timber, as well as Maori wood crafts and 'curios'.

Refreshment Buildings

This being Cork, eating and drinking were important elements to the social side of the Exhibition. There were six restaurants and three bars, including an 'American Bar' (6.20). In general, the design of these merits little comment; some were quite small, almost mere gazebos of canvas. In the case of the Temperance Restaurant, for example, the best the *Irish Builder* could say about it was that it was a 'large and well equipped building, thoroughly adapted for its purposes'. The American Bar was an octagonal tent-type structure, with red and white striped walls, and a roof covered with blue stars on a white background. This plain and simple bar specialized in cocktails, and did a very good 'Manhattan'[59] and 'Gin Sling'![60] Yet more were pre-fabricated structures, which will be dealt with in the next chapter. Despite the presence at the

6.20
Chalet Restaurant & American Bar.
The exhibition had five restaurants and three bars, including a temperance hall, but the Chalet (left) was the grandest. It was here that visiting dignitaries ate. It was one of the most eye-catching of the expo buildings. The American Bar, complete with Star-spangled banners and fiery cocktails, is in the centre, with a cigar stand to the right. (© NLI)

The fountain's design is credited to Henry Cutler, and no doubt he was responsible for the overall form, structural design and hydraulic operation. However, it seems probable that the details of the decoration were left to John Hegarty and his team of craftsmen, who are credited as builders. As we have seen, they recreated Cormac's Chapel in plaster, and were attuned to the rudiments of Celtic design, whereas Cutler was unlikely to have been. The fountain's structure is (as it still stands) reinforced white Portland cement concrete, whilst the upper-most tier is cast iron. In 1902, Portland cement-based concrete was very much a new material, not just in Ireland but worldwide. *The Builder* first introduced their readers to it in an article in 1900, and the first bridge to be built of the material in Ireland was completed in 1909.[76] The manufacturers of the raw material (The Irish Portland Cement Co Ltd, Dublin) included four marble plaques on the fountain to promote themselves: two in Irish and two in English. As well as being an early example of reinforced concrete in Ireland, it is also a very rare example of a quasi-secular structure being built in the Celtic Revival style. This style was generally used for ecclesiastical buildings and monuments.

6.23
Fr Mathew Memorial Fountain, 2010.
Aptly named after the 'Apostle of Temperance' the fountain originally stood in front of the Industrial Hall. Its decoration was made by John Hegarty from mortar. The Irish Builder noted its 'Celtic character' and 'very satisfactory outline.' The fountain was placed in an ornamental lake in 1913 and the upper tier was added later. It is one of the earlier reinforced concrete structures in Ireland. The fountain was restored in 2013. (© Tom Spalding)

However, those looking for architectural purity in the design of the fountain would be disappointed. Whilst being no doubt picturesque, its design includes elements of Celtic 'La Tène' decoration, mixed with later, knotwork-inspired motifs, such as one might find on the Ardagh Chalice. Distinctive Irish lettering around the perimeter of the second tier proclaims 'Father Mathew Memorial Fountain' in English. The four columns supporting this tier with their twisted, so-called 'Solomonic' design are distinctively Romanesque and similar ones can be seen in Cormac's Chapel. One can also identify simpler patterns based on squares ('diaper-work'), or even quasi-Baroque 'dolphins' and the goatish face of the god of hedonism, Pan. Pan is considered to be responsible (or if you prefer, guilty) for inventing the panpipes, and is most inappropriate on a monument to Temperance!

The Gaelic League and the Gaelic Pavilion (*Innis Fáil*)

The Gaelic League was to have a central role in the development of an Irish Village at Cork, but we have seen how the project fell through. Despite this, it is worth examining its architecture as it is so characteristic of its time. It was proposed initially that a number of different villages 'representative of various provinces' should be built, but this was later scaled back to one. The exhibit would consist of 'typical country cottages, whitewashed and thatched, but neat, and then a more pretentious building',

6.24.
Proposed Gaelic Pavilion (Innis Fáil).
Innis Fáil was to be a key part of the exhibition, and intended by the Gaelic League to be a showcase for Irish language and culture. It was proposed that clean-living country people be relocated there for the summer as living exhibits. In the event the scheme fell through, but it was still being publicized as the exhibition opened. The large building behind the round tower was to be a temporary museum.
(© CPM)

where lectures, music and dances could be held (6.24). A museum was planned to house 'historical, literary, and archaeological treasures' and the Gaelic League undertook to 'provide one or two intelligent families' from Irish-speaking areas to demonstrate handicrafts. It was also suggested that families from the three Irish-speaking provinces (Leinster was excluded) could be accommodated in separate cottages.[77] Judging by the publicity image which was widely distributed (indeed, which continued to be used in publicity material after the Exhibition opened),[78] the layout of the site was arranged around a village square and cross-roads. It seems the aim was to make the experience as authentic as possible and even street furniture (a pump and fingerpost sign, presumably in Irish) was to be installed. The 'museum' building illustrates some Arts and Crafts influence, whilst the cottages are more in the Irish vernacular. To the rear of these, small plots were provided, as well as a decorative bandstand. Unlike the Chicago exhibits mentioned in Chapter 4 (4.7, 4.8), the designer did not seem to plan to reproduce any famous buildings: there was neither a Donegal nor Blarney Castle. However, the master plan included distinctly Irish structures in the form of a Round Tower, and a church tower with stepped battlements. The former is quite similar to that in Timahoe, Co. Laois, which features a Romanesque door-case. Writing about the round tower in the *All Ireland Review*, Herbert Honahan explained, that it 'will be a real [*sic*] Irish Round tower which will be designed from the best examples in the country … From the top the observer will have, spread before him the magnificent panorama

of the grounds and exhibition buildings, the beautiful river and ancient city.'
Working somewhat against the authenticity of a 'real' tower, it was planned
that 'from the top of [it] at night a searchlight [would] cast its rays over the
grounds'.[79] The entire enterprise was to be built on marshy ground below the
Vincentian Church in Sunday's Well and was to be connected to the main
site via a new pedestrian bridge.[80] The scheme was later scaled back to a single
'Gaelic League House' plus lecture and concert halls.[81]

Although this in turn did not come to pass, members of the League did
contribute to other aspects of the Exhibition, such as hosting Irish dancing
performances and (as we have seen) by judging the completion for the Opening
Ode in Irish.[82] In the end the archaeological exhibits were accommodated in
the Art Gallery and in the DATI's stand, but a single Irish Labourer's cottage
was built. However, this had a slightly different aim.

The Irish Labourer's Cottage

Designed by Robert P. Gill, of Co. Tipperary, the Irish Labourer's cottage was
part of the DATI exhibit, and was intended as a model homestead for small-
holders. The house as built was based on cottages designed by Gill for the
Board of Guardians of the Nenagh (Poor Law) Union for £100,[83] and had
a kitchen/living room and three bedrooms. It was fitted out by two upper-
middle-class women as an example of how 'the humblest home may be made
comfortable and clean in an inexpensive manner'.[84] This was not the first time
a Cork Exhibition had featured an 'ideal home'. In 1883 thirteen models
of designs for a Labourer's Cottage were entered in a completion sponsored
by Waterford MP Henry Villiers-Stuart. The aim was that it be built for 50
guineas (about £5,500 today!).[85]

The decoration of the kitchen/living room in the 1902 cottage included
a tiled floor (to be painted weekly with 'Venetian red')[86], white-washed
walls, blue cotton curtains and a 'home-made scarlet quilt' on the bed. The
décor was declared to be 'altogether charming', by the *Freeman's Journal*. The
building was single-storied, arranged on a rectangular floor-plan. It seems
the bedrooms were connected by a corridor at the rear of the building. The
external walls appear (from the single remaining photograph) to have been
of timber or rendered brick, and a single chimney stack protruded through
the roof. The roof itself was slated, with a tiny porch over the front door.
The material is noteworthy. Whilst it had been proposed to use traditional

thatch for the Innis Fáil houses (foreign visitors would have expected nothing less from a 'real' Irish village) the spokeswoman for the DATI explained to patrons that, in a modern home, 'thatch was both troublesome and expensive', and thus should be avoided.[87] In contrast to the League's intention to show how Irish culture was compatible with the modern world, when it came to architecture, it seems the League considered that the old ways were best.

Perhaps as a gesture to the Gaelic League, the 'resident' of the Irish cottage was a 72-year-old Irish-speaking Kerrywoman, Mrs Courtney,[88] and a number of concerts and dances were held at the cottage under their auspices. The organizer of these events, P.J. Hannan of the Irish Agricultural Organization Society, explained that by getting involved, the participants would be 'doing their part towards making them all better Irishmen and Irishwomen than they had been'.[89]

The resident/exhibit was apparently often to be found in conversation with other Irish-speakers,[90] and the use of Irish spoken and written (albeit in a small way) was a characteristic of the exhibition, not seen in previous Cork shows. A noted local writer, Julia Crottie, recorded how she could hear knots of people practising their new-found language skills around the Central Bandstand and elsewhere. She marvelled at this, writing that 'looking back ten years it is difficult to realise the altered conditions of the present day ... At that time, the mere suggestion that they knew Irish would be deemed an insult to most middle-class folk.'[91] She also cautioned against the 'intolerance and rancour' of some purists, such as a 'bustling, loud-voiced man' who expostulated his views on people 'meddling and tinkering' with old Irish songs, as they were 'the genuine article'.

Other Celtic Revival influences

Aside from these examples, the influence of the Celtic Revival could be seen on a number of commercial stands and exhibits. In the printing trade, framed dedications and testimonies with a border of Celtic interlace were common, Guy and Co. showed books printed in Irish,[92] Carroll and McGrath (trading as Crotty & Co) displayed their *sliotar* and *camán* used for hurling.[93] Scientific instrument makers, Yeates & Sons of Dublin, decorated their 'Erin' range of barometers with emblems peculiar only to Ireland, such as the Round Tower, Celtic Cross, Irish Harp, and 'Irish Wolf-Dog &c' mentioned in Chapter 4.[94] Some of these were made from Bog Oak, regarded by many as a singularly

6.25.
The King's Cup.
A masterpiece of the
goldsmiths', silversmiths'
and jewellers' handicraft
(which) takes the form of
a copy of the celebrated
Ardagh Chalice, on
a large scale and is
guaranteed by Messrs.
Johnson to be of genuine
Dublin manufacture'.
Edmond Johnson was
one of Ireland's foremost
silversmiths, and had made
a number of chalice replicas
before this one, which was
three times as big as the
original and larger than
today's Sam Maguire Cup.
Elsewhere in the exhibition
he showed a selection of
other replicas, including
one of the Cross of Cong.
(© CPM, from *Army & Navy
Illustrated*, 19 June 1902.)

THE KING'S CUP.
To be raced for at Queenstown on July 18.

The roles played by the individual architects are illuminating. Arthur Hill was a Protestant and an Irishman. In his early twenties he had developed a strong interest in Hiberno–Romanesque buildings. Indeed, he won two silver medals from the Royal Institute of British Architects for his drawings of Irish churches in the 1870s,[105] including a monograph of Cormac's Chapel in 1874. However, his buildings at the Exhibition all avoid Celtic motifs and, in the case of the President's Pavilion in particular, make strong reference to modern English buildings. J.F. McMullen, who was responsible for the Fr Mathew Pavilion, was an Irish Catholic and is known primarily for his great Celtic Revival masterpiece, the Honan Chapel, but showed no interest in incorporating Irish design elements into his work at the Expo. Both architects would, doubtless, have been aware of the continuing Celtic Revival. Recent projects in this style in the Cork area included a neat Hiberno–Romanesque chapel, set on a picturesque island at Gougane Barra and dedicated to St Finbarre. This was designed by another Cork architect, Samuel Hynes, whom both men would have known.

Ironically, Henry Cutler (an Englishman) took the credit for, and may well have been the instigator of, the Celtic decoration on the Memorial Fountain. Whilst its authenticity is to be doubted, the level of detail is remarkable, down to the use of an Irish letter-form for the (English) commemorative inscription. The group responsible for the most striking Celtic-inspired designs (the DATI offices and aquarium) were genuine enthusiasts for Irish art and craft, but it must also be remembered, were working for an arm of the British state.

It is partly because of its appropriation by the British establishment that the Celtic Revival style had lost some of its emblematic power by the Edwardian period. It had entered the mainstream and been adopted by the government and some in the ruling classes,[106] and this goes some way to explain its marginalization as an inspiration for official symbols, even on coinage, after independence in 1922. An example of this appropriation is the following. When Edward VII offered to pay for a Cup for a sailing competition at the Exhibition, to be presented by the Royal Munster Yacht Club, it was decided 'that the cup shall take the form of an enlarged replica of the famous Ardagh Chalice' (6.25). To this end, a 16lb (7kg), 2ft (60cm)-tall silver-and-gold cup decorated with enamel beads was made in Dublin.[107] In selecting the chalice as a model the club was 'actuated by the desire to have the cup thoroughly Irish in design'. [108] The combination of British royalty and Celticism is striking. In another example seen in Dublin, at a St Patrick's Day ball in Dublin Castle before the First World War, members of the Gaelic League were to be seen dancing 'the Connaught Jig' with soldiers of the Royal Irish Rifles![109]

Building Changes in 1903

In the second season of the Exhibition, a number of changes were made to the buildings in the exhibition grounds. As a companion to the Irish Labourer's Cottage, a Normandy Cottage was built (6.26). It was based on a vernacular Norman design and built to French specifications by imported French labour. The cottage and its grounds were intended to show 'the great skill and ability of the French peasant'[110] (presumably as compared to the local variety). To this end 'a Norman peasant', a Monsieur Nicolle, his wife and child (suitably dressed in their traditional costumes) were 'induced to come and take charge of the plot for six months', [111] where they worked and slept. They can be glimpsed in a Cork Camera Club photo in the possession of Cork Public Museum. The two-storeyed house had a timber frame, with the sections between the woodwork covered in a cement render, and had a characteristically deep-hooded roof over one gable. It was praised for its neat architecture and use of internal space. One writer hoped that its presence would 'lead to the improvement of the architecture of our homes in the rural districts',[112] but the lack of Norman buildings in the Irish countryside today suggests that the idea was not taken up. However, after the close of the show, the building was moved from its original location (approximately the northeast corner of the current UCC rugby pitch) to the east side of the main gate of what became Fitzgerald's Park. It served as the home for the Park-keeper until it was removed.

The Canadian government exhibits were removed from their pavilion, which was modified externally and renamed the 'Western Pavilion', the Fr Mathew Pavilion was emptied and housed a 'teleautograph' and photography exhibit in 1903

6.26
Normandy Cottage, 1903. Two alternative ideal rural homes were presented to visitors. An Irish Cottage stood near the present Western Road entrance to the Mardyke sports grounds. It was a simple 3-bed bungalow with a small porch. In 1903, it was joined by the Normandy Cottage (shown) with the intention of drawing comparisons between the two. The builder was a M. Bergot of Caen. Irish visitors were intrigued by the tenants' wooden clogs, copper cooking pans and that they ate rabbits.
(© Tom Spalding)

(see the following chapter for details). The Office Building and one of the pre-fabricated tea houses (the Tír na nÓg) mentioned above were removed, but several other structures related to the Amusements section were added.

Conclusion

On examining images and descriptions of the buildings of the Cork Exhibition two conclusions can be drawn. The visitors were treated to a built environment which was truly representative of its age. The mish-mash of architectural styles, showing influences from the Classical world, the Near East and vernacular buildings sat within a site which plainly showed the influence of the current mode of laying out exhibitions and reflected practice in America and France. Such a range of influences was common in late Victorian and Edwardian buildings and came from a greater awareness of the extent of Britain's colonial dominions and, conversely, a greater appreciation for local architecture. The influence of the foreign shows on our own was, however, mediated by local needs and financial realities. Current politics and nationalism led to the adoption of some Celtic Revival influences, and the amount of cash available dictated the size, style and scope of the buildings and attractions.

In several cases it is hard to distinguish between the architecture of the exhibit buildings and the exhibits themselves. This is almost a defining characteristic of Exhibition architecture, and could still be said of World's Fairs today. A good example of this is the DATI's exhibit-cum-exhibition centre, and although Cormac's Chapel had almost become a cliché by 1902, it was appreciated by many visitors, no matter what their political allegiance. The Normandy Cottage is another example, and its parallel can be found in re-created 'Folk Villages' such as Bunratty in Co. Clare, or, on a grander scale at Disney's Epcot theme park in Florida. The latter features a World Showcase, where 'Guests' can share the 'culture and cuisine of eleven countries' including Italy, Japan, Morocco, France, United Kingdom and Canada.

Notes

1   He married in early middle age, *c.*1904, and had a family in Belfast.

2   As his Census return form shows. See Irish Census' 1901 and 1911 available online, http://www.census.nationalarchives.ie.

3   Archives of his work in Belfast primarily relate to the construction of engineering projects, such as abattoirs and water treatment, as well as social housing. See also his entry in the Dictionary of Irish Architects, www.dia.ie.

4   *The Builder*, 18 October 1902, p.337.

5   *The Engineer*, 2 May 1902.

6   *Irish News (Belfast)*, 28 April 1902.

7   'City YMCA', *Belfast Newsletter*, 23 June 1902.

8   This pavilion was requisitioned as a grandstand for the period of the Exhibitions, and still stands today.

9   This split between 'pastoral' and 'formal' was also a feature of the Chicago Exhibition. See B. Harvey, 'Architecture for the Future at the Charleston Exhibition, 1901–1902', *Perspectives in Vernacular Architecture*, 7 (1997), p.122

10 The summer of 1902 was wet, and 1903 was worse.

11 The Gallery itself was a legacy of a previous Glasgow Exhibition in 1888.

12 Whilst Mackintosh's overall designs were rejected, he did provide designs for four exhibition stalls.

13 *The Builder*, 6 April 1901, p.333.

14 See Harvey, *Charleston Exhibition*, p.126.

15 The area of west London called 'White City' commemorates the 1908 Franco-British exhibition which was so-called.

16 *The Builder*, 6 April 1901, p.334.

17 This technique continued to be used in Cork for making domestic ceilings until at least the late 1930s.

18 *Belfast Newsletter*, 6 July 1901.

19 *Irish Builder*, 27 February 1901 and 5 May 1901.

20 P. and J. Kinchin, *Glasgow's Great Exhibitions; 1888–1901–1911–1938–1988* (Bicester: White Cockade Publishing, 1988), p.83.

21 *Cork Constitution*, 23 January 1902.

22 Ibid.

23 'Greater Cork Exhibition Committee', *Cork Examiner*, 15 July 1904, ref: Frankenberg s Cable Co.

24 *The Builder*, 4 October 1902, p.293.

25 Called the 'Palace of Commerce', see Harvey, *Charleston Exhibition*, p.124.

26 *Cork Constitution*, 3 August 1901.

27 See P. and J. Kinchin, *Glasgow's Great Exhibitions*, p.84.

28 *The Builder*, 8 May 1902, p.1,227. The buildings were 'carried out with economy and care'.

29 *Irish Builder*, 10 April 1902. The buildings cost £5,000 and were constructed by Samuel Hill & Co.

30 *Belfast Newsletter*, 28 April 1902.

31 *Pall Mall Gazette*, 29 April 1902.

32 *Evening Herald*, quoted in the *Cork Constitution*, 29 April 1902.

33 *The Engineer*, 2 May 1902.

34 *The Northern Whig*, 2 May 1902.

35 *Irish Builder*, 22 May 1902, p.1,255.

36 F.E. Dixon, 'Dublin Exhibitions: Part 1', *Dublin Historical Record*, 26, 3 (June 1973), p.94.

37 James Miller of Glasgow, Walker's mentor, seems also to have been involved. Miller had a long career in expo design, working on Glasgow's 1938 Exhibition, aged 78. See *Building News*, 82, 2 May 1902, p.626 and P. and J. Kinchin, *Glasgow's Great Exhibitions*, pp.142–3.

38 *Cork Constitution*, 2 July 1902.

39 N. Bolotri and C. Laing, *The World's Colombian Exposition; the Chicago World's Fair of 1893* (Chicago IL: University of Illinois Press, 2002),

p.30. Mass media and illustrated magazines had made the dissemination of ideas about architecture and design a great deal easier than had been the case heretofore.

40 *Stratten's Directory*, 1892, p.200. He perhaps was attracted to Cork due to the boom in church building at the time. Amongst other work, he had also made railings, gates and lighting for the Crawford School of Art in 1890.

41 After the Expo, one seems to have been retained near the Cricket Club Pavilion for a decade or so.

42 H. Long, *The Edwardian House* (Manchester: Manchester University Press, 1993), p.168.

43 E.N. Kaufman, 'The Architectural Museum from World's Fair to Restoration Village', *Assemblage*, 9 (June 1989), p.21.

44 *Cork Examiner*, 23 January 1904.

45 Canadian National Archives, *Report of the Minister of Agriculture for the Dominion of Canada for the Year Ended October 1902*, p.vii.

46 J. Ghosh and V.J. Pryce, 'Canadian Immigration Policy: Responses to Changing Trends', *Geography*, 84, 3 (July 1999), p.234.

47 Canadian National Archives, *Report of the Minister of Agriculture*, p.vii They went on to exhibit independently at St Louis and Osaka, Japan.

48 *Cork Constitution*, 31 May 1902.

49 *Cork Examiner*, 14 February 1902.

50 In Wolverhampton too, the Canadians engaged local British architects Walker & Ramsay.

51 'The Cork Exhibition', *Irish Builder*, 5 June 1902.

52 See references to the Paris Exposition in A. Service, *Edwardian Architecture* (London: Thames and Hudson, 1977).

53 For example door knobs, letter-boxes and grilles made of pressed, wrought or cast metal remained popular into the 1930s.

54 *Belfast Newsletter*, 28 April 1902. The building

has since been painted pinkish-red.

55 *Cork Constitution*, 18 June 1902, quoting T.E. Barry of the *Freeman's Journal* (Sydney, Australia).

56 *Irish Builder*, 8 May 1902, p.1,227.

57 Ibid., 3 December 1903, p.5,015.

58 Ibid., 8 May 1902, p.1,227.

59 'Mr O'Donoghue on the Opening of the Exhibition', *The Weekly Examiner*, 17 May 1902.

60 *Cork Examiner*, 9 June 1902.

61 *The Builder*, 18 October 1902, 83, p.337.

62 *Illustrated London News*, 3 May 1902.

63 *Pall Mall Gazette*, 29 April 1902.

64 Long, *The Edwardian House*, p.37.

65 Ibid., p.140.

66 Ibid., p.85.

67 *Cork Examiner*, 23 January 1904.

68 J.J. Meagher, 'Irish Art Renaissance', *Irish Builder*, 22 May 1902.

69 Completed 1134AD, this was also one of the main influences for McMullen's 'Honan Chapel'. See J. Sheehy and G. Mott, *The Rediscovery of Ireland's Past* (London: Thames and Hudson, 1980), p.142.

70 B. Lawlor, *The Irish Round Tower* (Cork: Collins Press, 1999), p.218.

71 The *Belfast Newsletter*, 28 April 1902.

72 *Irish News (Belfast)*, 28 April 1902.

73 *Irish Builder*, 8 May 1902.

74 Now called the National College of Art and Design.

75 *Cork Constitution*, 26 May 1902.

76 At Mizen Head, Co. Cork, since destroyed.

77 H. Honahan, 'Cork International Exhibition, 1902', *All Ireland Review*, 2, 42 (21 December 1901), pp.348–9.

78 e.g. in the *Belfast Evening Telegraph*, 1 May 1902.

79 'Donahoe's Magazine', October 1901, cited in *Catholic Union Times*, 27 May 1902.

80 This part of the development eventually did

come to pass. The intended crossing was to be close to the weir where the present Mardyke Bridge (2005) now stands.

81 'The Gaelic League – Executive Committee', *Freeman's Journal*, 10 January 1902, p.4.

82 For example, Ald. Wm. Phair, V.P. of the Cork Branch played the *uilleann* pipes at the Labourer's Cottage on the 27 May 1902 (*Cork Constitution*), and a Mr Kelly of the League organized a dance which attracted 1,000 people (*The Nenagh Guardian*, 2 August 1902). Local branches from Naas and Navan led visits to the expo, but it seems that these were semi-private efforts, as was a visit by H.J. Courtney, accompanied by 'prominent members of Gaelic League branches in Dublin'. (*Kildare Observer*, 16 August 1902, *Anglo Celt*, 19 July 1902, *Freeman's Journal*, 6 August 1902) Judging by the League's journal *An Claidheamh Soluis*, the Dublin organization officially ignored the exhibition, preferring to put their energy over the summer into organising their annual *Feis* competitions.

83 Later called Nenagh Urban District Council, *The Speaker*, 23 August 1902.

84 *Hearth and Home*, 28 August 1902.

85 W.K. Sullivan, J. Brenan, and R. Day, *Cork Industrial Exhibition 1883, Report of Executive Committee, Awards of Jurors and Statement of Accounts* (Cork: Purcell & Co., 1886), p.373.

86 *Freeman's Journal*, 15 August 1902, p.9.

87 *The Speaker*, 23 August 1902.

88 'Mr H.J. Courtney, Dublin, at the Cork Exhibition', *Freeman's Journal*, 6 August 1902.

89 *Cork Constitution*, 10 July 1902 and Nenagh Guardian 2 August 1902.

90 *Freeman's Journal*, 23 August 1902.

91 J. Crottie, *Irish at the Exhibition, Cork Examiner*, 17 July 1902.

92 *All Ireland Review*, 31 May 1902.

93 *All Ireland Review*, 24 May 1902.

94 Anon., *Official Catalogue Cork International Exhibition 1902* (Cork: Guys, 1902), p.49.

95 M. Lenihan, *Pure Cork* (Cork: Mercier Press, 2011), p.33.

96 Generally written 'Céad Míle Fáilte' and often translated as 'One Hundred Thousand Welcomes'.

97 *Cork Examiner*, 12 May 1902.

98 Walter Tomlinson quoted in Kaufman, *The Architectural Museum*, pp.20–39.

99 J. Turpin, 'Exhibitions of Arts and Industries in Victorian Ireland: Part 1', *Dublin Historical Record*, 35, 1 (December 1981), p.7.

100 Dixon, *Dublin Exhibitions: Part 1*, p.100.

101 A. Pred, 'Spectacular Articulations of Modernity; The Stockholm Exhibition of 1897', *Geografiska Annaler: Series B*, 73, 1 (1991), p.67.

102 Such as at the Centennial Exhibition of 1876, Philadelphia. See Kaufman, *The Architectural Museum*, p.23.

103 From 'America the Beautiful', a patriotic song written by Katharine Lee Bates in 1893. Part of the inspiration for the song was the author's visit to the Chicago Exposition.

104 See Harvey, *Charleston Exhibition*, p.126.

105 *The Builder*, 28, 22 October 1870, p.853, and 32, 8 August 1874, p.662 cited on www.dia.ie

106 It was even used for decorative effect on the helmets of Royal Irish Constabulary helmets.

107 'Arrival of the Royal Cup in Cork', *Cork Examiner*, 28 May 1902. The cup was made by Edward Johnson Ltd.

108 *Irish Builder*, 5 June 1902, p.1,278.

109 'We Twa', memoires of Lady Aberdeen quoted in Sheehy and Mott, *The Rediscovery of Ireland's Past*, p.105.

110 *Irish Weekly Independent and Nation*, 30 May 1903.

111 Ibid.

112 *Cork Examiner*, 4 July 1903.

7.1

View of the Grand Avenue.
This image appears to show the exhibition just
prior to opening, as suggested by the partially-
completed stall of Cash & Co on the right (now
called Brown Thomas) & the relaxed attitude
of the shop assistants. (© CPM)

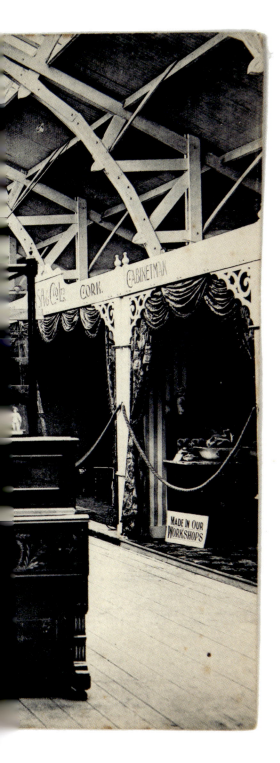

7

The Educational & Industrial Exhibits

Tom Spalding

After entering the iron gates of Cork's International Exhibition, and moving on into the grounds, there was a great deal for visitors to see. Aside from the eye-catching rides and amusements which we will deal with later, the stalls and commercial exhibits in the Industrial and Machinery Halls were crucial to the success of the Exhibition (7.1). This chapter sets out to answer three questions relating to the exhibits on show, namely: how 'international' was it, how 'industrial' was it and lastly, how innovative were the exhibitors and how were their innovations presented?

Firstly, it is fair to say that many of our visitors would be impressed simply because few would have had a similar experience prior to this point. The Exhibition was international in character and featured over 500 exhibitors, with representatives from twenty countries. These included British colonies such as Canada and New Zealand, but also China, Japan and Turkey. In the case of the former pair, dedicated pavilions were made available to display their wares.

As explained in the previous chapter, the Canadian government had gone to great expense to illustrate the boggling richness of their country. In Cork, visitors could see food and produce piled high: 'chicken, turkey, goose, duck … potted meats, sausage; raspberries, strawberries, damson plums … beans, petit pois, tomatoes', 'pyramids of Canada's "Club" rye whiskey' and so on. The assault on the senses continued with a 'display of cereals … set up in arches, pyramids, sheaves and bunches, festooned and wreathed in many different forms'.[1] To make the right impression, the Canadians had employed what we might now call a 'merchandiser' to take 'charge of the agricultural and general decorations'.[2] On the other side of their 5,000ft^2 (460m^2) hall, a display of the mineral and timber wealth of the Dominion was presented, including Klondike gold nuggets worth $15,000. Needless to say, this exhibit was supervised by an attendant. It seems the man was also kept busy fielding questions, mostly about agriculture, and distributing 'thousands of leaflets'.[3] The aim of the exhibit's organizers was to dispel the prejudice that 'Canada is essentially a land of ice and snow', and to present it in the most attractive light. This view was perhaps quite widespread. Writing less than a decade earlier, the veteran nationalist Denny Lane hoped that intending emigrants would stay at home and 'not beneath the chills of Canada … so fatal to the children of Irish parents'.[4] However, the presence of the Canadians illustrates how Ireland was integrated within the Empire and how, through those connections, it could access foreign markets and import luxury goods in seemingly limitless variety. Conversely, it would have suggested possible avenues for Irish exports. It certainly impressed some visitors: Michael Ronayne a 'prominent farmer' from Castlemartyr, was 'thunder-struck with the quality of [the] grain', whilst a local MP, Capt. A. Donelan, rated the pavilion as 'one of the chief attractions at the Cork Exhibition'.[5]

The Japanese government exhibit was also large and stretched between two avenues of the Industrial Hall. It was sponsored by the Japanese government at a time when the country was rapidly modernizing, developing its armed forces and looking overseas. Early in 1902, the Japanese had signed a military alliance with Great Britain and Ireland, producing (what one authority calls) 'a sense of grateful friendship' on behalf of the Japanese.[6] In the summer, as we shall see later, they cemented this relationship by sending a naval flotilla to these islands, members of which came to visit the Exhibition.

Across the expo cutting-edge technology was demonstrated to visitors, including moving pictures and telecommunications. Whilst much of this was not new per se, it is certain that many of the visitors would never come into contact with it before. For example, although the telephone had been present in Cork since at least 1892,[7] there were still very few in the city ten years later. Even in the Irish capital there were only eight public phones, as late as 1900. The two 'Public Call Offices' available to visitors in the Industrial Hall would have presented many ordinary people with their first encounter with the instrument. New ideas were also shown in the fields of electricity generation (a De Laval steam turbine), illumination (by the novel 'Welsbach' system for gas or by electric means) and food processing (especially the drying and preservation of excess produce). As mentioned in Chapter 6, the red-and-green-coloured fairy lights strung amongst the trees of the Mardyke made a huge impression on visitors spending time dining, 'courting', strolling or listening to music in the evenings. Although electricity had been demonstrated at Cork's 1883 Expo, many working-class homes were not to be connected to the electricity grid until the late 1940s. Unless they had visited a large American city or London's West End, those at the Exhibition would never have experienced this feeling of 'daylight at night'. The 1,000 lamps on the front of the Industrial Hall created 'an exceedingly pretty effect', with 500 more 'in use lighting the banks of the river and the trees about the grounds'.[8] Inside visitors

7.2
Main Exhibition Switchboard.
The giant marble switchboard, 16' x 10', installed by Porte & Co & the electrical generating machinery were exhibits in themselves. Raised on a 3' platform & surrounded by 'a massive brass railing' there was more than an element of theatre about it. (Courtesy Michael Lenihan)

experienced the glow of 2,000 more electric lamps on the individual stands, plus 180 powerful arc-lights for general lighting throughout the buildings. In a visit to the Wolverhampton Art and Industrial Exhibition which also took place during the summer of 1902, *The Builder* had inspected its electrical installation and was particularly struck by its arrangements. As the Cork show used a very similar centralized power supply, it seems safe to assume that the Cork plant could also be considered 'state of the art' (7.2).[9]

An exhibit of (human) baby incubators, imported from the Continent and supervised by a Monsieur Leotarde, where 'the development to maturity of three or four infants' could be observed, was a big 'hit' at the show.[10] History does not record the place from which the lucky neonates came, but the large Magdalene home across the river from the grounds, or the nearby Erinville 'lying-in' hospital, could have been the source. This kind of attraction combined the best and worst of the exhibition tradition, namely real advances in science and technology which would benefit mankind as well as a voyeuristic experience where people could be viewed as little better than objects. In this way they were similar to the anthropological exhibits previously discussed.

The Role of the Department of Agriculture and Technical Instruction

A significant, if less eye-catching, innovation was the involvement of the State in the exhibition. In Cork, the Irish Department of Agriculture and Technical Instruction (DATI), under Horace Plunkett, played a key role. Indeed, according to the correspondents of English newspapers such as the *Manchester Guardian, The Times* and the *Yorkshire Post*, the contribution of the DATI was the single most innovative thing about the Cork Exhibition. *The Times* explained how 'nowadays' exhibitions 'differed from one another only in size,' but the 'peculiar importance' of Cork's Exhibition 'consists in the fact that it is intended to present to the visitor … an object-lesson in the present state, and future conduct of, Irish industry and commerce'.[11] *The Daily Chronicle* went as far as to say that 'the Department may be said to dominate the exhibition',[12] whilst a French visitor came away with the impression that the Expo was 'almost entirely occupied by the Irish Department of Agriculture and Technical Instruction'[13] and the officials of the Canadian Department of Agriculture considered it 'by far the most instructive and practical exhibit'.[14]

A leading historian of Irish Exhibitions has written that 'the absence of State initiative – even up to the 1907 [*Dublin*] exhibition – is in marked contrast to Government policy in England and the Continent.'[15] He is right to say that the 1902 Expo was not a government initiative, but they were not shy in supporting it. The DATI had invested approximately £25,000 (c.£2.5 million) in their exhibits, amounting to about a quarter of the total cost of the enterprise. They saw their industrial role as two-fold: (a) the demonstration of industries which were unknown or had lapsed in Ireland with the aim of introducing them and (b) showing how existing small businesses could adopt new technologies from abroad to increase their profitability. To address the former aim, the DATI set up machinery for making carpets, hosiery, pottery, glass, clocks, paper-boxes, straw hats, wood carving, toys, artificial flowers, baskets and so on. In addition, the organization imported workers from several European countries and Great Britain to operate the machines:[16] hat-makers from Luton, weavers from Coventry, cloth-workers from Leeds, carpet-makers from Canterbury and a Staffordshire potter. One of the most beautiful working exhibits was the demonstration of Della Robbia luxury Arts and Crafts ceramics (7.3). The firm's Art Director, Harold Rathbone, and three of his artists travelled from Merseyside to make and decorate them, in some cases using Irish clay.[17] The concept of importing expertise from abroad to inspire indigenous entrepreneurs and investors had a long heritage in Irish exhibitions, but never before had the State taken a direct hand in its promotion. It seems that some of this effort may have borne fruit, in the short term at least. It was reported in March 1903 that following a demonstration of carpet-making at Cork, 'three industries [were] established in Ireland, one of them being in a workhouse in a poor district of Sligo'.[18]

7.3
Della Robbia ceramic vase. Della Robbia ceramic vase made by Charles Collis & Hannah Jones on site at the exhibition. The firm worked in a variety of styles; this is one of their more Art Nouveau-inspired designs. (© CPM)

An example of the second aim of the DATI's industrial policy was implemented in its work in the textile industry. In 1901 the DATI had identified a particular need to upgrade small, barely profitable, textile mills. To this end they showed 'new uses for Irish wools and new machines by which [these] mills can be rendered much more efficient'.[19] Another example of this aim was an Industrial Conference hosted at the expo by the DATI and Cork Corporation from 22 to 24 October 1902. Here, experts from Britain and Ireland, as well as Switzerland, Austria and Germany, spoke on subjects as diverse as glass manufacture, electric power, tanning and bog reclamation, in many cases with the aid of slide presentations.[20]

As in the case in the American Irish Villages, aristocratic and upper-middle-class women played a strong role at the Exposition in promoting

the paper pointed out to readers that 'the stream of emigration is still flowing rapidly'.[34] The Department's staff enthusiastically embraced the role of apostle for the new creed of training. With the support of the Irish Agricultural Organization Society and clergy throughout the land, it arranged for 100,000 rural-dwellers to visit the model farm, as will be detailed in Chapter 8.[35] The man in charge of the overall project was William Macartney-Filgate, a Dublin Castle 'mandarin'. (He can be seen alongside the redoubtable Lady Aberdeen in 4.6, steering her around the fishponds.) He was a Londoner, a Protestant, upper-middle class and single. It is revealing that on census night 1901 he was at his club on Kildare Street. Nonetheless, he pursued his role diligently and was remembered as 'a very amiable person' by Br Dominic Burke.[36] As mentioned in Chapter 5, he had advised on the initial planning of the Cork Exhibition and had been in charge of the Irish exhibit at Glasgow in 1901. He had met the Cork delegation there and fielded enquires at Glasgow on their behalf from 'Foreign and Colonial' exhibitors wishing to come to Cork in 1902.

Thomas P. Gill was in charge of the day-to-day running of the DATI agricultural exhibits. His background was more typical of the intended audience for this part of the show. He was a Catholic from Co. Tipperary and could speak Irish and English. In addition, he had spent some time in his twenties in the US and Canada.[37] In what was perhaps a little bit of nepotism, T.P. also happened to be the brother of Robert P. Gill, the designer of the Irish Labourer's Cottage in the DATI exhibit we met in the previous chapter.

The Industrial Exhibits

When one reviews the Exhibition Catalogue, it is full of names of many brands and companies still familiar to us today. These include: Fry's chocolate, Jacob's biscuits, Colman's mustard, Goodall's sauces ('Yorkshire Relish and Goodall's Household Specialities'), Guinness, Murphys, many other breweries and Bushmills Whiskey. In the retail sector the names Easons, Fannin Healthcare ('Artificial Limbs, Surgical Instruments, Trusses, etc.') and Elverys were present. Some companies, such as Belleek china and Schweppes soda water did not have their own stands, but were represented on the respective stalls of their sales agents (7.5). Local Cork firms such as McKechnies cleaners, Charles McCarthy (plumbers), Denis O'Sullivan and Co., the makers of brushes (now called DOSCO), and Guys the printers were present.

There was a huge range of industry sectors represented: firms operating in construction, chemicals and home-wares sat cheek by jowl with makers of leather goods and tobacco. In previous Irish exhibitions the goods had been arranged in strict groups, like families of animals in a zoology textbook. Visitors were supposed to compare a dozen different brands of honey, hardware or what have you, and draw educated conclusions from this. However, this could make for a dull display, and the jumbled arrangement used in Cork was supposed to break any tedium. Indeed, this approach was copied in a later Irish exhibition, in Dublin in 1907.[38]

However, the general experience of visitors to these stalls was to be limited to studying carefully arranged displays or making polite enquiries: in only a very few cases could the merchandise be sampled (7.4, 7.8). The Dutch firm of Van Houten's Chocolate held the concession for selling hot chocolate at 1d (c.40p) a cup including a biscuit, and chocolate bars.[39] The firm is still trading today, and had operated a large concession stall at the Glasgow Exposition.[40] Although people may have

7.4
White's Oatmeal Stall.
Many of the stands were quite unimaginative, but this Belfast firm had 'erected a cooking apparatus' on theirs to allow the staff to serve samples of Irish porridge to visitors & they had thatched the roof with Irish oats to reinforce their message.
(Courtesy Michael Lenihan)

been aware that this was intended to be an Industrial Exhibition, it would have felt to some like a giant shopping arcade. However, whilst the rules of the Exhibition allowed for the showing of prices, they generally forbade the selling of goods from the displays. This presented visitors with a tantalizing consumer paradox: the effective promotion of shopping as a leisure activity, without allowing the gratification of easy access to the goods. To make matters worse, many manufacturers took the approach of overwhelming callers to the stalls with mountains of products on display, creating a seemingly limitless cornucopia which achieved its impact by repetition or displaying a wide range. For example, Jacob's biscuit and cake stand was described as follows: 'amongst the 200 or more varieties, may be seen the well-known Cream Crackers' also Walnut Cream, At Home, Five O'Clock Tea, Arrowroot, Oxford Lunch, their new royalist ranges, the King's Own and Coronation, 'a rich shortbread with

GRAND AVENUE.—Attractive display of Builders' Ironmongery, Baths, Ranges, Grates, Spades and Shovels, Joinery Work, Wood Turning, and Wood Fibre for Packing, exhibited by Messrs. THE CORK TIMBER & IRON CO., LTD., KYLIE'S STREET, CORK.

AVENUE K.—Messrs. J. PERRY & SONS, LTD., 89 to 91, PATRICK ST., CORK.—Exhibit of High-Class Ironmongery, Mantelpieces in Marble and Wood, Stable Fittings, Patent Grates, Lamps, &c.

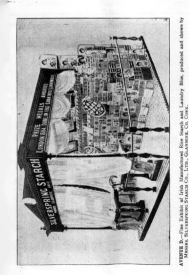

AVENUE D.—Fine Exhibit of Irish Manufactured Rice Starch and Laundry Blue, produced and shown by Messrs. SILVERSPRING STARCH CO., LTD., GLANMIRE, CO. CORK.

AVENUE E.—Elegant Exhibit of Drawing-room, Dining-room, and Bedroom Furniture, shown by MR. M. RYAN, 36 & 37, KING STREET, CORK.

7.6a & b Top
Model of Jacobs' Biscuit Factory, 1907.
Jacobs' stand featured 'various machines
in miniature ... made at great expense'
in London. The idea was reprised for the
Dublin expo of 1907 as seen in this model.
It is very similar to that demonstrated at
Cork, and may contain elements of it. This
model is presently in the collection of the
Irish Architectural Archive.
(© Tom Spalding)

7.7a - c. Right
Clockwise from top left: The lacquered
ashtray came from the Japanese exhibit
and the view it shows of the exhibition is
quite fanciful. The silk piece was produced
at the exhibition, probably on the DATI
stand & shows Blarney Castle. The elegant
vase was mass-produced, probably abroad
& given an applied transfer decoration.
(© CPM & Courtesy N. Murray
& M. Teegan)

a glacé cherry in centre' and so on.[41] The backdrop to the stand was a wall of colourful biscuit boxes 7ft (2m) high, in an arrangement like giant building blocks. The cakes were arranged in glass vitrines, as one would see protecting priceless artefacts in a museum. In another case was a scale model of one of their newest biscuit factories (7.6a & b). The commercial nature of the exhibit was emphasized by the advertising posters set around it.[42]

The intention however was not to tease without gratification: orders could be taken, and with the consent of the Executive Committee, the stall-holder could sell goods to visitors, so long as they were non-display items.[43] This appears to have been quite a common occurrence, especially in relation to commemorative souvenirs, which might still be found in many 'good rooms' in Cork to this day (7.7a – c, 6.11). Consumers could also purchase larger goods, such as pianos.[44]

Import substitution was a significant trend at the show, as it had been at previous Irish exhibitions. For example, Irish-grown and -processed pipe tobacco, sold under the enticing 'Lonely Ploughman' brand, could be viewed in the DATI area. (The growing of Irish tobacco had been supressed in the seventeenth century in order to support that industry in the colony of Virginia.) Irish-made bicycles, agricultural machinery (especially from Co. Wexford), furniture and umbrellas were also displayed. Irish clothing was an important element of the Exposition, with the press trumpeting approvingly that 'no Irishman need go outside Ireland for his underwear or linen, ties or handkerchiefs'.[45] Aside from the clear patriotic encouragement to buy Irish, the supposedly superior quality of Irish goods was stated by many exhibitors and newspapermen. For example, the furniture of a local man, Michael Ryan, was contrasted with 'the flimsy shoddy so largely imported [which was] pleasing to the eye, but next to useless for wear'.[46] The 'fine specimens' of Irish-produced building stone and slate had caught the eye of *The Builder*, but they warned that the 'there would … be a larger market for these if the quarries were better worked, for it is complained that the supply is not reliable'.[47] As we have seen, there was also strong evidence for the continuing revival of 'peasant' crafts, predominantly in textiles: tweeds, woollens, crochet and lace.[48] Much of the latter was produced by women under the regime of various religious orders in Cork and further afield, whilst the woollens were generally made by men, working in cottage industries in the west of Ireland. Pride in Irish-made goods was also clear on the stall of Pearse and Sons, who created marble sculptures and altars at their works in Dublin (7.8). Patrick Pearse, and his brother William, the future 1916 revolutionaries, had inherited the business at the time of the Expo. They displayed their company's name in Irish and English and were at pains to point out that all their work was 'executed on our own premises by Irish artists'[49] and that 'inscriptions in Irish [were] a speciality'.[50]

7.8
A page from *The Illustrated Cork Exhibitor* 1902
Super-aeration, soap, sticks and altars.
Patrick Pearse's father had come from England in the 1860s to work in the church building boom. He died in 1900. Despite Pearse's personal reservations about the show, the family entered this stall (bottom left) at Cork. The family's enthusiasm for things Irish is clear in the signage and literature at their exhibit.
(Courtesy Michael Lenihan.)

THE ILLUSTRATED CORK EXHIBITOR, 1902.—SOME NOTABLE EXHIBITS.

AVENUE I.—Super-Aeration Machinery for supplying sterilized Iced Mineral Waters, drawn from bulk, Exhibited by the Sole Agents—Messrs. Kiloh & Co., Ltd., Patrick Street, Cork.

AVENUE 1.—Exhibit of Umbrellas, Sunshades, and Blackthorn Sticks, Manufactured by Messrs. F. Smyth & Son, 75, Grafton Street, Dublin.

AVENUE I.—Messrs. Pearse &Sons, 27, Great Brunswick St., Dublin, consisting of a High Altar in Irish, Carrara, and Sicilian Marbles; Baptismal Font and Credence Table; also Statue of the Sacred Heart. All Designed and Executed by Messrs. Pearse at their Works in Dublin.

AVENUE F.—Exhibit of Soaps, including "Finlay's Silkstone Soap," Candles, and Glycerine, and the raw materials used in the manufacture of these articles, shown by Mr. Alex. Finlay, Soap, Candle, and Glycerine Manufacturer, Belfast.

41

'A Hopeless Failure'? *The Irish Builder*, 19 June 1902

Despite all the excitement of the opening day and the breathless coverage in the press, not all the exuberance of the Exhibition's supporters rang true. Whilst there were some foreign exhibits, the vast majority (93 per cent) were from what the BBC still occasionally refers to as the 'home nations' of the British Isles (see Appendix 4). Nearly two-thirds were from the island of Ireland. However, due to the jumbled nature of the exhibitors already alluded to, Irish exhibits were not exhibited alongside British ones in a single bloc, which might have suggested a tacit support for the Union by the organizers.[51] A focus on local produce was not unique to this exhibition. At Glasgow in 1888 for example, two thirds of the exhibits came from Scotland, many from the area between Glasgow and Edinburgh.[52]

With the notable exceptions of the Japanese and Canadians, the foreign exhibitors were generally not national governments, as one would have found at Paris or Glasgow, but enterprising individuals from Syria, France, the Austro-Hungarian Empire and Turkey. It is likely that, given the abundance of International Exhibitions in western Europe at this time[53] and the nature of the goods they displayed, many (if not most) of these foreigners were travelling craftsmen on the Expo 'circuit', or as one person put it; stalls of 'knick knacks vended by cosmopolitan traders'.[54] Examples include a Foo Chah Lee of Shanghai, who showed 'Picture Frames, Vases, etc.' of oriental make, whilst Elea Lubascheff (of Ekaterinburg, 1,000 miles east of Moscow) sold 'Russian Artistic Cast Iron and Ural Stones'.[55] Given the lead taken by the Americans in the holding of exhibitions and the muscular growth seen in their industries at this time, as well as the attempts of the Cork organizers to play the Irish card and lure Americans 'home', one would expect a good number of US firms to be represented. In fact there were only three (or five if a British agent for the Vertical Feed Sewing Machine Co. and an Irish stall with a harvester from the McCormick Harvesting Machine Co are included).[56]

This was recognized by the more astute journalists covering the fair. The *Freeman's Journal* sought to put a positive gloss on this, explaining to its readers on the 19 August that:

> Amongst the things that most forcibly strike a visitor … is that in spite of its International scope, the Exhibition has remained genuinely Irish in character. In spite of the Egyptian Theatre and the 'sorceress' from Cairo who offer 'chuc chuc'[?]

to the passers-by; in spite of the lively little Japanese salesmen, who push their wares so industriously in the Industrial Hall, and run about chattering broken English as glibly as a sailor from Marseilles; in spite of the pushful Yankee who takes your photograph on a postcards 'while you wait' and of the suave Frenchmen who press souvenirs upon you with that mingled deference and gallantry which is their birthright … the Exhibition remains in its essence an Irish exhibition.[57]

The *Journal* went on to applaud the Gaelic tinge of the Exhibition, especially in the fields of music and art. However, one could argue that far from being international, the Expo was not even truly national in character. Fifty per cent of the total number of exhibitors came from the province of Munster, i.e. within 95 miles (150km). Indeed, 43 per cent originated from within Cork City and County. Strikingly, 40 per cent of the Cork City exhibitors came from just four streets! Despite assertions to the contrary in the press, only twenty-two of Ireland's thirty-two counties were represented, and some rural counties (e.g. Carlow, Offaly, Mayo and Meath) appear to have contributed exhibits which could be classed as little more than 'sales of work' arranged by the local clergy, although this may be a little harsh. It was not just the under-developed parts of the country which performed poorly. The effort of the Munster cities of Limerick (eight exhibitors) and Waterford (just four) was particularly weak given their industrial bases and proximity to the show. As one would expect, industrial Ulster was better represented, a fact not lost on the Belfast press of both persuasions, who proudly editorialized about 'their' exhibitors. Arguably the most famous Lagan-side firm, Harland & Wolff shipbuilders, were present in the form of 'splendid' models of the *Teutonic* and the *Majestic*. At this time, the firm and other Belfast shipbuilders were launching 150,000 tons of shipping per annum.[58] As well as H&W, other major Belfast engineering firms on show included: Musgrave & Co., manufacturers and patent-holders for stoves and radiators, who had showrooms in Frankfurt and Paris and were suppliers to half the crowned heads of Europe; Davidsons & Co., who dominated the tea-processing industry and were in the process of diversifying into fans for power generation, heating and ventilation; and the Belfast Ropework Co., which ran the 'largest single ropeworks in the world' at the end of the nineteenth century.[59] The city and surrounding area mustered thirty-seven other exhibitors, mostly coming from the food-and-drink, construction (including building materials) and textiles sectors. Dublin, meanwhile, sent a creditable seventy-eight firms, many of whom were involved in the same areas as their northern brethren, but also with a strong representation of printers, stationers and photographers. Aside from the well-known brands mentioned above, other firms from the capital included the brush manufacturers IS Varian & Co., the publishers MH Gill & Co., Paterson's matches and Rathbornes, the candle-makers.

Whilst there were some notable examples of new or emerging technologies on show, there were (at least, with the benefit of hindsight) some glaring absences. The areas of technology which came to dominate Europe over the next fifty years were not present – for example, no mechanical transport (apart from steam trains) and certainly no evidence of advances in aeronautics. As one would expect, the Glasgow festival of 1901 had featured that city's extensive shipping industry as well as machine guns and armaments by Alfred Nobel and a series of motor-car trials.[60] There was little evidence in Cork of telecommunications or healthcare, and the only armaments on display were by one Belfast firm showing sporting guns.[61] Whilst moving pictures were exhibited, there is no sign that recorded music was demonstrated, even though phonographs had been available in Ireland for several years. Lastly, the service sector, which came to dominate the late twentieth century, was poorly represented (representing about 10 per cent of the Irish exhibitors). However, this is perhaps to be expected, given that this show was primarily aimed at enhancing Irish manufacturing industry and agriculture.

Despite the generally positive tone taken at the time by the local, national and international gentlemen of the press, there was some negative commentary. A French reviewer visiting in August was disappointed at the lack of variety at Cork, reflecting the comments of the *Freeman's Journal*, but from a different point of view. 'This exhibition' he huffed 'describes itself as international although the only example of exoticism in it is the Cairo Street' (see Chapter 8).[62] Criticism also came from closer to home. The *Irish Builder* fumed that 'as a serious industrial effort the Cork Exhibition does not count' and that 'the general character of the exhibits is to the last degree disappointing'. Furthermore, they took exception to the organic nature of the arrangement of the exhibits: 'the "Vulcanite Roofing Company" … is sandwiched between Price's Candles and a millinery exhibit!' they sniffed.[63] In a later piece they

Other exhibitors had a merely national profile, with operations around the country. Examples include: Robertson, Ledlie, Ferguson & Co., (branches in Belfast, Cork and Waterford, employing 250 'hands') and R & J McKechnie, the cleaners and dyers, who had offices in Dublin, Cork and Limerick and were 'represented by agencies ... from Bray to Bantry'.[73] Furthermore, many of the smaller firms at Cork had previous experience of expos at home and abroad and proudly showed their competition medals on their stalls like old soldiers on a military parade. In their press advertisements and commercial directories, exhibitors frequently included images of their exposition awards, as well as their location and date. Some, such as McKechnies, still had theirs from Dublin's 1853 Exhibition on their stand, and many showed theirs from Cork (1883). One particular distillery had a cabinet of whiskey glasses used by various crowned heads and celebrities to sample their brand of the 'water of life' at their exhibition stands over the years.[74] The firm of Deasy & Co., Clonakilty, showed their 'first-class highest award, diploma and medal' which had been presented for their porter in 1893 at the World's Fair, Chicago.[75] There were other Irish firms which were veterans of Paris and Glasgow as well, illustrating both how well-established the rituals of international exhibitions were, and how some Irish firms were becoming integrated into global trade. For example, the Guinness exhibit in Cork, which primarily consisted of a large-scale model of their St James's Gate brewery, had previously been on display at both Paris and Glasgow. McKenzies (agricultural suppliers of Camden Quay, Cork) had exhibited in Paris, and it was noted approvingly that their goods were displayed at home 'exactly as exhibited at the Paris Exhibition'.[76]

The Cork organizers had been clear from the beginning in their 'Rules for Exhibitors' that 'it is not intended to issue any awards', and indeed none were awarded. This may have been done in the spirit of 'fair play' or perhaps been a financial decision, given the amount of work to judge and award such prizes. At Cork's 1883 Expo, over £300 (£30,000) was spent on medals, and hundreds of prizes were given.[77] Given the clear importance businesses attached to these medals as promotional tools (7.9), this may have been a factor in why some foreign firms stayed away, and an oversight on the part of the organizers.

7.9
Advertisement for Plunkett's Maltsters. This firm had a strong export market & in common with many others were proud of their various exhibition medals from around Europe.
(Courtesy Michael Lenihan)

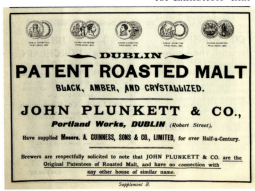

An Industrial Exhibition?

As to the question, posed at the top of this chapter, as to whether this event might properly be called an 'industrial' exhibition, the evidence points to the affirmative. Unlike the exhibitions held in Dublin between 1853 and 1882, where the primary exhibitors were retailers, rather than manufacturers,[78] the majority (72 per cent) of the *c*.320 Irish exhibitors at Cork were the makers of some, or all, of their merchandise (7.10). If those retailers who proudly stated that their wares were Irish-made (if not actually manufactured by them) are included in the figure above, it rises to three-quarters. Department stores, such as Switzers of Dublin, made an effort to make this clear to visitors (7.5). Other Dublin department stores (Arnott's, Clery's, etc.) had stayed away, but the big Patrick Street stores from Cork were there in force. That Arnott's should not be involved, given the involvement of senior members of that family in the Expo, is a mystery; perhaps they felt that the presence of their business Cash & Co. of Cork was sufficient.

Many of these stores, whilst primarily involved in retail, retained significant numbers of staff on their premises to custom-make clothing, especially shirts. It must be admitted that aside from the large department stores, a number of

7.10

Munster Arcade Stall. Some exhibitors were primarily involved in retail, such as Robertson, Ledlie, Ferguson & Co. (the Munster Arcade). However, here they emphasized their shirt-making business complete with three seamstresses at work. Staid as these displays may seem to us, they were standard fare at international exhibitions.

(Courtesy Michael Lenihan)

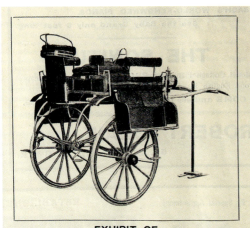

EXHIBIT OF

Messrs. CROSS AND SONS,

18, 19, SULLIVAN'S QUAY, CORK.

**Cross's Patent Improved Irish Jaunting Car
with Driver's Seat Behind.**

No. 309, AVENUE O.

7.11

Advertisement for Cross & Sons.
This firm received a patent for a modified jaunting car
which embodied many refinements, including placing the
jarvey at the rear, rather than the front. Another Cork maker,
James Regan, showed a patent 'Ralli' Car & took over fifty
orders in the first month of the expo.
(Courtesy Michael Lenihan)

the other 'manufacturers' included above were also
retailers first and manufacturers second. Lastly, it
should also be explained that the activities of some
of the other firms we include as 'manufacturers',
such as the many convents making lace, or small
sweet-makers serving a local market, were limited in
scale and perhaps not truly 'industrial' or capable of
penetrating export markets.

However, lest we be too harsh on these nascent
manufacturers, it is clear from the exhibition
catalogues and press clippings that a significant
minority of the Irish stands were demonstrating
patented technology, or at least, new methods
for doing things. Examples included a new rear-
driven jaunting car from Cross of Cork (7.11) as
well as innovations by other vehicle manufacturers,
a semi-automatic weaving loom aimed at training
tradespeople and Kapp & Peterson's patented
tobacco pipe. Belfast firm Davidson and Co.
showed their range of 'Sirocco' high-speed fans
(7.12)[79] and Wood's Pavement and Construction
Co. of Skibbereen had laid their patent-wood
flooring throughout the exhibition buildings
and 'granolithic' concrete used for the steps of
the Industrial Hall, by way of promoting their
invention.[80] One of the innovations which caught
the eye of many visitors was the 'Sunbeam' Acetylene
Gas Co. of Coleraine and Belfast. The inventor
of their gas-making process, Mr Williamson,
had received a patent for an automatic system of
generating, storing and igniting acetylene gas for
domestic and industrial illumination. The *Irish
Builder* confidently predicted that in spite of all
the enemies of gas lighting, this technology 'must
come to the front as the premier light of the near
future'.[81] Williamson and his colleagues believed

that gas was superior to electricity for lighting, and they weren't to know they were pursuing a technological dead end. Indeed, they had no doubt been encouraged that their work was beneficial when they won a prize at the Paris Expo for their work.[82]

There were other innovations from Belfast: Johnston (umbrellas, sunshades and walking sticks) were planning to introduce silk weaving for their products, for the first time in Ireland (7.13),[83] whilst R Christy and Co. showed their 'improved garden tents, without cords or centre pole in three sizes'.[84] In the Machinery Hall, visitors could see the new American 'Linotype' printing process demonstrated on the Cork Examiner stall and, on Messrs McKenzie's exhibit, 'an improved masticator manufactured at their Engineering Works'.[85] The Irish engineering industry was well represented. Although many of the firms were small, some, like Pierce of Wexford, showed strong signs of innovation. Based on the efforts of these firms, *The Times* predicted (sadly wrongly as it turned out) that 'Wexford promises to become the Birmingham of Ireland'.[86] As well as their 'famous "Victor" mowers', Pierce also exhibited their own-brand bicycles. A rival Cork manufacturer showed at least seven different models of bike, including the Royal Irish Constabulary 'path-racer' with 'its new pattern dropped frame and straight forks which looks a marvel of speed, and weighs only 19½lbs [9kg]'.[87] A less practical vehicle was the floating bike presented by a Limerick man. The machine had two floats and was intended to be propelled by paddles worked by the pedals.[88]

7.13

The exhibit of Johnston's umbrellas of Belfast & Dublin.

This was one of the more imaginative exhibits. It included a model of Blarney Castle, pre-fabricated from blackthorn walking sticks in Belfast. Inside visitors could experience the crystal 'Wonder Room'. The presence of the castle at exhibitions was by now something of a cliché.

(Courtesy Michael Lenihan)

In the field of building construction, several innovations were presented. The frame of the Art Gallery was constructed entirely of fireproof wood, 'as used in the construction of British and American warships'[89] and clad in corrugated iron. The wood was fireproofed by a patented process whereby it was treated with various chemicals including acid and ammonia.[90] The constructors were Humphreys of Knightsbridge, who had built the (British) Colonial and Indian sections at the Paris Exposition, for which they won a gold medal.[91] It possibly may not have been a pretty building, and no photographs of its exterior are known to survive, although it can be partially glimpsed behind the main Industrial Hall (6.5).

Two other English firms supplied pre-fabricated (or 'portable') buildings to the Exhibition Committee. These were not entirely a new idea for Cork; in 1851 a local firm had provided a 'corrugated and galvanised iron house' to the British Army to house 200 convicts and two years later a wooden prefab was sent from Cork to Australia. [92] In the 1860s the US Civil War had increased the profile of pre-fabrication as it was adopted by both armies to

7.14

Portable House & Café.
The Portable House Co. of
Fleetwood, Lancs, supplied
this L-shaped, half-timbered
building to act as a temporary HQ for exhibition staff.
The Irish Builder reckoned
it would be 'suitable for a
gentleman's shooting box
or seaside bungalow'. It cost
£800, & was disassembled
after the 1902 show. The
firm also supplied the Tír na
nÓg tearoom which may be
glimpsed on the far left.
(Courtesy Michael Lenihan)

house their men.[93] However, the products erected in the exhibition grounds were a world away from these Spartan military examples. The Portable House Co. erected two buildings at Cork, but their offices for the Cutler and his team was the more significant. Like the President's and Lord Mayor's Pavilion mentioned in an earlier chapter, this building revived many features of English vernacular architecture. These included the projecting gables and 'oriel' windows, red Broseley roof tiles, 'half-timbering' and multi-paned windows. It also introduced some more contemporary design features such as large porches *cum* verandas at the front and rear (7.14).[94] As we will see in a later chapter, buildings in this style were to have a long-lasting effect on Cork's architecture, even if the pre-fabricated system was not adopted. At the end of the show, the prefabs were removed from the site and their fate is unclear. However, within four years, two of the firms involved (John McManus & Co., who built the 'Colleen Bawn' tearoom, and the aforementioned Humphreys) had opened Dublin offices to serve the Irish market. The latter specialized in 'Iron Hospitals' and had built several across the country by 1907.[95] Concrete made with Portland cement was also demonstrated in Cork, in its reinforced form for the Fr Mathew Memorial Fountain, and for paving slabs around the grounds.

1903 Exhibits

The second year of the Exhibition showed considerable changes in the exhibits and introduced some new innovations. Some firms returned for the 1903 season, but instead of the 503 exhibitors listed in the catalogue in 1902, there were now only 190, and many of these were private individuals. The exotic element was boosted by an Indian Section. The London firm of Ardeshir & Byranji showed examples of Indian Art Ware and Embroidery. This firm's business was based on retailing Indian 'fancy goods' such as brass tea trays, sandal-wood carvings, vases and candlesticks imported from the sub-continent.[96] They had many years of experience in displaying at British exhibitions.[97] The DATI had populated about a fifth of the main Hall in 1902, but did not return for the second season. They donated their outside exhibits to the Exhibition Committee, and their internal space was filled with various worthy exhibits of science and industry, archaeology and history, natural history (especially stuffed animals), raw materials, forestry and flora, a schools exhibit and a lecture hall.

The floor area of the Women's Exhibit was doubled, the space filled with thirty-nine exhibition cases, and it became a more significant element of the show. The description of their presentations ran for over twenty pages in the exhibition catalogue. The exhibits, however, were very similar to the previous year. Whilst lace and crochet predominated, there was more of an emphasis on antiques, but also modern applied art from the Celtic Revival 'Dun Emer Guild', as well as loans from the Royal School of Art and Victoria and Albert Museum in London.

Some new foreign exhibitors came, such as Hovis bread, but the overall impression was of a large bazaar. There were many more fancy goods stalls and small concerns. One of these, which became a successful and long-lasting Cork business, was the sweets and Turkish Delight stand of Hadji Bey et Compagnie. Its founder, Harutun Batmazian, was a member of Turkey's persecuted Armenian Christian minority. He set up in business on MacCurtain St, and later production moved to 7 Parnell Place.[98] His firm survived until the mid-1970s, but the brand was revived in 2010.[99] The newly founded

Cork Industrial Development Association held an exhibition of goods made in Cork City and County, consisting of over fifty firms, most of who had been involved in the previous year. This group was founded by some leading Cork industrialists, but also involved several 'advanced Nationalists' including Liam de Roiste, later a Sinn Féin TD for Cork. The national aim of the 'made in Ireland' spirit seen in 1902 was also made explicit in a further 'Industrial Development' exhibit. Products were classed in four categories. The first class were those made in Ireland of Irish materials, the last (and presumably least desirable) classification consisted of those made abroad of foreign matter.

In terms of new innovations, the 1903 Exhibition introduced the city to the radioactive element radium, 'the latest wonder of the scientific world'. It was used to demonstrate X-Rays, although the protection offered for visitors from the material was rudimentary in the extreme.[100] A forerunner of the fax machine, the 'teleautograph' which allowed a person to sign documents remotely, was also shown. This product had first been demonstrated ten years previously at Chicago. The motor car made a huge impression at the 1903 show, as racers involved with the Gordon Bennett trophy stopped off here (see Chapter 9).

Lastly, a new water-borne transport link from the nearest tram stop was built to aid access to the grounds. This 'Gravity Canal' was the brainchild of Henry Cutler, although the design was based on something he had seen at the Glasgow Exhibition. Essentially, it was a pair of aqueducts running 200 yds (c.180m) each way along the Mardyke. After climbing to a platform 6ft (1.8m) above the pavement, passengers would settle into a small boat and, due to the gentle incline, drift serenely towards their destination. They were deposited at a basin near the main gates raised 3ft from the ground. Returning passengers would board the vessels for the journey back to the tram stop. The empty boats would then be winched back up to the starting platform. This system is the basis for all modern theme park water rides, and tame as it may sound to us, it was hailed as 'an undoubted novelty'[101] and 'a grand side-show' in itself.[102]

Conclusion

In summary, though the Exhibition was industrial, astute observers would have noticed that the strength of Irish industry still lay in its traditional areas, and that apart from a number of northern firms, the country was falling behind

British and Continental technology. Nevertheless, those seeking evidence of what was frequently referred in the All Ireland Review and elsewhere as 'the Irish industrial revival' could find some comfort. The innovations shown by at least some of the Irish firms, the emphasis on local production throughout the show and especially the work of the DATI were laudable. There was a tangible sense that this event, at the beginning of a new century, was going to be the start of something significant. The intended result of all of the Cork Exhibitions was to kick-start national improvement and (aside from the criticisms outlined above) there was to be no place for negativity. Following on from the efforts of the DATI and others, the *Cork Examiner's* correspondent hoped eventually 'to see … Irish technical schools equal to any in the world, scientific agriculture everywhere introduced, and the flow of emigration arrested by flourishing industries'.[103] It would take a long time and much water under the bridge before this was to come to pass.

Notes

1   Anon., *Official Catalogue, Cork International Exhibition 1902* (Cork: Guys, 1902), p.31.

2   A Mr Hay, Canadian National Archives, *Report of the Minister of Agriculture for the Dominion of Canada for the Year Ended October 1902*, p.vii.

3   Canadian National Archives, *Report of the Minister of Agriculture*, p.262.

4   D. Lane, 'The Irish Industries Association', *The Irish Monthly*, 21, 239 (May 1893), pp.237–41.

5   Comments in Visitor's Book, Canadian National Archives, *Report of the Minister of Agriculture*, p.264.

6   R. Storry, *A History of Modern Japan* (London: Penguin, 1982), p.138.

7   Robert Scott & Co. Ltd became South of Ireland agents for the 'Consolidated Telephone Construction and Maintenance Co. Ltd., London' in 1892. See *Strattens' Dublin, Cork and South of Ireland Directory* (London: Stratten & Stratten, 1892), p.176.

8   *Irish Builder*, 9 October 1902.

9   The installation was completely independent of the city's supply. The nearest grid supply point was at the Band Field, near the current main entrance to UCC. Cork City and County Archives Institute, Cork, ESB Holdings, U620, Box 39 Letter from Cork Electric Tramway and Lighting Co. to F. Daly, 27 November 1905.

10 *Cork Constitution*, 28 May 1902.

11 *The Times*, 3 May 1902.

12 *Daily Chronicle*, 19 June 1902.

13 C. Schindler, 'En Irlande' (Paris, 1903), in J. Fischer and G. Neville (eds), *As Others Saw Us* (Cork: Cork University Press, 2005) p.105. In fact the DATI indoor exhibit consisted of 30,000ft^2 (20 per cent of the Industrial Hall) one tenth of which was the Women's Section. The work of the Irish Department also included gathering statistics which allowed Ireland's trade to be studied independently of that of the United Kingdom from 1904 onwards. This information was of great interest to those wishing to make the case for Home Rule or full independence.

14 Canadian National Archives, *Report of the Minister of Agriculture*, p.261.

15 J. Turpin, 'Exhibitions of Art and Industry in Victorian Ireland: Part 2: Dublin Exhibitions of Art and Industries 1865–1885', *Dublin Historical Record*, 35, 2 (March 1982), p.51.

16 H. Plunkett, *Ireland in the New Century* (London: J. Murray, 1904), p.285.

17 F. McDonald, *Analysis of Pottery Vase made on Site at the Cork International Exhibition 1902*, Unpublished MA Year 1 Thesis (Dublin: National College of Art and Design, 2011).

18 'The Canterbury Weavers', *Whitstable Times and Herne Bay Herald*, 7 March 1903.

19 *Belfast Newsletter*, 1 May 1902.

20 Advertisement 'Cork International Exhibition', *An Claidheamh Soluis*, 18 October 1902.

Speakers included: M. Boveri of Baden, Switzerland, Wilhelm Exner (Vienna) and J. Tissington (Tatlow). The DATI also used the Expo as an opportunity to launch a second edition of their *Ireland, Industrial and Agricultural* (1901).

21 The general committee included three duchesses, six marchionesses and twenty-nine countesses.

22 M. Luddy, 'Women and Philanthropy in Nineteenth-century Ireland', *Voluntas: International Journal of Nonprofit Organisations*, 7, 4 (1996), p.358.

23 Anon., *Official Catalogue 1902*, pp.26–30.

24 Anon., *The Illustrated Cork Exhibitor* (Dublin: Wilson, Hartnell & Co, 1902), p.22.

25 Ibid, p.57, advertisement for Lansdowne Tweeds.

26 'Cork Exhibition – the Technical School Exhibits', *Irish Builder*, 5 June 1902.

27 'Visit of Irish Trades Union Congress', *Cork Examiner*, 22 May 1902.

28 D.V. Kelleher, *James Dominic Burke; A Pioneer in Irish Education* (Dublin: Irish Academic Press, 1988), pp.143 & 146.

29 See Plunkett, *Ireland in the New Century*, p.285.

30 P. and J. Kinchin, *Glasgow's Great Exhibitions; 1888–1901–1911–1938–1988* (Bicester: White Cockade Publishing, 1988), p.86.

31 J.F. Maguire, *The Industrial Movement in Ireland as illustrated by the National Exhibition of 1852* (Cork: John O'Brien, 1853), p.9.

32 W.E. Coe, *The Engineering Industry of the North of Ireland* (Newton Abbot: David & Charles, 1969), p.132.

33 *All Ireland Review*, 17 May 1902.

34 *Belfast Newsletter*, 1 May 1902.

35 See Plunkett, *Ireland in the New Century*, p.286.

36 See Kelleher, *James Dominic Burke*, p.144.

37 Census of Ireland, 1901, records for Gill (aged

42) and Macartney-Filgate (37).

38 S. Rains, *Commodity Culture and Social Class in Dublin 1850–1916* (Dublin: Irish Academic Press, 2010), p.189.

39 Anon., *Official Guide, Cork International Exhibition 1902* (Cork: Guys, 1902), p.26.

40 See P. and J. Kinchin, *Glasgow's Great Exhibitions*, pp.47 & 59.

41 See Anon., *Cork Exhibitor*, pp.26–7. Jacob's were biscuit makers to 'Her late Majesty Queen Victoria'.

42 Ibid., p.36.

43 This arrangement had also been a feature of the 1853 Dublin Exhibition. See Rains, *Commodity Culture*, p.34.

44 Brian Lawlor recalls that his grandparents purchased a piano at the exhibition. B. Lawlor, *Rosenheim and Windermere* (Bantry: Somerville Press, 2011).

45 *All Ireland Review*, 21 June 1902.

46 *All Ireland Review*, 6 September 1902.

47 *The Builder*, 83, p.337, 18 October 1902.

48 This had been a trend in Irish retail for about twenty years. See Rains, *Commodity Culture*, p.95.

49 See Anon., *Official Catalogue 1902*, p.53.

50 See Anon., *Cork Exhibitor*, p.33.

51 This had been a contentious issue in Irish exhibitions since 1852.

52 See P. and J. Kinchin, *Glasgow's Great Exhibitions*, p.28.

53 1902 saw exhibitions in Wolverhampton, Dusseldorf and Turin, where C.R. Macintosh exhibited.

54 See Anon., *Cork Exhibitor*, Supplement E.

55 These were probably semi-precious stones such as malachite.

56 On McKenzie & Co.'s stall in the Machinery Hall.

57 'Cork Exhibition', *Freeman's Journal*, 19 August 1902.

58 Coe, *Engineering in North of Ireland*, p.91.

59 Ibid., pp.74 & 120.

60 See P. and J. Kinchin, *Glasgow's Great Exhibitions*, p.71.

61 Joseph Braddell & Co, Belfast, largest manufacturers in Ireland in 1893 & makers of shotguns and 'Ulster Bulldog' revolvers. See Coe, *Engineering in North of Ireland*, p.15.

62 See Schindler, En Irlande; *As Others Saw Us*, p.105.

63 *Irish Builder*, No.1018, 22 May 1902, p.1,256.

64 *Irish Builder*, 19 June 1902.

65 'Cork Exhibition', *Irish Builder*, 5 June 1902.

66 *Irish Builder*, 9 October 1902.

67 Editorial, *Lincolnshire Echo*, 7 May 1902.

68 See Plunkett, *Ireland in the New Century*, p.288.

69 See *Stratten's 1892*, pp.280–1.

70 See Anon., *Cork Exhibitor*, p.51.

71 *All Ireland Review*, 17 May 1902, Vol. 3, #11, p.165.

72 C. Rynne, *The Industrial Archaeology of Cork City and its Environs* (Dublin: Stationery Office, 1999), p.159.

73 See *Stratten's 1892*, p.195.

74 *Cork Constitution* 17 May 1902, The firm was Dunville & Co. Ltd (Whiskey), Belfast.

75 Anon., *Official Guide 1902*, p.17.

76 *All Ireland Review*, 21 June 1902.

77 W.K. Sullivan, J. Brenan, and R. Day, *Cork Industrial Exhibition 1883, Report of Executive Committee, Awards of Jurors and Statement of Accounts* (Cork: Purcell & Co., 1886), pp.295–431.

78 Rains, *Commodity Culture*, p.75.

79 Anon., *Official Guide 1902*, p.25, the firm also had branches in London, Manchester, Glasgow, Bristol and Newcastle-on-Tyne.

80 'Cork Exhibition', *Irish Builder*, 5 June 1902. According to the *Southern Star*, 6 June 1901, the pavement material was invented by Mr Wood and was 'made from a superior hard whinstone' like flint or basalt.

81 *Irish Builder*, 8 May 1902, p.1229.

82 See Anon., *Cork Exhibitor*, p.48.

83 Ibid., p.26.

84 *All Ireland Review*, 6 September 1902.

85 *All Ireland Review*, 21 June 1902.

86 *The Times*, 3 May 1902.

87 'Irish Cycle Company' est. 1889, Patrick St, Drawbridge St and Anglesea St, Cork see *All Ireland Review*, 28 June 1902.

88 *Cork Examiner*, 30 May 1902.

89 Anon., *Official Guide 1902*, p.32.

90 *Irish Builder*, 8 May 1902, No.1017, p.1,227 & *The Builder*, 83, p.168, 23 August 1902 'Fireproof Wood' by W.C. Dickinson.

91 See Anon., *Official Catalogue 1902*, p.12.

92 R. Herlihy, *Tales from Victorian Cork 1837–1859* (Cork: Red Abbey Publications, 2012, p.104.The firm was McSwiney & Co, the site Spike Island, see also p.217.

93 English and Scottish firms such as Handyside of Derby and Macfarlane of Glasgow were world leaders in prefabricated cast iron structures by this time, but these were generally not residential. cf. M. Higgs, 'The Exported Iron buildings of Andrew Handyside & Co. of Derby', *Journal of the Society of Architectural Historians*, 29, 2 (May 1970). For the US, see M.J. Darnall, 'Innovations in American Prefabricated Housing: 1860–1890', *Journal of the Society of Architectural Historians*, 31, 1 (March 1972), pp.51–5.

94 Anon., *Official Guide 1902*, p.43 (ill.).

95 *Irish Builder*, 13 January 1906 & 20 April 1907. The Iron hospitals were in Clonmel, Waterford and Rathmines. Humphreys went on to be the exclusive constructor for the 1907 Dublin International Exhibition. See also, *Irish Builder*, 3 December 1904, p.827, Advert for McManus 'Iron and Wood Buildings' of every description. 'John McManus has supplied to HM Government the largest order ever executed for Iron Buildings exceeding in value a quarter of million sterling.'

96 *Irish Times*, 21 May 1898, quoted in Rains, *Commodity Culture*, p.159.

97 See P. and J. Kinchin, *Glasgow's Great Exhibitions*, p.37.

98 'New Lease of Life for Cork's Age-Old Sweetmeat', *Cork Examiner*, 26 May 1971. Ogilvie & Moore took over the manufacture of Turkish Delight.

99 http://hadjibey.ie/history.html available 20 February 2013.

100 Anon., *The Official Catalogue and Guide, Greater Cork International Exhibition 1903* (Cork: Guys, 1903), p.24. The sample was held in a small brass tube and it appears that people were allowed to handle it. See also, *Cork Constitution*, 13 August 1903.

101 *Cork Examiner*, 28 May 1903.

102 See Anon., *Official Catalogue and Guide 1903*, p.48.

103 'Visit of Irish Trades Union Congress', *Cork Examiner*, 22 May 1902.

No. **36**

Cork International Exhibition,

1902.

Season Ticket.

THIS Ticket entitles Subscriber to admission to the Exhibition at all times when open to the public, with the exception of Opening Day, and six other days of which due notice will be given.

NOT TRANSFERABLE.

This Ticket is issued subject to all regulations of the Executive Committee, made or to be made, and will be forfeited if lost, lent, or transferred, and must be shown on each occasion of entering the Exhibition.

Signature of Holder *Barry M. Mullen*

34 Grey Street No. 36

R. H. Atkins Hon. Sec.

GREATER CORK
INTERNATIONAL EXHIBITION
1903.
SEASON TICKET.

8
Tourism, Royal Visits, Amusements and Entertainments

Daniel Breen

Exhibitions and Tourism: If You Build it, They Will Come!

The rapidly changing world of global innovation and progress that had inspired International Exhibitions also created an industry devoted to travel and pleasure-seeking. By no means did they develop independently of each other; in fact they enjoyed a mutually beneficial relationship almost from the start. Popular tourism was initially a British invention, catering for an emerging urban working class that desired to escape the humdrum of their everyday life and 'get away from it all'.

The grandfather of modern tourism was a devout Baptist and Temperance Society member, Thomas Cook, a name still synonymous with travel today.[1] In 1841, he organized a trip between Leicester and Loughborough (11 miles, 18km) to bring a group of 570 teetotallers to a temperance rally. A band was employed to entertain the passengers on the round trip and the service cost one shilling (c.€4.40). Cook had seen a market for excursion holidays and over the following decades he developed and expanded his operations. The nineteenth century brought much-needed reform to working practices, with the introduction of several Factory Acts designed to limit child labour and regulate hours and wages. The increased free time and disposable income of the working classes, as well as the emergence of extensive transport and communication networks made holidaying both fashionable and affordable. International Exhibitions proved to be one of the most popular destinations for all classes. Thomas Cook was one of the first to exploit their appeal by bringing 165,000 people to the Crystal Palace, and four years later he pioneered foreign package holidays by ferrying a group from Leicester to the 1855 Paris Exposition. For Cook, excursion holidays were a divinely inspired

8.1:
Season Tickets 1902 & 1903.
Barry McMullen of 34 Mary St, Cork City, purchased this 1902 season ticket. McMullen was a builder and lived with his two sons, his daughter-in-law and granddaughter. One son, James (aged 41 and unmarried), was the architect who designed the Father Mathew Pavilion in the exhibition. He was also heavily involved in the Gordon Bennett time-trial event in 1903.

social crusade intended to bring the educational aspects of travel to ordinary people.[2] The durability of the International Exhibitions is, amongst other things, testament to their long-lasting popularity as a tourist destination. The attendance records for major International Expositions provide truly astronomical figures. Six million visited the first international exhibition in Hyde Park, eleven million came to Paris in 1867, and over one hundred million people in total journeyed to fill the grounds of America's pre-First World War Fairs. In 1900, Paris welcomed fifty million visitors, even though the French population at the time only numbered thirty-five million. The twenty-first century continues to demonstrate that exhibition fervour still shows no sign of abating, as Shanghai 2010 recorded a staggering seventy million visits.[3] Serving this amount of people requires detailed planning and co-operation between travel agencies, rail and ferry services and exhibition organizers.

During the formative years of modern Irish tourism, Thomas Cook and (later Thomas Cook and Son) helped promote Ireland as a popular destination in Britain. Cook began excursions to Ireland in 1849 and was by 1888 able to offer tours throughout Ireland by rail, steamer and coach, and welcomed his first American tourists in 1895. However, Cook was in constant conflict with the Irish railway companies, who wanted to run their own excursions, cutting Cook out of the loop. He set up his first Irish office in Dublin in 1874 and had three further offices in Belfast, Cork and Queenstown by 1900; it is a former employee of Cook's Dublin office, Frederick W. Crossley, who is credited as the 'engine' of Irish tourism in the later decades of the nineteenth century.[4] In 1891, Crossley resigned his job from Thomas Cook and Son, as he felt he was not receiving the support he needed to develop Ireland's embryonic tourism industry. In her book *Irish Tourism 1880–1980*, Irene Furlong highlights that tourism in Ireland during most of the nineteenth century suffered from a lack of well-known attractions, a complete dependence on foreigner visitors and 'deficiencies of accommodation, amenities and transport facilities, along with an image of lawlessness and political unrest'.[5] Crossley aimed to bring together groups and individuals who could benefit from the untapped potential of Irish tourism with the founding of the Irish Tourist Association in 1894. He and his fellow members 'wished to dispel the impression of Ireland as a wild and uncivilised region through effective advertising'.[6] Committees were set up in Belfast and in 1896 a Cork committee was formed under the auspice of the

Earl of Bandon. In June of the same year, Crossley organized a large meeting of the Irish gentry and political classes in London to discuss and promote Irish tourism. It received much attention and coverage in the British media, serving Crossley's desire to bring Ireland's potential to a larger audience. In many ways, Crossley and Irish exhibition organizers shared the hope that they could improve the international and national perceptions of the country and what it had to offer.

As early as 1852, the Cork Exhibition attracted many visitors from Great Britain, thanks to cheap tickets organized by the Chester and Holyhead Railway Company.[7] As he had done for visitors to the Crystal Palace, Thomas Cook took 'thousands' of British people to visit the 1853 Exhibition in Dublin.[8] By the time of Cork's second exhibition in 1883, advertisements in the official illustrated guide detailed tourist routes from Britain and regular passenger services between America and Ireland.[9] Due to the work of men like Crossley and the influence of Thomas Cook's agency, organizers of the 1902 and 1903 Exhibitions were in a favourable position to exploit the improved rail and ferry services to Cork, its improved tourist accommodation and the city's enhanced public amenities. Aside from descriptions of the exhibition grounds and its attractions, the official guides (8.2a & b) gave over a good deal of their content to advertising shipping services of the Dominion,

8.2a:
Tourism and Cork's Exhibitions.
The development of a tourism industry alongside the international exhibition movement was a symbiotic relationship. The 1902/3 Exhibitions proved no different. Local hotels, restaurants and transport companies reaped significant profits from the events. It was estimated that the exhibitions brought £1.25 million (£125 million) into the local economy.
(© CPM)

The Munster Hotel,

COBURG STREET, CORK.

Private

Dining and

Sitting

Rooms.

Wedding

Orders

at

Shortest

Notice.

FAMILY AND COMMERCIAL.

TURNER'S HOTEL,

CORK

(Opposite Berwick Fountain).

FIRST-CLASS FAMILY

COMMERCIAL HOTEL.

Restaurant Attached.

TABLE D'HOTE, 2 till 3, and 6 till 7-30.

Electric Light. Night Porter.
'BUSES ATTEND ALL TRAINS AND STEAMERS.

E. T. Turner,
Proprietor.

HOTEL METROPOLE, CORK.
A Splendid Modern Hotel. Electric Elevator. Promenade Roof.

Cunard and White Star Lines as well as tourist packages offered by both Irish and English rail companies. Details of these packages were regularly published in newspapers, highlighting both the scale of connections between Cork and foreign cities and the impressive public transport services available at the time in the city. The City of Cork Steam Packet Company, for example, offered British tourists packages to Cork and vice versa (including both ship and rail) from London, Bristol, Milford Haven, Newport, Plymouth, Cardiff and Southampton.[10] Even the Boston-based *Donahoe's Magazine* arranged packages for interested Irish Americans who wanted to patronize the Exposition.[11] The advertising crusade in America was no doubt aided by the membership of the US Consul to Queenstown (Cobh) D. Swiney in the Executive Committee.[12] Many of the special packages arranged for foreign visitors allowed at least two weeks' stopover in Ireland before their return journey, permitting adequate time to sample what the rest of the country had to offer. The exhibition guides also contained useful information for tourists such as train, tram and jaunting car routes and rates as well as promoting the city as a travel hub and a base for those who may have wanted to travel further afield,

8.2b:

Tourism and Cork's Exhibitions.

The development of a tourism industry alongside the international exhibition movement was a symbiotic relationship. The 1902/3 Exhibitions proved no different. Local hotels, restaurants and transport companies reaped significant profits from the events. It was estimated that the exhibitions brought £1.25 million (£125 million) into the local economy. (© CPM)

experiencing towns and attractions across Munster like Queenstown, Youghal, Ballycotton, Bandon, Limerick, Killarney, Lismore, Fermoy, Glengarriff and Clonakilty (8.3). Following its regular appearances at foreign expositions, the 'world famous' Blarney Castle was now promoted as a necessary destination for all tourists. The illustrated guide published by Guy & Co Ltd entitled *Cork International Exhibition and South of Ireland Souvenir* is so similar to modern-day tourist brochures that it would hardly look out of place at a Bord Fáilte event today (8.2a).[13]

By the autumn of 1901, however, some concerns were raised in the press and at committee meetings as to whether there was enough accommodation in the city to cater for the increased influx of tourists. Fears had been roused following a visit to Glasgow Exhibition by Fitzgerald and members of the Executive Committee in June 1901 where they learned first-hand that, if Cork's exhibition hoped to attract the visitor numbers needed to make it a success, guest accommodation was an issue that needed immediate attention. Three of Cork's well-known hotels, the Victoria, Imperial and Metropole, committed themselves to improvement works to increase their accommodation.[14] Arthur Hill, as well as busying himself on the exhibition grounds, also supervised improvements to the Metropole Hotel on King's Street (now MacCurtain Street). In early September 1901, Atkins, the Exhibition's secretary, wrote a letter that was published in all local newspapers asking all parties who had private lodgings or rooms to let to submit their details and charges to his

8.3:
Rotunda of the Industrial Hall.
The importance of the tourist element to the whole enterprise is evident from the fact that the first stalls a visitor would see are run by the Great Southern & Western and Midland Great Western Railways.
(© NLI)

Unceasing Round of Amusements.

COME & VISIT THE

Cork International Exhibition

NOW OPEN.

THE LORD LIEUTENANT ON THE EXHIBITION:

Speaking to the Trinity College graduates in Dublin on May 30th, his Excellency the Lord Lieutenant of Ireland, Earl Cadogan, said :—" I hope that every lady and every gentleman in this room will, before the season is over, make it their business, as well as their pleasure, to go and see what, in my opinion, is **ONE OF THE MOST REMARKABLE EXHIBITIONS** that has ever been held, probably in any country. It is impossible to exaggerate the ability and the success with which the arrangements for that Exhibition have been carried out, and I am quite sure it will **WELL REWARD A VISIT,** which I hope, you will all feel disposed to pay it."

The **EDUCATIONAL ADVANTAGES** are of immense importance to Farmers and others, who should not fail to visit the Exhibits of the Department of Agriculture and Technical Instruction. Agricultural Experts on the Grounds who will give information and instructions to Visitors FREE.

Look out for *CHEAP EXCURSIONS by all Railways,*

8.4:
Advertising the Exhibition. Leaflets and posters were sent throughout Ireland and abroad to attract as many visitors as possible. The emphasis of an 'Unceasing Round of Amusements' at the top of the pamphlet is telling.
(© Clonakilty Museum)

office.[15] He hoped to furnish these details to the foreign press so as to allow visitors to plan accommodation before leaving their native lands. One of the most intriguing structures associated with the Exhibition was Gordon's Hotel, built where the modern-day Erinville Hospital was located (see Chapter 6).

Exhibition organizers, and especially the DATI, arranged special excursion packages in conjunction with railway companies to allow hundreds of thousands of Irish people to visit the Exhibition. Specially priced train tickets which also included entrance to the Exhibition were offered and towns and cities across the country availed of these arrangements and organized large excursion groups to visit Cork (8.5). Over the 1902 August Bank Holiday

EMPLOYEES, LEE BOOT MANUFACTURING CO. CORK. 1902 EXHIBITION.

for example, thousands of visitors came through the exhibition gates on excursions from Limerick, Portarlington, Dublin, Laois, Carlow, Claremorris, Templemore and Castlebar. In fact, Fitzgerald estimated that 27,000 people visited on the Bank Holiday Monday alone.[16] Later that month, a group of 500 people travelled to the Exhibition from Clonakility aboard specially organized trains. The business owners and tradesmen in the town had all agreed to give their workers the day off so that they could visit the Mardyke.[17] Many of the rural and urban working-class groups that travelled to the Exhibition were usually supervised by their local priest. Examples include a 350-strong group from Nenagh who visited under the charge of Fr Crowe, while a group of 800 from Bandon were supervised by Fr McSwiney, Chaplain to the Bandon Presentation Convent.[18] At a grass-roots level, the clergy played an important role in ensuring their congregations were able to visit the Cork Exhibition so as to benefit from the educational exhibits and demonstrations on display in the Western Field.

The most important clergyman engaged in both years of the Exhibition was renowned scientist and educational reformer, Brother Burke, though Revd P.J. Dowling, Vice-Chairman of the Cork Technical Institute, was a Vice-President for the 1903 season. Despite the absence of the Church hierarchy, there was a strong undercurrent of religious and moral sentiment at the Exposition.

8.5:
Dwyer's Lee Boot Factory Employees.
This detail shows some of the 104 female and 100 male staff on a visit, paid for by their employer in 1902. The women, particularly, are dressed en fête. Such 'works outings' were encouraged by the exhibition organizers, and were a memorable day out. (© CPM)

8.7:

Who Could Be Seen on the Exhibition Grounds?
A wide variety of people and cultures that could be seen on the banks of the River Lee during the exhibition: both foreign and local, & from all social classes. The emphasis on the unusual illustrates the blurred line between exhibits and employees. Illustrations like this underline how exhibitions tended to promote people as curiosities, celebrating the exotic and the strange, as well as the Victorian fascination for 'types', so apparent in 9.5. (© CPM)

The growth in newspaper readership in our period of study accelerated a celebrity culture. Wherever members of the royal family, important foreign dignitaries or internationally renowned philanthropists travelled, the press and public were sure to follow (though it lacked the intrusive traits of the modern *paparazzi*). It became imperative therefore for the organizers of Cork's Exhibitions to entice as many of these 'celebrities' to the Mardyke as possible. Not only did they guarantee newspaper coverage for the city but their presence helped affirm the months of hard work invested in the project. For Fitzgerald and others, attracting King Edward VII to Cork was crucial to fulfilling the Exhibition's potential to focus positive international attention on the city. Cork's earlier exhibitions had not attracted royal visits and in many ways this matched the limited scope of the undertakings. In 1903, the Executive Committee had surpassed previous organizers by bringing a man Fitzgerald termed as the 'greatest living Sovereign and the most popular Sovereign in the world' to its exhibition.[25] The planned arrival of the royal family symbolized the confidence of its organizers and the stature of what they had achieved on the Mardyke. It did not hurt either that royal visitors tended to stimulate local and British interest and increase attendance.

Prior to the King's visit in August, other members of the royal family had undertaken the pilgrimage to Cork. These included the Duke and Duchess of Connaught (the King's brother), as well as their children, Prince Henry of Prussia and Princess Margaret of Connaught in 1902 (8.8a & b). Many prominent Anglo-Irish politicians, some of whom we have already met, such as the Lords Lieutenant of Ireland, the Earls of Cadogan and

Dudley and their wives, had visited the exhibition grounds on numerous occasions. The Chief Secretary of Ireland, George Wyndham, and his wife, Countess Grosvenor, made a private and unofficial visit to the Exhibition in early September 1902. They were personally welcomed by the Lord Mayor but the visit drew some criticism from United Irish League corporation members as a protest at Wyndham's continued role in implementing the Irish Coercian Act of 1881.[26] In the weeks before the official opening in 1902, two leading figures of Irish nationalism, John Redmond and William O'Brien, called in on the Mardyke to see for themselves how preparations were progressing. They expressed their unconditional support for the project and were heartily cheered by the workmen present. It is clear therefore that by the time King Edward arrived in Cork, the Exhibition was enjoying healthy patronage from all sides of Anglo-Irish political life.

8.8a & b:
The Visit of the Duke of Connaught and Prince Henry of Prussia, 8 May 1902.
The Duke performed two important functions that day: he opened the new bridge that linked the Western Road to Donovan's Road and he also officially opened the Water Chute. The Duke and Duchess enjoyed a tour through the grounds and a pleasure cruise on the river (in the State Electric Barge, the Shamrock).
(© Michael Lenihan & CPM)

The day after the closing of the second season, the *Cork Constitution* published a roll call of the most illustrious visitors.[27] As expected, royalty and political figures dominate the list but several unusual and unexpected names do appear. Chief amongst them were the rear-admiral, officers and crew of the Japanese fleet. On 21 August 1902, two Japanese warships, the *Asama* and the *Takasago* steamed into Cork Harbour to attend the Exhibition.[28] They had been en route from England, where they had attended King Edward's coronation celebrations, as well as promoting the newly signed Anglo-Japanese Alliance mentioned in Chapter 7. Four hundred crew members were transported free of charge to the Exhibition from Queenstown (Cobh) by the Cork and Passage Railway Company. The *Cork Constitution* described these naval guests as 'bright, intelligent lot, somewhat below the average British tar in physique'.[29] The 'Jolly Japs' had little or no English between them and watching them try to communicate with stall holders was 'most amusing'.[30] They seemed to have particularly enjoyed the Machinery Hall and the bars, and took great pleasure from the Water Chute. Later that afternoon, Admiral Goro Ijuin and his officers were personally shown around the grounds by Lord Mayor Fitzgerald (8.9). After the tour, the officers were treated to dinner at the Chalet Restaurant followed by speeches and other pleasantries at the Lord Mayor's Pavilion. During the course of the speeches, Admiral Ijuin thanked his hosts for their hospitality and hoped in the near future Irish manufacturing products would become better known in Japan, strengthening commercial and cultural links between both countries.[31] The oriental visitors departed from the grounds to the cheers of the large crowd which had gathered to observe them. The Japanese had brought an element of the exotic to the Mardyke and must have caused quite a sensation amongst the native onlookers.[32] Another 'exotic' visitor to the Exhibition was the Maharajah Scindia of Gwalior, ruler of a small region in northern India. His presence is explained by his appointment as King Edward's honorary aide-de-camp in 1901, a title he received for his support of Britain in putting down the Boxer Rebellion.[33]

In the autumn of 1902, two prominent guests from Australasia called in on Cork's exhibition. These were Richard John Seddon, Prime Minister of New Zealand, and Cardinal Moran, Archbishop of Sydney. Seddon, New Zealand's longest serving leader (1893–1906), had a powerful influence on the country's politics during the late Victorian period. A staunch imperialist, he also arrived in Cork after first attending the coronation of King Edward in

8.9:
Insignia of the Commander of the Order of Sacred Treasure.
After the exhibition, the Emperor of Japan bestowed this honour on Fitzgerald 'in recognition of courteous attentions shown to our naval officers and others and of valuable services rendered to the Japanese Squadron on the occasion of their visit to this country, 1902'.
(© CPM)

London. A famously rotund man, Seddon, on entering the Industrial Hall, weighed himself on a penny-slot machine which recorded the impressive figure of almost twenty stone (*c.*127kg).[34] He was particularly interested in the New Zealand exhibits that were housed in the Lord Mayor's Pavilion. Cardinal Moran visited the Exhibition while in Cork receiving the Freedom of the City. He had a personal interest in the material displayed in the Father Mathew Pavilion as his uncle, Cardinal Cullen, Rector of the Irish College in Rome, was a friend to the late temperance crusader. Again, as with other important visitors, he received a guided tour through the grounds by the ever-present Lord Mayor Fitzgerald.

King Edward VII and 'Rebel Cork'

> *Oh everywhere there's gladness*
> *For up the River Lee*
> *Their Majesties are coming*
> *Dear 'Rebel Cork' to thee!*
> *Perhaps – well – yes – we earned it,*
> *But soon, as will be seen*
> *A true Cead Mile Failte*
> *Will greet our King and Queen!*
> – First verse of a poem printed in the *Cork Constitution*, 30 July 1903

The visit of King Edward, his wife, Queen Alexandra, and their daughter, Princess Victoria, to the Exhibition on 1 August 1903 was the social event that left every other in the shade. It was a publicity coup, promoting Cork as a modern and civilized city, especially in the British media, as well as earning kudos for the organizers and politicians involved.[35] By the time of her death in 1901 Edward's mother, Queen Victoria, led a reclusive lifestyle, secluded from the outside world. She did visit Ireland in the year before her death but it was a spur-of-the-moment decision that caught many in Ireland by surprise. The Queen was received cordially and enthusiastically wherever she went but the visit did highlight the growing tension between various factions of Irish nationalists as to how best to 'greet' her.[36] In the end any opposition petered out due in part to the Queen being viewed as an old woman who should not be subjected to harassment, and perhaps more importantly, the divisions that existed within Irish nationalism prevented any co-ordinated protest being organized. Her reign in Ireland witnessed great changes in politics and attitudes towards the monarchy and for many prominent nationalists she remained the 'Famine Queen', and to them her 1900 visit was nothing more than recruitment campaign to enlist Irishmen for the Boer War.[37]

However, the news of the imminent arrival of the new monarch in 1903 was generally viewed in Ireland as a good omen for the future of Anglo-Irish relations. King Edward, or 'Bertie', was generally seen to be a friend of Ireland, genuinely interested and eager to bring peace and prosperity to its people. In his two-volume biography of King Edward, Sidney Lee highlights how it was rumoured at the beginning of his reign that Edward hoped to tackle the Irish Question.[38] Though this was an exaggeration of Edward's goodwill towards nationalist Ireland, (as he did not support Home Rule), he was committed to improving social and political conditions in the country. King Edward came to the throne at 59 years of age and was king for only nine years before his death in 1910. In this short time, he came to symbolize the optimism of the period and served as a figurehead for a more inclusive, open and popular monarchy.[39] Edward was indeed a popular monarch, both at home and abroad, and earned the nickname 'Uncle of Europe' for his cordial and diplomatic relationships with many other European rulers.[40]

News of the death of Pope Leo XIII reached Ireland just as the Edward's visit started in Dublin. The King enhanced his reputation amongst the Catholic community by immediately sending his condolences to Cardinal Logue in Armagh. Horace Plunkett, in reviewing the King's visit, attributed this gesture as 'proof of his knowledge of Irish conditions'.[41] His visit to Cork came at the tail end of the official tour of Ireland that also included stops at Dublin, Belfast, Derry, Kerry and Galway. However, it must have been with some trepidation that King Edward disembarked on Victoria (now Kennedy) Quay to begin a day-long excursion through Cork City. He had visited the city once before as the Prince of Wales in 1885 but on this occasion, he was subjected to a less-than-enthusiastic reception, as the citizens of Cork booed and hissed him (4.12). Taking their cue from the contemporary political and social unrest in the country, they also waved black flags to signal their disgust as he made his way through the city.[42] In 1903, the atmosphere had very much improved, yet the regal visit did reveal the continued complex and varying attitudes towards the monarchy, Irish–British relations and Irish Independence. Unionists were understandably thrilled with the visit, staunch nationalists and radicals opposed it, but moderate nationalists and many Home Rulers believed the King should be accorded a friendly and respectful welcome without stooping to excessive 'posing and posturing'.[43]

Overall, the royal jaunt around Ireland was positively received, and the King and Queen were greeted with a warm and welcoming reception wherever they went. The entire operation was staged with the pomp and pageantry associated with royal excursions, incorporating processions, speeches, presentations and a very visible police and military presence. In Cork, as the royal family disembarked from the HMS *Vivid*, they were welcomed by the 'frantic acclamation and the waving of handkerchiefs'.[44] They were met by a delegation that included the Lord Mayor, the Duke of Connacht and the nineteen Unionist councillors. Though the newspapers refer to the popular and enthusiastic response received by the royal family in Cork, it was clear that thirty-five nationalist councillors were absent from the initial welcoming party. The *Freeman's Journal*, which was generally positive about the royal trip, warned its readers not to be overly seduced by the 'rosy cloud of promises, *and* vague blessings for Ireland'.[45] It summed up the age-old position for the majority of nationalists towards the monarchy that 'Irish loyalty must be secured by the concession of Irish liberty.'[46] This sentiment was not based on the antipathy towards King Edward, but on the frustration at the lack of progress in securing Home Rule for Ireland.[47]

While there were no protests on the scale of the 1885 visit, it would be wrong to take this as an indication of unequivocal loyalty towards Edward. One leading Cork nationalist, Liam de Roiste, saw this lack of protest as a result of the 'ten thousand armed men … five or six thousand armed police, [and] a host of detectives and spies', being present in the city at the time of the visit. It is clear from newspaper accounts that the royal processional route was lined with officers and infantry of various British and Irish regiments who guarded the quays and the side streets.[48] De Roiste also complained that the prominent military and police presence was such 'no protest can be made: no sound but that of "loyal" cheering come to his ears. Even if the city were seething with "disloyalty", Edward will not be permitted to see any display of it.'[49] William L. Cooke, who as a child lived on the Western Road, recalled his father telling him years later about how their house was stoned and windows broken because they displayed Union Jacks in celebration of the royal visitation.[50] Another man by the name of Arthur Jones was sentenced to seven days' imprisonment for tearing down some of the street decorations. On being sentenced, he claimed that he was 'sorry for rebel Cork' and that he would repeat his actions upon his release.[51] As for de Roiste, he decided along with some of his nationalist friends, including Terence MacSwiney, to cycle to Crosshaven to escape the 'flunkeyism and toadism' on display. On their way out of the city, they encountered the royal procession on the Grand Parade near the 1798 Memorial Stone. In his diary, de Roiste wondered to himself if the King knew what that monument stood for or if he was aware of how the statue of King George II that had previously occupied that spot had 'met a watery doom?'[52] It is clear the 1903 visit brought to the surface the viewpoints of more radical and hard-line nationalists. Though in the minority, de Roiste points to the direction Irish politics would take in the coming decades:

> Well, 'Ned's' visit is ended now, thank God. Our work for the building up of the Irish nation must go on: and will go on. The outward gilding of the day may have seemed splendid to those to whom it appealed; but the inward spirit that is Irish Nationality will palpitate when the tinselling of 'loyalty' for England's King are rotted.[53]

On examining the newspapers and photographs taken at the time, we see the 'loyalty' described by de Roiste. The reports and images reveal a city excited and willing to enjoy the patronage of Edward (8.10). The day was divided into four distinct engagements. On landing at Victoria Quay, the royal entourage immediately made their way to Cork Park on the Marina, where the King presented new colours to the 2nd Battalion of the Royal Irish Regiment and the 2nd Battalion of the Royal Munster Fusiliers. They travelled straight from Cork Park to the Mardyke, arriving at twenty minutes past one. Their stay on the exhibition grounds incorporated an official ceremony in the Concert Hall (8.11), a twelve-course luncheon in Shrubbery House (8.12) and a guided tour through the grounds in the royal carriage (Fitzgerald walked beside them) (8.13). They enjoyed watching members of the Executive Committee careen down the Water Chute and observed Irish dancing and music on the Western Gardens near the Irish Labourer's Cottage. They left the grounds at around 4pm and made their way to the Glanmire Station, where they were officially

From top:
8.10:

En Route to the Exhibition Grounds.

King Edward's jaunt through the streets attracted attention from the general public even if there was not universal support for his empire. Besides the royal family and the Lord Lieutenant, there were three other carriages carrying the Duke of Connaught, Major General McCalmont, Sir Neville Chamberlain and numerous members of the royal household-in-waiting. Accompanying them were an escort of the Royal Horse Guards and the band of the King's Royal Rifles. The lavish decoration and bunting hung on St Patrick's Street would indicate that there was significant loyalty in the city. Many residents and business owners along the processional route sold vantage-point viewing from their windows or roofs. (© CPM)

8.11:

The King and Queen's Official Reception.

In the Concert Hall, a special dais covered with a red cloth was built in front of the usual stage to accommodate the royal reception. Admission to the Concert Hall was set at 10 shillings (£50) while ordinary entry to the grounds was set at five times the usual price at 5 shillings (£25). This commercial exploitation may account for the fact that the Concert Hall was half empty. (© IAA)

8.12:

A Royal Lunch.

King Edward and Queen Alexandra enjoyed a 12-course meal with an assortment of wines (quite a normal sitting for royalty at the time) in what is now Cork Public Museum. Eighteen people including the Lord Mayor, Lady Mayoress, the Earl and Countess of Dudley, the City and County High Sheriffs and Henry Cutler joined the King and Queen for the meal. The image shows the King and Queen ready to continue their tour of the exhibition grounds. (© CPM)

8.13:

The King Inspecting the Exhibition Grounds.

After lunch, the royal carriage made its way through the grounds with Lord Mayor Fitzgerald walking alongside, on the King's right. Note the RIC policemen forming a protective guard beside the King's carriage. (© IAA)

met by representatives of the Great Southern and Western Railway Company and other important figures, including Horace Plunkett. They took the royal train to Queenstown, where they were once again met by local representatives before boarding the royal yacht, *Victoria and Albert*, to leave Ireland after what was regarded as an extremely successful tour.[54] The cordial mood was summed up in a speech given by Fitzgerald in the Concert Hall, where he believed the historic atmosphere 'long charged with ancient memories of sorrow' was losing ground to a new era of positivity where 'old conflicts [were] abating, old animosities [were] appeased, and old bitternesses [were] dying away'.[55] King Edward shared this sentiment by telling the audience that his visit to Ireland had given him a 'clearer insight into some conditions of Irish life than he had before possessed, and he should rejoice if, as anticipated, it was productive of practical benefit to the country'.[56] In a letter addressed to the people of Cork and published in local newspapers, Edward stated that the memory of his visit to Cork would 'remain a happy possession'.[57] For men like Horace Plunkett, Edward had shown the Irish people during his Irish sojourn that he could be their King and that he 'prides himself on being the ruler of Ireland'.[58]

The conspicuous and genuine efforts by some involved in Cork's local government to use the 1903 royal tour as a foundation for future prosperous and peaceful relations between both countries fitted perfectly with the agenda of the Exhibitions on the Mardyke. Both were celebrations of the presumed benefits of Home Rule and the possibilities it offered Ireland and any potential growth and progress. The 1903 visit was also a strong and potent exercise in colonial relations that was carefully stage-managed to show the King as a benevolent ruler, personally interested in Irish affairs. The fact that Fitzgerald was subsequently awarded a Baronetcy for his efforts on the Mardyke and Horace Plunkett was knighted for his services to Ireland, symbolized how Cork's 1902/3 Exhibitions were supported by the British establishment.[59] In the DATI exhibits and the regal endorsement of the exposition, a 'road-map' for Ireland's industrial, educational, and especially, its political recovery was laid out.

Exhibition Amusements: Technology, Pleasure and Profit

By the beginning of the twentieth century, anyone attending a significant exposition expected to be both educated and enthralled in equal measure. Whilst they prepared for the 1902 season, Cork's organizing committees were well aware of the public's appetite for amusements and attractions; after all it was one of the main reasons the Mardyke was chosen over the Cornmarket (see Chapter 5). Though education and technical instruction were viewed as an exhibition's most laudable features, it was the promise of fun and exotic diversions that generated the biggest excitement amongst exposition customers. These diversions included a heady mix of high culture, populist entertainment and sporting events that were very much of their time. From the gallery of paintings and historical artifacts to the frequent choral and orchestral concerts and fairground attractions on the Western Field, Cork's Exhibition, as with other international examples, offered something for all classes and discriminations. Early Exhibition organizers resisted bringing amusements within their official range of events, preferring to keep them at the periphery. Despite this, playgrounds of hedonistic delights sprang up next to the official grounds. At New York's 1853 'Crystal Palace' exhibition, for example, the 'unofficial' entertainment section was said to consist of 'grog shops, gambling dens, side-shows, cock-fight arenas and other haunts of dissipation that perturbed respectable citizens'.[60] By France's second international exposition in 1867 and the first German-language exhibition in Vienna in 1873, planners had begun to accommodate more pleasure-seeking attractions that did not fit the rigid focus on education. Organizers

help cope with numbers hoping to splash down in the Lee. A reporter from the *Nenagh Guardian* devoted a long article to a visit of more than 350 of the town's citizens to the Exhibition on 28 July 1902. The following description in his own words captures the technological thrill of the Water Chute:

> From a platform some sixty [*sic* seventy] feet high a series a parallel planks are laid cross-wise on heavy bars of timber running down into the water. Down these planks a double line of steel rails also run. On these rails a pair of cars [boats] run; one set of rails carrying the cars into the water and the other set carrying them up again. From the platform below, the intending passengers take their seats in an ascending car, and on reaching the upper platform they are transferred to the descending one, and all being ready, the vehicle is sent forward on its downward journey, and the wheels being well greased and the rail worn smooth with frequent usage, the car rushes down with terrific speed, gaining increased momentum with every yard, and finally plunging onto the water, throwing up clouds of spray from the contact.

The Water Chute did not require sophisticated machinery to operate but simply relied on the principle of gravity. Cars (or you could call them boats) would carry passengers on rails up a gradual ascent where a seat is taken in one of the descending cars. The boat would then be launched down a 250 feet ramp at an exhilarating speed and hit the water below with a 'gliding, skimming motion'.[73] The *Nenagh Guardian* reporter concluded his account of the ride describing the experience as:

> awful but attractive, and with those who have once experienced its 'pleasures' the feeling is that they would like to keep at it all day. The spectator who, for the first time, sees the car rushing down expects when it reaches the water that it will plunge to the very bottom, the pace is so great, but it doesn't – it merely shivers a bit (like a vessel when struck by a heavy sea), and then glides on until the effect of the impetus is over, when the man in charge brings it back to the bank.[74]

8.14:
Facing page
The Water Chute.
This was the most popular and visually arresting amusement on the site, underlined by the number of photographs that were taken of it. The views offered from the top of the Chute would have also been a key aspect of its appeal. For many Corkonians, the thrill of rushing down the slide and bobbing across the surface of the water would also have proved too tempting to resist. The choice of the Mardyke as the location meant that the organizers could take advantage of the River Lee for various modes of entertainment and sport. (© CPM)

The passengers were then offloaded at a landing stage further down river.

Apart from the rush and excitement of riding the Water Chute, there was another reason it proved so enticing to visitors. The Chute offered those who ventured to the top a bird's-eye view of the exhibition grounds and the wider cityscape. This was also what made the Ferris Wheel, Eiffel Tower and other colossal exhibition structures both thrilling and awe-inspiring. Standing at the top of the Water Chute, one could not but be impressed at what had been achieved on the Mardyke (frontispiece). From the ornate main gates across to the Irish Labourer's Cottage in the Western Field, something very special had been accomplished, never to be repeated in the city's history. From this high point one could see the university buildings as well as St Fin Barre's Cathedral in the distance, reminding visitors how much has improved in Cork over the previous century. Monumental amusements like the Water Chute gave the observer, both literally and figuratively, a new perspective of their modern world and in the words of the cultural historian Astrid Böger helped them 're-imagine their relationship to the surrounding culture'.[75]

A study of the pictorial evidence of the Water Chute would lead one to think that there was little concern for 'health and safety', but there were automatic brakes and grippers in place to prevent any runaway vehicles. Despite the safety features in place, accidents could not be prevented from happening. In early June 1902, upon entering the water at the bottom of the slide, a boat containing several eminent citizens, including members of the Executive Committee, suddenly sprang a leak. Luckily, the occupants only suffered a good soaking, but it was sarcastically reported that the Royal Humane Society[76] 'have not yet decided how many gold medals they intend to distribute among the large assemblage on the river bank who continued to laugh with the utmost heartiness'. The incident did not seem to deter anyone, though, as 1,200 people shot the chute during the following day. The Water Chute was officially opened by the Duke of Connaught and Prince Henry of Prussia on 8 May, as the ride had not been completed by opening day. The royal party made their way to the top of the slide but did not partake in the ride. Even though the Water Chute was the most expensive ride on site (six pence compared to three pence for most others), it was patronized by approximately 160,000 people over both years of the Exhibition, making it the most profitable attraction.

Switchback Railway

The success of the Water Chute was nearly matched by another popular ride on the Western Field, a fore-runner to roller coasters known as the Switchback Railway (8.15). It was made possible through application of the latest technology intended to bring excitement to all classes at affordable rates. The origins of these attractions can be traced to seventeenth-century rides made of wood and ice known as 'Russian Mountains'.[77] The French popularized their own versions of Russian Mountains during the eighteenth and nineteenth centuries. However, America is the birthplace of the roller coaster as we understand them today. La Marcus A. Thompson is credited with building the first Switchback Railway at Coney Island in 1884.[78] He charged five cents a ride and collected in the order of $600 a day. It was an instant hit and its success ensured that the roller coaster became an American cultural icon. Thompson shared some of Thomas Cook's philanthropic motivations. For Thompson, many of society's ills and vices could be substituted with 'something better, something clean and wholesome'.[79] Switchback Railways and his other attractions brought

'sunshine that glows bright in the afterthought and scatters the darkness of the tenement for the price of a nickel or dime'.[80] In 1887 Thompson introduced his most famous attraction, the 'Scenic Railway', in Atlantic City. This ride is a close relation to that which was built on the Mardyke. Since his first Switchback Railway, Thompson had been granted thirty patents, improving many aspects of his gravity ride. The safety designs he and his engineer, John Miller, introduced are now standard in all modern roller coasters. Success enabled him to form the LA Thompson Scenic Railway Company to sell and export his rides nationally and internationally.

Expositions were significant sources of revenue for the company as confirmed by a 1910 catalogue that stated 2.8 million men, women and children had enjoyed his ride at the 1908 Franco-British Exhibition. The same catalogue claimed eight million people had patronized his rides across the United States during 1909.[81] Glasgow had Switchback Railways at both their 1888 and 1901 Exhibitions which, as we have seen, directly inspired its inclusion at Cork. The Switchback Railway installed on the Western Field was described in the official catalogue as a 'large scale' structure that had never 'been before attempted in Ireland'. It was also noted that it contained the latest device known as the 'Kick', which would add 'further excitement to the

8.15:
The Switchback Railway. This attraction must have been an impressive sight for anyone visiting the exhibition. The people in the image next to the attraction give us some idea of its scale. The image also shows the two parallel tracks that comprised the ride. Note the unfinished Canadian Pavilion in the background with the rudder proclaiming 'Toronto' projecting from the windmill. (© CPM)

pleasures which the journey affords'.[82] The ride consisted of two platforms roughly 295ft (90m) apart that were joined by two undulating rail-tracks. A carful of passengers, having paid three pence each, would leave from each side and begin the journey to the opposite platform, travelling at about six or seven miles an hour. The exhibition guide recommends the experience on the Switchback Railway as a suitable 'nerve tonic'.[83] However, a tragic accident occured on 28 June when one William Mellerick, who worked at Carlisle Fort in Cork harbour, but lived on Harper's Lane (now St Paul's Avenue), 'through some mishap or other … lost his hold and was precipitated from the car, first to the rail-track, and finally to the ground'.[84] He later died from the head injuries he sustained. These rides clearly involved a certain amount of risk, but this formed part of their attraction.

Cinematograph

A word of warning. The cinematographer operator will take a series of snapshots in the gardens today … Ladies, you have received due notice. Don't blame us if you don't look pretty. See that your hats are on straight, and wear a bewitching smile. We have always said that you are beautiful. Don't give the cinematograph man a chance of finding us out.
– *Cork Examiner*, 7 June 1902

The important part played by the Exhibition in bringing cameramen to Cork to capture the city at the height of its confidence cannot be overstated. We have made much of the role film technology played in the opening day but its influence can be seen throughout the Exhibition season. Cinemas were still a relatively new feature of life, as the Lumiére brothers had only publicly shown the first film in France six years earlier.[85] Companies had been coming to Ireland to film since 1896 but these visits were limited to Belfast and Dublin.[86] To have secured the services of renowned showman George Green and Mitchell and Kenyon was a feather in the cap of the exhibition organizers (2.5). The twenty-two films pertaining to Cork survive from their archives, capturing a variety of aspects of everyday life that lend to a better understanding of the city's social history at the beginning of the Edwardian period.[87] All the films were shot with the express purpose of being shown by the two cinematographs (cinemas) based in the city at the time. One was in the Assembly Rooms on the South Mall, and was run by the Irish company the Thomas-Edison Animated Photo Co. The second cinematograph showed films in the Concert Hall on the exhibition grounds and was run by George Green and his manager, Thomas Moore.[88]

George Green (8.16), originally from Preston but synonymous with Glasgow, was one of 'the most influential fairground showmen of the late Victorian era' (and yet another connection between the Glasgow and Cork Exhibitions).[89] He operated fairground rides through Scotland and Northern England with his brother John and he installed the first cinematograph show on a fairground in 1898 and would later pioneer early forms of cinema-theatre. By the time of his death in 1915, he had established ten 'picture palaces' in various towns and cities throughout Scotland. The *Showman* announced in its 21 February 1902 issue that Green had purchased 'the finest possible machinery and accessories' for its engagement at the Cork Exhibition. The article readily endorsed Green's reputation by suggesting:

> It may safely be assumed that what he does not know of the bad and good points in all details of the art of cinematography is scarcely worth worrying about, and his selection of the machine that is to represent him at the Cork Exhibition will be based on his long experience and deep study of the working of many of the best known makes.

8.16:
George Green (1861 - 1915) Considered one of the most successful showmen of his generation, Green was one of the first to pioneer the fairground cinema. During his career, he also established a chain of picture houses across Scotland as well as a film rental company. Following his death, his sons expanded the family business and were still operating throughout Scotland well into the twentieth century.

Over the months of May, June and July 1902, Green and Moore filmed at various locations and events in the city (see Appendix 5). They captured the opening day parade, the visit of the Duke of Connacht and Prince Henry on 8 May, and filmed 'staged' events like a fire rescue near the Cornmarket, described in the *Cork Examiner* as 'Cork Fire Brigade turning out to a big fire and their work thereat'.[90] They also visited the Mardyke on a number of occasions to shoot footage of athletic events, and other sporting activities. The most popular types of films sought by cinematograph operators at the time were busy street scenes and the 'Factory Gate' films captured outside factories and work premises. These films recorded large groups, who would be encouraged to come and see themselves at the cinematograph later over the following days and weeks. The thrill of seeing yourself on the big screen would have been hard to resist. The Mitchell and Kenyon archive from Cork has scenes from Patrick Street, King Street, Grand Parade and one 'factory gate' film shot outside the Lee Boot Company (now Square Deal) on Washington Street. Alongside the collection of locally shot footage, George Green would have also had many fictional and comedic films available to him to show his audiences. He most likely purchased these from other film companies or salesmen and would have already shown them on numerous occasions throughout England.[91] Looking at the cinematograph shows that had been held in Dublin from as early as 1896, we see that their programmes included a wide variety of foreign-produced short films.[92] The cinematograph in the Concert Hall only cost three pence to visit but the historical legacy left to Cork by Green is priceless.

Amusements for the 1903 Season

At the National Library Ireland, hidden amongst a collection of letters received by Count Plunkett (5.11) as exhibition secretary, are a number of hand-scribbled notes by Plunkett himself. The notes detail themes and topics he wanted to raise or discuss and were presumably written before or even during an Executive Committee meeting. On one page is listed the amusements they hoped to bring to the city in 1903:

> Houseboats
> Boat Race – Water Fete
> Captive Balloon
> Swiss Village – 6d to Panorama
> Captain Cody in June (Olympics)
> Monorail
> Motor Races – Spirit Motors
> Cycle Races – Motor cycles?

Fitzgerald, Plunkett and the committees, buoyed by the success of 1902, strived to 'push the boat out' for the upcoming season. Though many of their concepts would remain still-born, the broad range conveys the sense of imagination and enthusiasm employed by the organizers. The amusements committee, for example, went as far as to contact renowned aeronaut Captain Stanley Spencer to see if they could hire his captive balloon ride. [93] This was a lighter-than-air balloon tethered to the ground with a restraining device, allowing patrons to experience a balloon trip without the fear of leaving the Mardyke altogether.

The monorail would have been a unique and fascinating addition to the site, as would the Swiss Village, but sadly neither of them materialized. There were also plans to bring over the big wheel that had been engaged at the 1902 'Paris in London' Exhibition at the Earl's Court.[94] In addition, the possibility of Colonel Bill Cody (Buffalo Bill) coming to Cork was a most exhilarating prospect. Buffalo Bill and his Wild West Show were an international sensation, performing throughout Europe and America in the Victorian and Edwardian periods. The show was the star attraction at the 1889 Paris Exposition and garnered worldwide acclaim for Buffalo Bill and his depiction of America's wild west.[95] As his show was on tour in Great Britain during 1902/3, enquiries were made to Cody's managers about bringing it to Cork. Due to the inclement weather in Ireland and his advancing age, Buffalo Bill would only come to Cork if he was guaranteed covered space for himself and his performers to shelter from the weather while staying in Cork (about 800 people were employed by Cody).[96] One of the most famous female performers in the Wild West Show was Annie Oakley, whose skill with a rifle thrilled audiences worldwide. Both Cody and Oakley had thrilled the crowds at the Paris Expositions in 1889 and 1900. Unfortunately, Cody and his show never made it to Cork, but in late August 1903, the Exhibition would host an American shooting show given by 'Miami – The Western Rifle Queen', a pale imitation of Annie Oakley.[97] On this occasion, as in other cases, our organizers had to rely on simpler, less ambitious and less costly amusements.

Cork's second season saw a continuation of many of the 1902 amusements, most notably the Water Chute and the Switchback Railway. The Distorted Mirrors attraction was re-branded the 'Palace of Illusions' and moved to another location on the Western Field while the various shooting galleries and river-based attractions also remained in place for 1903. Some new attractions were added including the Gravity Canal (mentioned in the last chapter), the Aerial Racer and an Exhibition Zoo. The 'Aerial Racer', similar to a zip line cable ride found in most modern adventure parks, ran parallel to the Switchback Railway in the Western Field. Visitors were urged to try 'the experience of a lifetime' although it was only deemed suitable for the 'sterner sex'.[98] Initially, the animal exhibit was limited to five camels and three elephants housed in structures built at the entrance to the Western Field.[99] They were intended to carry children from one end of the gardens to the other. The 'Camel House' was located next to the Palace of Illusions, where howls of laughter erupting from the Palace 'had a peculiar effect' on the camels, who according to the *1903*

Official Guide were more used to the 'deathly stillness of the Arabian desert'.[100] Alas, a week after the opening, one of the camels passed away 'after a short illness' and was transported to UCC, where it was 'honoured by being dissected'.[101] By the end of July, the animal population on site had expanded into a virtual Noah's Ark, including two sea-lions, a hyena, a group of young lions, a sloth, a bear, a Russian wolf, snakes, various birds and a kangaroo, as well as a fine collection of primates.[102]

Conclusion

Though there were many aspects of the 1902/3 Cork Exhibitions that set it apart from its predecessors, it is in the area of amusements that the most dramatic differences can be seen. The range and scope of what was offered on the Mardyke was, even by modern standards, impressive. As a result of the lessons learned from the evolution of the exhibitions during the previous half century, Cork's organizers possessed an understanding of what Edwardian audiences would have expected from their undertaking. Though all involved in the 1902/3 project wholeheartedly hoped the Exhibition would bring the industrial and agricultural improvements Ireland so badly needed, they were also equally aware that the exhibits and demonstrations designed to achieve this had a short-lived appeal for exhibition

8.17a – c:
Illustrations of the Amusements and Entertainments. These series of illustrations depict the range of amusements enjoyed by exhibition visitors. The image of the exhibitions grounds at night is particularly interesting as no night-time photographs of the site are known to exist. (© CPM)

visitors. Without the collection of side-shows, rides and the many cultural attractions that we will explore in the next chapter, the Exhibition would have lacked the excitement and social enjoyment that undoubtedly brought a vast amount of repeat visitors through the entrance gates. Without them, the 1902/3 Exhibitions would have been much less memorable events (8.17a – c).

On a final note, in examining the King's visit and the 1903 opening day ceremonies (Chapter 4), one can appreciate in retrospect just how unique and special the 1902 opening day was in bringing the majority of the political and social community of Cork together for a common purpose. Many of the subsequent official events held in conjunction with the Exhibition only served to illustrate the underlying political differences in the city. It would seem that the strong feelings expressed by some at the 1883 exhibition opening or the Prince of Wales's 1885 visit had not gone away.

Notes

1   At the time of writing in early 2013, Thomas Cook was undergoing serious re-structuring, as the company struggled in the tough economic climate. They were forced to close 195 of its high-street travel agencies, resulting in the loss of 2,500 jobs.

2   I. Furlong, *Irish Tourism 1880–1980* (Dublin: Irish Academic Press, 2009), p.9. In a treatise on tourism entitled *Physical, Moral and Social Aspects of Excursions*, Cook stated that tourism's greatest benefit was that it would 'unite man to man, and man to God'.

3   The official attendance figures must be taken with a pinch of salt as they fail to account for repeat customers, site workers or exhibitors. Though it is clear that millions of people did travel from abroad to visit these World's Fairs, the majority of visitors would in reality have been local and national in origin.

4   See Furlong, *Irish Tourism 1880–1980*, pp.18–19.

5   Ibid., p.19.

6   Ibid., p.21.

7   *The Times*, 12 June 1852.

8   See Furlong, *Irish Tourism 1880–1980*, p.17.

9   See H.C. Hartnell, *Illustrated Guide to the Cork International Exhibition 1883* (Cork: Guys Bros, 1883), advert section xv–xvii.

10 *Cork Examiner*, 9 October 1902.

11 Ibid.; 30 August 1901; 26 December 1902.

12 *Cork Daily Herald*, 6 July 1901, details a speech given to the Executive Committee by Mr Swiney, in which he stated he had contacted the US State Department regarding the Exhibition and how he would contact leading newspapers in the main American cities to advertise the event. He would also approach shipping companies with the view to setting up specially priced tickets and services to Cork.

13 This sixty-seven-page publication only devoted fifteen pages to images and description of the Exhibition, while the remaining pages provide tourist information about Cork City and the surrounding province.

14 *Cork Constitution,* 20 December 1901.

15 The advert ran in *Cork Constitution, Cork Examiner* and *Echo* from 2–7 September 1901.

16 See *Cork Constitution,* 5–8 August 1902. Fitzgerald quotes this number during an Executive Committee meeting that details that Regatta and the Bank Holiday weekends had been extremely successful.

17 A copy of the petition signed by Clonakilty businessmen and tradesmen can be found in Cork Public Museum. There are also a number of associated documents detailing communication between Clonakilty's civic leaders, the DATI and the Cork, Bandon and South Coast Railway.

18 *Nenagh Guardian,* 30 July 1902; *Cork Examiner*, 17 August 1902.

19 *Nenagh Guardian,* 2 August 1902.

20 *Cork Constitution,* 5 March 1902.

21 Ibid.

22 *Cork Examiner,* 26 February 1902.

23 In 1894, Crossley had begun a publishing company to print propaganda-esque literature in the form of a monthly journal entitled the *Irish Tourist.* He hoped to achieve two aims: 'to make better known to the world Ireland's charm and beauty, and to attract multitudinous visitors', see Furlong, *Irish Tourism,* p.20.

24 According to official published records, the 1852 Exhibition recorded 129,031 visitors, while the 1883 event attracted 229,960 people.

25 *Cork Examiner*, 7 August 1903. The 1853 International Exhibition in Dublin had attracted Queen Victoria and her family while the Prince of Wales, the future King Edward VII, officially opened the 1865 Exhibition.

26 *The Cork Constitution*, 10 September 1902 British and Irish newspapers reported that at a meeting of Cork Councilors, Lord Mayor Fitzgerald refused to allow a motion from UIL members that condemned his conduct in welcoming the Chief Secretary to the Exhibition. Fitzgerald defended his actions by stating that he had acted as Chairman of the Exhibition and not as Lord Mayor of Cork. In a speech delivered in Cork, Michael Davitt accused Fitzgerald and the Executive Committee of 'flunkeyism' and described the actions of Fitzgerald as another example of how the exhibition was being exploited by Unionist interests. He was particularly disgusted by the fact that three varieties of potato recently grown in the DATI plots were called after three British 'heroes' from the Boer War. See *Northants Evening Telegraph,* 10 September 1902.

27 *Cork Constitution,* 2 November 1902.

28 *Cork Constitution,* 22 August 1902. The *Asama* was the lead ship of an early class of armoured cruisers of the Imperial Japanese Navy. It saw action during the Boxer Rebellion, the Russo-Japanese War and World War I. It was decommissioned during World War II as it was deemed too old-fashioned to be retro-fitted. The *Takasago* was a cruiser of the Imperial Japanese Navy. It too played a part in both the Boxer Rebellion and Russo-Japanese War. It was however, the last major Japanese warship lost in the war. It was sunk by a mine in December 1904.

29 Ibid.

30 Ibid.

31 Ibid.

32 The following day, 350 more crew members travelled to the Exhibition accompanied by their own band. It was by all accounts a 'novel treat' for all who witnessed it. This day also saw Fitzgerald and a select group of Executive Committee members make a return visit to the Japanese warship *Asama* as guest of Admiral Ijuni. They received a guided tour of the impressive ship.

33 The Boxer Rebellion was an anti-foreign and proto-nationalist revolt in China that took

place between 1899 and 1901, opposing foreign imperialism and Christianity. It was violently and brutally put down by an eight-nation alliance, all with their own interests in China, including Britain, Japan, Russia, US, Germany, Italy, France and Austria-Hungary.

34 *Liverpool Mercury*, 3 September 1902.

35 A cursory search through the online database of British Newspaper Archives reveals how national and regional newspapers reported extensively on King Edward's visit in 1903. All accounts emphasized and underlined the positivity surrounding the trip that boded well for future Anglo-Irish relations.

36 See Murphy, James *Abject Loyalty*, pp.276–89.

37 Ibid.

38 S. Lee, *King Edward VII, A Biography Vol. 2* (London: Kessinger Publishing, 1927), p.166.

39 To get further information on the interesting and entertaining life of King Edward, see Ridley, *Bertie: A life of Edward VII* (London: Chatto and Windus, 2012). It details his turbulent and hostile relationship with his parents and how he was denied any proper responsibilities by Queen Victoria, who blamed him for the death of her beloved Albert. Free from official constraints, Edward toured Europe, ate, drank, gambled, partied and lived life to its fullest. Even after his arranged marriage to the Danish Princess Alexandra, his notorious playboy lifestyle continued unabated. Despite his reputation, he was a shrewd and tactful diplomat and took a keen interest in bringing the monarchy more in line with the modern world, and more importantly, the needs of his subjects.

40 King Edward VII deserves a great deal of credit for managing Anglo-French relations at the time and his official, but self-organized, visit to Paris in 1903 helped usher in a new era of cordial relations between both nations. Another reason he was known as the 'Uncle of Europe' was the fact that he was related to nearly every major European ruling monarch at the time.

41 See Ridley, *Bertie*, p.167.

42 Ibid., p.242. The Queen and her staff in Buckingham Palace genuinely had some misgivings about the visit of the Prince and Princess of Wales to Ireland during the rise of Irish nationalism during the 1880s. The reception in Cork was reported back to the Queen as 'a bad dream'. The carriage was assaulted with boos and hisses from 2–3,000 people waving black flags, shouting 'no Prince but Parnell'.

43 *Freeman's Journal*, 29 March 1903. In Dublin, its corporation voted not to present the King with an official address. An article, 'When the king came to town' (*Galway Advertiser*, 12 May 2011), details how the visit of King Edward VII to Galway caused a variety of reactions across the city and county.

44 *Cork Constitution*, 3 August 1903.

45 *Freeman's Journal*, 29 March 1903.

46 Ibid.

47 Murphy, James *Abject Loyalty*, p.297.

48 Ibid.

49 Liam de Roiste, *Diary A1 July 29 1903* (Cork City and County Archives). In our opinion, de Roiste was exaggerating the level of anti-monarchist sentiment in the city. Even if there were less of an armed presence on the streets, any nationalist protests would have been limited to a minority group. Also, the atmosphere of Anglo-Irish relations was far more friendly in 1903 than it had been twenty years before, rendering a mass nationalist protest unrealistic.

50 William Levington Cooke was four at the time of the royal visitation and wrote down his reminiscences in 1965. He noted several other memories of the exhibition, highlighting how much of an impact the

Exhibition would have had on young children of Edwardian Cork.

51 *Nottingham Evening Post*, 31 July 1903.

52 Ibid., 1 August 1903. A cenotaph was erected in honour of Irish nationalists on the Grand Parade in 1898, that later evolved into the present-day National Monument in 1906. Previously, there had been a painted statue of George II erected on the site that was 'removed' in 1862. The statue gave its name to the Irish translation for Grand Parade, *Sráid an Chapaill Bhuí* (Street of the Yellow Horse).

53 See de Roiste, *Diary A1 1 August 1903*.

54 See Murphy, *Abject Loyalty*, p.297; Lee, *King Edward VII*, pp.169–70.

55 *Freeman's Journal*, 3 August 1903.

56 *Edinburgh Evening News*, 3 August 1903. When Queen Elizabeth II gave her state speech in Dublin Castle on 18 May 2011, she echoed many of King Edward's sentiments. She, like him, acknowledged the troubled past between both islands but hoped for a better and brighter future.

57 *Freeman's Journal*, 3 August 1903. This is a quote from an open letter to the people of Cork published in the local newspapers. King Edward would compose a similar letter to the people of Ireland re-emphasizing the new dawn in Anglo-Irish relations.

58 S. Murphy, James, *Abject Loyalty*, p.297.

59 A Baronet was a title below that of a baron, but above that of a knight. It meant that Fitzgerald's male decedents would inherit 'Sir' until the end of time or at least when the male line ends.

60 A. Böger, *Envisioning the Nation: The Early American World's Fairs and the Formation of Culture* (Frankfurt-on-Main: Campus Verlag GmbH, 2010), p.38.

61 *Cork Constitution*, 3 August 1901.

62 Ibid., 12 June 1901.

63 P. and J. Kinchin, *Glasgow's Great Exhibitions 1888, 1901, 1911, 1938 and 1988* (Bichester: White Cockade, 1988), pp.90–2.

64 *Cork Examiner* 2 September 1901.

65 Ibid. The proposed role for the miniature locomotive in 1902 was fulfilled by the Gravity Canal in 1903.

66 Anon., *Official Catalogue, Cork International Exhibition 1902* (Cork: Guys, 1902), pp.115–17.

67 Ibid., p.115. It appears the 'Cairo' side-show was an indoor experience located within the Turkish Bazaar (situated next to the Canadian Pavilion).

68 *All-Ireland Review,* 21 December 1901.

69 Anon., *Cork International Exhibition and South of Ireland Souvenir* (Cork: Guys 1902), p.14.

70 The amusements were brought to a halt on the evening of Monday 20 July to solemnly mark the passing of Pope Leo XII, who had died earlier that day – one of the rare occasions they were not making money.

71 Cartnell, *The Incredible Scream Machine – A history of the Roller Coaster* (Bowling Green OH: Amusement Park Books, 1987), pp.19–33.

72 S. Rains, *Commodity Culture and Social Class in Dublin 1850–1916* (Dublin: Irish Academic Press, 2011), pp.144–5.

73 Anon., *Official Guide, Cork International Exhibition 1902* (Cork: Guys, 1902), p.37.

74 *Nenagh Guardian*, 31 July 1902

75 See A. Böger, *Envisioning the Nation*, p.38.

76 *Cork Constitution,* 9 June 1902. The Royal Humane Society was founded in London in 1774 and continue to this day issuing awards to life-savers whose acts of courage have saved people from drowning.

77 Cartnell, *The Incredible Scream Machine* This chapter details the evolutionary history of roller coasters and the birth of popular amusements rides in general across Europe.

78 For more detail on Thompson, see Cartnell,

The Incredible Scream Machine, pp.43–54, where the life and times of the 'Father of Gravity' is excellently illustrated.

79 See Cartnell, *The Incredible Scream Machine*, p.49.

80 Ibid.

81 Ibid., p.49.

82 Anon., *Official Guide 1902*, p.37.

83 Anon., *Official Guide 1902*, p.37.

84 *Irish Independent*, 30 June 1902.

85 V. Toulmin, S. Poppie and P. Russell (eds), *The Lost World of Mitchell & Kenyon-Edwardian Britain on Film* (London: BFI, 2004), p.33.

86 Ibid., p.93. For more information, visit the Irish Film & TV Research Online website at www.tcd.ie/irishfilm

87 The Mitchell & Kenyon collection, which contains over 800 films, was discovered in 1994 during building work at an old business premises in Blackburn belonging to Mitchell & Kenyon.

88 V. Toulmin, S. Poppie and P. Russell (eds), *The Lost World of Mitchell & Kenyon,* p.98

89 Ibid.

90 *Cork Examiner*, 22 May 1902.

91 One witness, William L. Cooke, who is mentioned earlier in this chapter, remembers seeing 'the first moving pictures in which gigantic shadows put dogs into a machine from which they drew out sausages. It terrified me.' This refers to a popular type of special effect film produced by many international film companies that appeared to show animals, usually dogs and pigs, being fed into a machine and emerging as sausages.

92 K. and E. Rockett, *Magic Lantern, Panorama and Moving Picture Shows in Ireland, 1786–1909* (Dublin: Four Courts Press, 2011), p.221. This book offers a fascinating history of moving picture exhibition in Ireland. What is particularly apparent is that Ireland was quick to follow European trends and adopt the cinematograph as a popular form of entertainment.

93 *Cork Constitution,* 23 January 1903. Captain Stanley Spencer came from an aeronautical family from London. His father and grandfather had built balloons before him, while Stanley engineered several capitive and long-distance balloon rides all around the world. He was most famous at the time for building and flying an airship over London in 1902.

94 Ibid.

95 See J. Jonnes, *Eiffel's Tower and the World's Fair where Buffalo Bill beguiled Paris, the Artists quarreled and Thomas Edison became a Count* (New York NY: Viking, 2009). This is a fascinating account into Buffalo Bill in Paris but also at how exhibitions captured the imagination of the public.

96 *Cork Constitution*, 3 January 1903. A letter was read at an Executive Committee meeting from Buffalo Bill's managers requesting the large space but sadly it was a request that could not be fulfilled by the committee.

97 Ibid., 13 August 1903.

98 Anon., *Official Catalogue 1903,* p.44. The reference to the 'sterner sex' should not be taken as overtly sexist but as an Edwardian course of action to preserve female modesty. If a woman wearing a dress, for example, zipped by on the Aerial Racer, people on the Western Field would have been treated to an eyefull of her undergarments!

99 Ibid., p.46.

100 Ibid.

101 *Cork Constitution,* 5 June 1902. The skin and head of the camel was to be given to Mr Rohu, a taxidermist, who would turn his skill to mounting the animal.

102 *Cork Constitution*, 30 July 1903.

THE CORK NATIONAL IND

9.1 **1852 Art & Archaeology Gallery.**
The 1852 Cork National Exhibition is
believed to be the first which featured a
dedicated art gallery. The exhibit featured
painting, sculpture as well as specimens
of archaeological objects & applied art. By
1902, the scale of the undertaking had grown
such that five galleries were required for the
exhibition collection. (D Breen's Collection)

BITION.—FINE ARTS HALL.

THE BOULD THADY QUILL[1]

Ye maids of Duhallow who're anxious for courting
A word of advice I will give unto ye
Proceed to Banteer to the athletic sporting
And hand in your names to the club committee
And never commence any skits on your programme
Till the carriage you see flying over the hill
Right down through the valleys and glens of Kilcorney
With our own daring sportsman the bold Thady Quill

At the great hurling match between Cork and Tipperary
('Twas played in the park on the banks of the Lee)
Our own darling lads were afraid of being being beaten
So they sent for bold Thady to Ballinagree
He hurled the ball right and left in their faces
And showed the Tipperary men action and skill
If they touched on his lines he would certainly brain them
And the papers were full of the praise of Thady Quill

At the Cork Exhibition there was a fair lady
Whose fortune exceeded a million or more
But a bad constitution had ruined her completely
And medical treatment had failed o'er and o'er
O, Mother, says she, sure I know what will ease me
And cure this disease that will certainly kill
Give over your doctors and medical treatment
I'd rather one squeeze out of bold Thady Quill

(Chorus)
For ramblin', for rovin', for football' or courtin'
For drinkin' black porter as fast as you'd fill
In all your days rovin' you'll find none so jovial
As our Muskerry sportsman, the bould Thady Quill.
– *Irish Ballad c.1905*

9
Exhibiting Culture – Displaying Art, Music and Sport

Daniel Breen and Tom Spalding

Leaving aside, for a moment, the array of industrial exhibits, the wonders of the latest machinery in action and the lure of thrilling rides and sideshows, the 1902/3 Exhibitions were also places to enjoy the simpler pleasures in life. The same employment and social reforms that had enabled the lower classes to take to the tourist highways had also introduced the concept of recreation time to Victorians and Edwardians. Free time could now be spent in local amenities, such as parks, galleries, concert halls and museums, whilst amateur societies offered lectures and demonstrations in a wide variety of subjects including photography, archaeology and science. The local public park, the hallmark of any modern city, was a mainstay in most Victorian town planning. It was a place to escape the dreariness of one's working life and to avoid the hustle and bustle of the streets. In many ways, they became the heart of local communities, where 'boating, playing ball games and simply walking, co-existed happily with the business of just relaxing in the sunshine'.[2] However, Cork did not, to this point, have such an amenity. Hosting the Exhibition on the Mardyke, a destination for promenading for the city's populace since the early eighteenth century, meant patrons could stroll the grounds, enjoy the many restaurants, cafés and bars and socialize with family, friends and fellow visitors in the most picturesque and pleasant of surroundings. Therefore, beneath the complex and constantly shifting business of arranging exhibitions was a solid foundation based on the fact that they provided a highly social communal experience. By the late nineteenth century, art, music and sport had become important in the lives of ordinary people in Cork, and the exhibition organizers were more than willing to exploit this.

The Art Galleries

Although science, technology and innovation were the core principles of all International Exhibitions, organizers also placed importance on displaying fine arts. Since their inception, organizers had exhibited fine art to 'avoid the charge of philistinism'.[3] To have a strong and flourishing culture with a rich artistic output was deemed by Victorians to be just as important as having a successful industrial economy. Exhibitions offered common ground where art and industry could meet as equals, with the intention that they could learn from each other. Art galleries were not necessarily more popular or more commercially successful than the industrial exhibits or amusements, but they gave the entire enterprise a level of cultural respectability. Interestingly, Cork was the first city to undertake this exercise in status-raising, attaching a dedicated fine art gallery to its 1852 Industrial Exhibition (9.1). Though there were paintings and sculptures scattered throughout the Crystal Palace event the previous year, Cork's exhibition was the earliest to set aside a space specifically for displaying art. According to J.F. Maguire, 'Fine Arts' were a necessary facet of modern life, and industrial expositions, as they 'refined, civilised, elevated and ennobled communities and countries'.[4] For Maguire, exhibitions provided an ideal opportunity to blend high-quality artistic techniques and styles with manufacturing processes, in what he called the mixing of 'beauty with practical utility'.[5] Internationally, it was the French who took this idea to a higher level, when they unveiled the first dedicated Fine Art Palace at the 1855 Exposition. Over the subsequent decades, exposition art galleries became artistic battlegrounds between countries, demonstrations of who had the 'best' artists or who had the most space to display their art. This competitive spirit, so utterly characteristic of the exhibition tradition, created an artistic forum through which style, content and national cultural identity could be discussed and criticized.[6] However, when it came to planning the great American expositions, organizers had less of a heritage in painting or sculpture to draw from. World's Fairs therefore, became incredibly important in helping to establish an 'American Culture' by familiarizing Americans with foreign art forms and encouraging their own creative impulses.[7] For smaller expositions like those in Ireland, impressive art galleries may have been even more necessary, because they helped compensate for the paucity of international and innovative industrial exhibits and lent an aura of civility to the whole affair.

Turning our attention to Cork, one found within the walls of the 1852 Art Gallery: paintings, interspersed with sculpture, architectural drawings, jewellery, silver work and the 'more elaborate and costly descriptions [*sic*] of furniture'.[8] In total 567 works were displayed celebrating deceased and contemporary Cork and Irish artists including James Barry, Nathaniel Grogan, Daniel MacDonald and Daniel Maclise, among many others. For practical reasons, there were fewer sculptures than paintings present. The sculptural highlight was the marble figure of the *Dead Christ* by John Hogan.[9] This iconic piece was displayed in its own room decorated with purple drapery, separated from other sculptures and specially lit for dramatic effect.[10] Elsewhere, as was mentioned in Chapter 4, an impressive collection of archaeological antiques were housed in a series of cases.[11] Though the Royal Irish Academy had been exhibiting Irish antiques to select audiences since the 1830s, 'Ancient Ireland' became more accessible after 1852 and became established as an integral element of Ireland's cultural milieu both at domestic and foreign industrial exhibitions.

Cork's 1852 template was applied a year later in Dublin where the Art Gallery housed an impressive installation of works by Irish and foreign artists.[12] Corkmen played a part in the art exhibits in other Dublin exhibitions, for example Sir Thomas Deane, Benson, Daniel Maclise and John Foley all sat on the Fine Art Committee for that city's 1865 event.[13] The same concept was rolled out at the other Irish national exhibitions during the nineteenth century, including at Cork in 1883. The great role played by art at industrial expositions pointed to the wider growth in art appreciation in Ireland and a movement towards making art more accessible to the public at large. The success of the fine art and antique sections of the 1853 Industrial Exhibition in Dublin was such that it directly led to the establishment of the National Gallery of Ireland in 1864 and the Museum of Science and Art (later the National Museum of Ireland) in 1877.[14] In Cork there was also a proliferation of art institutions during the nineteenth century from the Cork Society for Promoting the Fine Arts in 1815 to the establishment of the Crawford School of Art and Gallery in 1885.[15] So it came to pass that by the time the 1902 Fine Arts and Archaeological Committee, headed by Vice-Chairman Arthur Hill, came to plan the Art Gallery, they had plenty of experience and knowledge at their disposal.

Fine Art and Archaeological Section

Hill's committee was prestigious and included the Presidents of the Royal Academy of Art, the Royal Hibernian Academy and the Royal Scottish Academy. In addition, Walter Strickland (a noted art critic from the National Gallery of Ireland) served on it, and it was advised on archaeological matters by local men, J.P. Dalton, Marcus Hartog and Sidney Seymour Lucas. Over 600 *objets d'art* were collected from within Ireland and abroad, as well as 186 photographs, to be displayed in their own section. The artworks mainly consisted of paintings, but also included some small sculptures and models and, as in former expositions, the galleries included a collection of archaeological artefacts and applied art (especially silverware), such as an eight-sided silver ceremonial mace dated 1696.[16] For many visitors, it was one of the highlights of the Exhibition. Before the galleries even opened it was written that 'the Arts Section would repay … the cost of a ticket to the entire Exhibition'.[17] The collection was praised by *Irish Builder* (who also reviewed applied and fine art in their journal) as 'undoubtedly the finest of its kind ever got together in Ireland and [being] alone worth going to Cork to see'.[18]

According to the Official Catalogue of the 'Fine Art and Archaeological Section', the work of over 280 artists was represented at the show, as well as an unknown number of photographers.[19] Whilst these artists represented an exemplary selection of late-Victorian British and Irish art, many of them have seen their reputations diminish since. A highly creditable 11 per cent of the artists at the show were women.[20] Rather than a review of the great art movements of the past, this was very much an exhibition of contemporary art. Two thirds of those presenting were living artists (although a number of them were advanced in years) and this emphasis on modern art had also been a characteristic of the 1853 Dublin Exhibition gallery.[21]

Unlike an exhibition at a municipal art gallery, the bulk of the work (64 per cent) was offered for sale. Prices listed in the catalogue ranged from £5 to £1,000. According to the *Irish News*, 'The Gallery [contained] pictures to the value of £200,000'.[22] Whilst being far from *avant garde*, some of the artists strove to produce work on the most up-to-date topics. For example, picture No.25 showed *The Irish Pavilion, Glasgow Exhibition*, held only the previous summer. The artist was Susan Crawford and the price, £25. As well as minor talents like Ms Crawford, the show also included the 'best masters of the modern British School'.[23] The Pre-Raphaelite Brotherhood, that quintessentially English movement, was represented by two of its founders, Sir John Millais and William Holman Hunt, whose *The Afterglow in Egypt* was described as 'magnificent' (9.2).[24] Many of the other artists displayed were associates of, or strongly influenced by, the Brotherhood. In addition the American painter, John Singer Sargent and a small number of continental artists were also represented.

There had always been a strong tradition of importing British art to Irish exhibitions; indeed as late as 1906 it was stated that 'in order to keep up a credible exhibition, about two fifths of the pictures … have to be invited from Great Britain'.[25] In Cork, it seems that this was also the case. Ninety-six (or about a third) of the artists were classed as 'Irish', but in fact many of these were based in England. Nonetheless, this was a strong showing of Irish painters, a number of whose reputations have, it may be said, stood the test of time. John, the father of William and Jack Butler Yeats, was represented by three works. Edith Somerville exhibited three illustrations for her series of 'Irish RM' books for which she is mostly remembered today. Better-known at present are the sculptor Oliver Sheppard, the painter Walter Osborne and what we might call the 'Big Four' of nineteenth-century Cork art: the aforementioned Maclise and Barry and the sculptors Hogan and Foley. Amongst the British sculptors at the exhibition, Hamo Thornycroft is perhaps best recalled today.

9.2

The Afterglow in Egypt, 1854, William Holman Hunt.

This image of an Egyptian peasant girl was painted during the artist's travels in the east. Its Orientalism chimes with other aspects of the Cork Exhibition such as the Cairo Street. The title is something of a mystery as it is not a landscape, but its colours are captivating. (© Bridgeman Art Library/Southampton City Art Gallery)

9.3

Gallery 1, 1902.
A portrait of Queen Victoria hung in the centre of the Art Exhibition. In front are two sculptures by Oliver Sheppard; a plaque representing the Children of Lír, & Innis Fodra (1901), which so captivated Patrick Pearse. This work had previously been moved from Gallery 2 to stand in front of the Queen in this gallery. The work is hung very densely, below eye-level & over doorways. (© Tom Spalding, with thanks to T. Allen & D. Ó Riain-Raedel)

The Exhibits

The exhibition was hung in five galleries, arranged in three wings, and a modern gallery-visitor would be immediately struck by the crowded 'Salon' style hanging of the pictures, with work cramped together and displayed at knee level and over doorways (9.3). A portrait by William M. Egley of the late Queen Victoria was placed at the heart of the exhibit and is likely to have been one of the first pictures visitors would see upon entering.[26] It, and a landscape, *Departure of Queen Victoria from Kingstown* (Dún Laoghaire)

9.4

Gallery 2, 1902.
This room held a collection of mostly English & Scottish oil paintings, as well as some Continental works. The nearest sculpture is *A Warrior Bearing a Wounded Youth* by Thornycraft & the central figure is Sheppard's *Fin-Foya* (1899). The building was constructed out of corrugated iron & 'fire proof' wood. This 90' x 30' gallery was the largest. Overall the galleries covered 1,800 ft². (© Tom Spalding, with thanks to Tim Allen & Dagmar Ó Riain-Raedel)

were lent by Edward VII. The organizing committee had scoured far and wide for art. As well as those lent for sale by the artists, pictures were also lent by many municipal galleries, primarily from the north of England, such as Manchester, Oldham, Blackburn, Liverpool, Preston, Bradford and Leeds as well as several others, and eight pieces from the collection of the Victoria & Albert museum.[27] In addition to the portrait of Victoria, the General Fine Art section included William Frith's *Derby Day*, so well regarded at the time that it apparently '[did] not need description' (9.5).[28] Also in this room was Millais's portrait of the noted engraver Thomas 'Oldham' Barlow, lent by the Corporation of Oldham.

Moving into Gallery Two, one would find a selection of British and foreign oils (9.4). To the modern imagination, the work of Monet, Renoir and other French Impressionists dominates our perception of late-nineteenth-century art. However, there were no works by these Frenchmen on show in Cork. The conservatism of the organizers, as well as the lack of modern French art, was not unique to this exhibition: for example, there were few pieces by the Impressionists in the significantly larger show put together in 1901 in Glasgow,[29] and a decade or so later an exhibition in the Royal Academy in London was praised for its 'solid and respectable' selection, which wouldn't ruffle any feathers.[30] Although it had been twenty years since the Impressionist's finest hour, their style was described in the *Cork Constitution* in 1902 as

9.6
A Children's Party or The
Birthday Party, *c*.1900,
Walter Osborne.
This late work by Osborne
is a charming image
of a birthday party and
captivated viewers with its
innocence & Impressionist
style. Whilst Impressionism
was almost a passing phase
in French art by this time, it
was still considered novel
to many visitors to the Cork
show. Osborne was one of
the many contemporary
Irish artists represented in
Cork. (Courtesy Wikipedia
Commons)

'audacious' and explained thus: 'the artists of the Impressionist school seek to produce effects by a mass of colour which is laid on by a few broad strokes'. The tone of this coverage suggests that in the eyes of the local *cognoscenti*, Impressionism was something quite novel. The paper went on to explain that there were some Irish and British painters who also worked in the style, as we will see. Each gallery featured a number of small sculptures or models and in Gallery Two, visitors could inspect *A Warrior Bearing a Wounded Youth* by Hamo Thornycroft, which had won a gold medal at the Royal Academy back in 1876.[31]

The third gallery concentrated on Irish Oils and was praised as a 'thoroughly representative collection'.[32] According to the *Cork Constitution*, it received 'a very large share of attention from every class of visitor'.[33] As was mentioned above in the context of American art, there was pointedly national aspiration to this gallery. The quality of the Irish work was said to be such that it would be 'indicative of civilisation and refinement in any nation'. Although a 'striking'

portrait of W.B. Yeats, by Alice S. Kinkead was praised, Yeats' father, John's portrait of the old Fenian John O'Leary was (perhaps deliberately) not mentioned at all in the review by the loyalist *Constitution*. This gallery also included the work of Walter Osborne whom, the paper reminded readers, 'is an Irishman … who is in the front rank of Impressionists'. He had spent time in Pont Aven, a popular resort for post-Impressionists in Brittany, and in Belgium, and had received a bronze medal for his portrait of Mrs Noel Guinness at Paris in 1900.[34] This provides a further example, if any were needed, of the ways which international exhibitions interconnected different cities and people across many fields of human endeavour. His painting *The Birthday Party (A Children's Party)* was singled out for particular praise in Cork (9.6).

The fourth gallery consisted of watercolours and black-and-white etchings and lithographs, many lent by *Illustrated London News* and *The Weekly Graphic*. As one might expect, many of these images had a strong imperial theme, a flavour of which can be garnered from their titles: *Attending to the Wounded of the Highland Brigade at Magersfontain, Conje's Boers Surrendering* and *Expedition against the Mad Mullah*. The final gallery covered photography. Whilst photographs had been shown at the Crystal Palace in 1851 and at Dublin in 1865, it was felt by contemporary viewers in Cork to be quite unusual to have so many photos on exhibition. One journalist covering the show believed it to be only the second time the art was given this level of exposure in recognition of its 'artistic claims', after Glasgow.[35] The work was said to be a 'revelation of what can be done in photography', especially the portraiture of Baron Arild Rosenkrantz, who also practised as a painter and stained-glass artist.[36]

Irish Nationalism in Art

Amongst the cases of applied art were some examples of Irish art from an altogether different period: specimens of weapons and implements of the 'Kelts' and a gold bracelet which, it was claimed, 'was bestowed on the bards of ancient Ireland'.[37] The cases also included modern reproductions of Celtic jewellery by Waterhouse of Dublin. Perhaps much of this material, some of it lent by the great Cork antiquarian Robert Day,[38] had been originally intended to be exhibited in Innis Fáil, the Irish Village. In addition to the portrait of Fenian John O'Leary, [39] Yeats exhibited a fine portrait of the constitutional politician, Isaac Butt, and a watercolour, *The Unicorn*. There were many landscapes and much work concentrating on more whimsical Irish themes such as Osborne's *The Man who had seen the Leprechaun*. It is perhaps indicative of the level of familiarity of the general public with Irish folk-tales that it was felt necessary to provide an explanation in the catalogue that a Leprechaun was 'a Fairy Cobbler'.

There was also on show some Irish art with a more nationalist inspiration. Oliver Sheppard, best known today for his sculpture *The Dying Cú Chulainn* in the GPO in Dublin, showed three pieces on Irish themes: a small sculpture *Innis Fodra (Fáil), The Island of Destiny* priced at £150, a plaster bronze *Fin-Foya (Sweet Voiced)* as well as a plaster bronze plaque *The Fate of the Children of Lír*.[40] In style, these pieces related to the work of Thornycroft and the modern British school, which according to John Turpin would have appeared decidedly 'naturalistic and up-to-date' when compared to the work of Hogan or Foley on show in a neighbouring gallery.[41] These works had avowedly Irish themes, the former in particular. *The Island of Destiny*, created within a year of the Exhibition, illustrated three figures: a dead or dying man, a handsome young woman and a boy, representing Ireland past, present and future. The symbolism was not lost on many viewers and had a particular effect on Patrick Pearse. His firm exhibited in Cork for six months in the building next door to the Galleries and he had a personal and professional interest in sculpture, however, it appears that he did not visit the Exhibition, and he claimed he first saw it at the Royal Hibernian Academy in 1901.[42] Writing in *An Claidheamh Soluis*, the journal of the Gaelic League, in 1906 Pearse was struck by the power of the sculpture when he stated that 'though the world would run red with blood, the cause of that woman (*presumably, Irish freedom*) shall triumph'.[43] The portrait of Queen Victoria also hung in this room and such mixed messages, what F.S.L. Lyons has called 'cultural fusion', were not unusual at this time in Irish life, as we have seen again and again in this book.[44]

Music

Central to the more placid pursuits available on the Mardyke and to Cork people in general, was music (9.7). It is no exaggeration to state that musical performance was omnipresent during both seasons of the Exhibition. In official openings and sporting events, royal visits and night-time entertainments, music played a dominant part in all proceedings and festivities. Its importance to the organizers was underlined by their expenditure of a substantial portion of the budget (about £9,000)[45] on the provision of music and the fact that the Exhibition's musical director, Theo Gmür, was the only office-holder to be paid a salary (£200 per annum). Since moving from his native Switzerland to take up the post of organist in St Peter's and St Paul's in 1881, Gmür had amassed an impressive résumé. He had been appointed Professor of Harmony, Counterpoint and the Organ at the Cork Municipal School of Music, as well as chief conductor of the school's choral society. Gmür's close working relationship with Cork's municipal authorities almost certainly ensured his appointment as musical director for the 1902/3 Exhibitions. Not only did Gmür have to conceive, arrange, rehearse and deliver musical programmes of impeccable quality, he also had to manage a 400-strong orchestra and choir as well as performing regular organ recitals as a soloist.[46] Gmür was one of several foreign musicians who came to ply their trade in the city by the Lee. The two factors that contributed to this influx of continental talent were the increase in the number of Catholic churches in the city, which needed experienced organists, and the establishment of the Municipal School of Music in 1878.

By the late 1880s, besides Gmür, the school had one Belgian, Leopold De Prins, and two Germans, Hans Conrad Swertz and Heinrich Tils, on its staff.[47] It had fallen to Swertz to organize and arrange the instrumental and choral music during the 1883 Exhibition. This conclave of continental musicians played a pivotal part in shaping Cork's cultural landscape by modernizing its church music, enhancing its educational facilities and inspiring a greater appreciation and enjoyment of music of all styles and taste. Gmür and his fellow immigrants supplemented their income by giving private lessons or tutorials, usually from their own home.[48]

The recorded history of musical appreciation in Cork City stretches back to at least the early eighteenth century.[49] The formation of amateur musical societies, 'glee clubs' and the public demand for high-quality concerts and performances meant that by the 1840s, according to Susan O'Regan, the city 'was established on the itinerary of the foremost European and British artists and confident local entrepreneurship had begun to privatise the organization of the most prestigious concerts'.[50] The Theatre Royal (situated on the site of the current GPO) served the concert-going public from the eighteenth century until the opening of the Opera House in 1877. Local and international soloists, orchestras and touring operas catering for all classes played to enthusiastic

9.7
Cork Working Men's Band, 1903.
This 36-man band stand on the Main Bandstand, in front of the silver cup they won in Dublin in 1897. They also won the band competition at the 1903 expo. In the first exhibition season this bandstand was reserved for professional & military bands. (Courtesy Des Kiely whose grandfather & great-grandfather are in this photograph)

and receptive audiences. Concerts were also held in other locations like the Assembly Rooms on the South Mall and on the old bandstand on the Mardyke which pre-dated the Exhibition. The nineteenth century saw the formation of popular local working-class bands, including the Barrack Street Band (1837) and the Butter Exchange Band (1878).[51] The soldiers, sailors and RIC men stationed in Cork and surrounding environs meant there was also a regular supply of military and regimental bands willing and able to entertain the city's populace. Official civic receptions, public holidays, sporting and other public gatherings utilized this wide variety of city-based bands at their disposal, bringing pleasure and enjoyment to all those concerned.

The rich pool of available talent in the city was something the organizers of Cork's various exhibitions were well aware of when it came to drawing up their musical programmes. Each group had made provision for a concert hall, a substantial organ and sufficient stage and floor space suitable for large concerts and recitals. At each exhibition the best available local, national and foreign talent was hired to form musical ensembles. For example, the choir at the 1852 opening day event was predominantly drawn from members of Dublin choral societies while the 1883 opening day orchestra was staffed by instrumentalists from Cork, Dublin, Belfast, London and Manchester (9.8).[52] In the absence of other amusements at the 1852 and 1883 Exhibitions, musical performances formed the bulk of the entertainment provided by the committee. In total there were 181 concerts and performances held in 1883 'in which', it was said, 'all classes of visitors must have found something suited to their respective tastes'. These included performances from the three principal musical bodies in the city at the time, the Cork Orchestral Union, Cork School of Music and the Cork Musical Society, as well as a multitude of local and regimental bands. One of the reported highlights of the 1883 season was the civilian and military band competitions held over two days in September.[53] The closing day performances were also something very special, as four regimental bands joined forces to perform a quadrille known as the 'British Army'.[54] It must have been an amazing sight watching the bands marching through the building with the 'Scotch pipers, drummers, fifers and trumpeters' causing a 'great furore'.[55] Though there were far more thrilling distractions on offer in 1902 and 1903 than had been the case at previous exhibitions, visitors would have still expected, indeed demanded, a similarly extensive and high-calibre musical programme.

The 1902/3 Music and Amusements Committees need not have been worried, as they were spoilt for choice. They were able to recruit a small exhibition orchestra made up of foreign musicians that was conducted by an Italian, Ferruccio Grossi.[56] The committee also hired local and military bands to perform on a regular basis throughout the season for a variety of events, no doubt easing the workload on Gmür. Aside from the Concert Hall and the three bandstands, concerts were occasionally held from the top of the Water Chute (!) and in the Chalet Restaurant. The area near the Irish Labourer's Cottage on the Western Field also staged concerts and *céilí* of Irish music, dance and song. The music played by these bands was unashamedly popularist and included pieces by classical composers like Wagner, Rossini and Verdi, marching band music by the contemporary American composer John Philip Sousa, as well as many British and Irish ballads and airs (see Appendix 6). To promote the numerous bands and performances on the grounds, a *Daily Programme* was published to keep the public informed. For example, on Wednesday, 24 September 1902 the public enjoyed four hour-long performances by the band of the 2nd Battalion, Royal Scots Fusiliers (two in the afternoon and two in the evening), on the central bandstand. At the Western Field bandstand, the Barrack Street Band played for two hours that evening while at 5pm, Mr Frank Muspatt gave a solo organ recital in the Concert Hall.[57] On a side note, the Scots Fusiliers finished their set with 'God Save the King', while the Barrack Street Band closed their performance with the piece 'St Patrick's Day', an unofficial national Irish Anthem in pre-Free State Ireland. Some bands like the RIC band often played both songs, so as not to offend any particular section of their audience.[58] On one occasion, the Berlin Philharmonic Wind Orchestra ended a concert with 'Let Erin Remember', which delighted the majority nationalist members of the audience. The loyalist spectators were left slightly embarrassed as they had stood with hats removed, in anticipation of either 'God Save the King' or the German national anthem.[59] Like every other aspect of the Exhibition, musical performance could become politicized.[60]

The Berlin Philharmonic Wind Orchestra was the most prestigious to appear in Cork, and their presence was an example of the great efforts the committee expended in securing international groups to play on the Mardyke. The Orchestra was hired for a week-long engagement in July 1902 and played three times a day to thousands of spectators who travelled from all across the country to hear such a marvellous band. Due to their popularity, they were invited back for another week 'at enormous expense', and they would return again to play the opening week of the 1903 season.[61] They were considered by many who saw them as the best musicians to ever play in Cork. According to the *Irish Times*:

> The performances are simply a revelation to music lovers – and they are no mean judges in the South – and the attendances in the vicinity of the band stand on which they play are immense. The band numbers some fifty performers and is mainly brass, a set of valve trumpets being added to the usual compliment of a military band and besides they have combinations made up of Pandean [Pan] pipes, bells, czimbals [cymbals] and some instruments long since out of use in our bands, which produce most striking and artistic effects. By common consent, there has never been such music heard in Cork, as the playing is full of musical fervour and soul. Never has a more thrilling performance of the Tannhauser Overture, of Oberon, or of Zampa been heard in Cork. One musician said to our representative, We thought we idealised what first class renderings should be, but I must say our ideals are but common place next to the marvellous interpretations given us by this band.[62]

Other foreign groups of note included Herr Kandts' Viennese Band, hired at £135 (£13,500) per week, the Blue Hungarian Band and from France, the

Orchestre de la Renaissance. In conjunction with the visit of the Japanese Navy in August 1902 (see Chapter 8), a Japanese military band entertained crowds on the exhibition grounds, inbetween the frequent rain showers. The band was described as 'a really clever combination and strikingly remarkable for its precision'. The *Cork Constitution* went on to say that they played some popular Japanese airs, which 'may be deservedly popular in Japan, but we confess that they were, more or less, wasted on ourselves, as we were utterly incapable of appraising them at their real value'.[63] Fortunately for this critic, their repertoire also included many European, British and Irish melodies. All the international bands undoubtedly helped increase attendance figures, but like the Art Gallery they also gave the Exhibition an air of cultural sophistication and prestige.

In our time, when music is freely and conveniently available on a multitude of formats, it is easy to forget just how important the social aspects of music were to our Victorian and Edwardian ancestors. The lives of Cork's citizens were greatly enriched by melody and song. Whether it was a social gathering in the drawing room of a middle-class family, or a public demonstration on the city's thoroughfares, music was the focal point for most, if not all, social interaction. In the wider context of Cork's commercial life during this period, one can detect a significant increase in music-related businesses in the late nineteenth century. In 1845, the city boosted five 'Music Warehouses' and nineteen 'Professors of Music' (teachers), as well as two singing coaches.[64] By 1891, this had increased slightly to twenty-five music teachers and three businesses that sold or made musical instruments and other related products.[65] By 1907, the numbers had almost doubled with forty-three teachers and sixteen retail businesses listed in that year's commercial directory. There were three local exhibitors displaying instruments in the 1902 Industrial Hall and one of them, Daniel Nunan (an organist at St Augustine's) was selling sheet music of the waltzes and marches he had specially composed for the Exhibition.[66] Though it would be difficult to prove that Cork's exhibitions helped create the large consumer music market present in the city by 1907, they certainly illustrated music's commercial potential.

Exhibiting Sport: Where We Sported and Played

Hosting the Exhibition on the Mardyke capitalized on its historical use as a haven for recreation and the presence there of clubs involved in cricket, tennis and boating. As we will see in Chapter 10, there is an intimate relationship between exhibitions and public parks, and the former regularly inspired the establishment of the latter. This is the case in Cork, where Fitzgerald Park stands on the site of the great undertaking of 1902 and 1903. Apart from the Mardyke, the other major centre of sport in the city at the time was an area near the Marina known as Cork Park.[67] Though home to the Cork Racecourse since the 1860s, Cork Park also began hosting rugby games in the 1870s. The GAA started holding Cork championship matches there in 1887, and the site began to assume the character of a full-time sports facility. Soccer was enjoyed in the city but would only become popular after Independence, due in part to its failure to become established in UCC.[68] Since its formation in 1884, the GAA enjoyed great support in Cork in both hurling and football.[69] Over both seasons of the exhibition, local championship matches were regularly held on the Mardyke between teams like Blackrock, St Finbarrs, and several others. Other sports like swimming, hockey and angling were also beginning to become more organized and thrive. By the opening of the Exhibition, Cork had a healthy sporting community catering to all social and religious persuasions.[70] The combined grounds of the Cricket and Boating Clubs, comprising about twenty acres, hosted the majority of sporting events connected with the 1902 Exhibition. Here, spectators were treated to hurling and football matches, athletic competitions, cycle races and tennis tournaments while music floated through the Mardyke grounds, a soundtrack to the spirit of friendly competition, both in industry and sport (9.9).

Recreational activities had become increasingly popular in late-Victorian Ireland, both for sport and leisure; and none more so than cycling. Initially associated with the urban middle class, bicycles were by now an affordable means of transport exploited by those wanting to take day-trips or simply get from A to B. In America, the bicycle business boomed in the 1890s, as it went from a $2 million pastime to a $32 million industry within the decade.[71] The average price of a bicycle there had dropped from around $100 in 1893 to $3–$15 in 1904, replacing the horse as the most popular means of private transport in the cities.[72] A similar pattern can be seen in Ireland and the rest of the developed world where cycling became an integral part of urban living.[73] Dublin became a centre of bike manufacture when Dunlop set up in the city in 1888. During the 1890s, twenty-five bicycle companies sprung up in the Irish capital and the city held a dedicated bicycle exposition in 1897. Between the years 1891–1907, the number of bike shops and agents in Cork City more than doubled, from four to ten, and the city had its own bicycle manufacturer; the Irish Cycle Company on Parnell Place. The formation of cycling clubs, biking tours and a subsequent loosening of social norms had a tangible impact on the ordinary lives of men, women and children in Ireland.[74] As we saw in Chapter 7, cycling and its associated commercial and sporting off-shoots were given a prominent place at the 1902 Exhibition. The official guidebooks listed the tourist-friendly cycling routes available from Cork for day trips or three or four day excursions throughout the county and as far as Kerry.[75]

9.9
Sporting Competitions. This detail of a Guy's panorama shows the east end of the site where sporting events were concentrated in 1902. The Cricket Pavilion served as a grandstand for cycling races & other sports. Tennis can be seen played in the centre of the image & water-borne events were catered for from the slipway of the Sunday's Well Rowing & Tennis Club. (© CPM)

One important characteristic of sport as displayed on the Mardyke and all other late-Victorian expositions was its internationalism. The development of modern sport was directly influenced by this facet of expositions and a natural bond was formed between them due to the mutual desire for international competition. Unsurprisingly, three of the first four modern Olympiads coincided with expositions: Paris (1900), St Louis (1904) and London (1908). Tellingly, even prior to the first Olympiad held in 1896 in Athens, exhibitions were often described using Grecian metaphors.[76] For example, the Crystal Palace exhibition in 1851 was exalted as the 'Olympic game of industry, this tournament of commerce'.[77] By the beginning of the Edwardian era, international and national athletic, golfing, boxing and football tournaments and matches became more feasible due to proficient sports administration, standardized rules, reliable communication and swifter modes of transport. At Cork, every effort was made to attract high-profile national, but more importantly, international competitions. These would ensure extra publicity and encourage more 'punters' through the gates. For instance, the Irish Amateur Athletic Association national championships were held on the Exhibition's sporting grounds on Saturday 21 June. Admission was one shilling and admission to the exhibition itself was available at a reduced rate of six pence. The day's programme included the 100 yard, 220 yard, half-mile, four mile, 120 yard hurdle races, as well as the hammer, the shot and the high jump. This was the first occasion the Championships were held in Cork.[78] Later in the summer (8–12 July) an international lawn tennis tournament took place at the exhibition which saw a record number of 125 entrants from across the British Isles, including Mr A.W. Gore, 1901 Wimbledon All-England Champion. The chief prize was the Cork Exhibition Challenge Cup, valued at £10 (*c.*£1,000 today). The scene was set in an article in the *Irish Times*: 'the weather was beautiful, the five courts played splendidly and there was a large and fashionable attendance of spectators, who watched with sustained interest, the progress of play'.[79]

By far the best patronized international event during the first season of the Cork Exhibition was the International Rowing Race held over three consecutive days at the end of July. This International Regatta attracted twenty teams from across Ireland, Britain and Europe as follows:

Division One, International Rowing Race:

Bann Rowing Club	Magdalene College, Oxford
Berlin Rowing Club	New Ross Boat Club
City of Derry Boating Club	Newry Rowing Club
Dublin Metropolitan	Shandon Rowing Club
Dublin University Boat Club	Shannon (Limerick) Rowing Club
Emmanuel Boat Club, Cambridge	University College, Oxford
Leander Club	

Division Two:

Athlunkard Rowing Club	Lincoln Rowing Club
Commercial Rowing Club	Pembroke Rowing Club
Cork Boat Club	Waterford Boat Club
Lee Rowing Club	

The teams competed in a series of heats over two days until the field was reduced to just two finalists who competed on the last day, 24 July. The races were held over a two-mile stretch of the Lee, starting opposite Dunkettle Railway Station and finishing at the Bandstand on the Marina Walk, near the Shandon Boat Club. On the eve of the regatta, 22,000 people passed through the exhibition turnstiles and no doubt many were visiting the city to experience what promised to be a splendid three days of rowing.

The credit for conceiving the International Boat Race belongs to the Lord Chief Justice of Ireland, Lord O'Brien of Kilfenora, who proposed the idea in July 1901.[80] The proposal to hold an exhibition in the city had spurred Lord O'Brien to gather around him a representative committee composed of members of the senior rowing clubs in Britain and Ireland to help arrange an international event.[81] The organizing of the regatta itself was left in the capable hands of the Cork City Regatta Committee, who had experience in managing the city's annual regatta.[82] Lord O'Brien was also instrumental in having an 'International Cup' specially made for the occasion (9.10). At a meeting of the International Boat Race Committee, held in Dublin's Four Courts in early February 1902, he announced that a sum of over £400 was subscribed to the event in order to manufacture the cup and cover the prize money for the eventual winners.[83] The subscriptions were limited to one pound and the list of donors was a 'who's who' of the contemporary British and Anglo-Irish upper class including Arthur Balfour, who would become Prime Minister of Britain in July 1902, Lord Ashbourne, the Lord Chancellor of Ireland and Sir Thomas Lipton, a wealthy tea merchant.[84] Though rowing was a pastime predominantly popular with the upper echelons of society, the fact that between eighty and one hundred thousand spectators packed the Marina to watch the final day's racing testifies to the sport's popularity amongst all classes.

9.10
Cork International Exhibition Rowing Trophy. This trophy by West of College Green, Dublin 'jewellers & silversmiths by special appointment to the King of Ireland' stood 3 ft 6 ins (1 m) high & weighed approximately 650 ounces (18½ kg). The Leander Club of Henley, Oxfordshire won it in 1902. It is currently insured for £165,000. (Courtesy Leander Club)

The final was contested between the Berlin Rowing Club and the Leander Club of Henley in England. Leander, founded in 1818, has claims to be the world's oldest rowing club. It was a hard fought and exciting race which saw Leander achieving victory by a single length. At the finishing line, both teams were 'quite done up' by the exertion but this is hardly surprising as the race was run in a time of 11 minutes and 11½ seconds, 51 seconds faster than any other over the previous three days.[85] At the prize-giving ceremony, Lady Bandon presented Leander's captain with the International Cup and each member of the team also received an engraved silver cup. The three days had passed without a hitch and would live long in the memory. The regatta proved to be an enormous success, one English newspaper remarking how this was the first time an English eight (rowing crew) had rowed in Ireland and that 'the regatta in Cork is a sporting fixture which has never had its parallel in any other country'.[86] In the days after the race, Lord O'Brien received a letter from Kaiser Wilhelm II thanking him for inviting the Berlin team to the race and hoping that the favour could be someday returned as 'such contests are excellent in promoting good feeling and friendship between the two countries'.[87] Aside from the International Cup races, there were also a number of junior and senior

8   Ibid., p.442.

9   This spectacular marble sculpture currently resides in St Finbarre's South, South Parish.

10 F. Cullen, *Ireland on Show; Art, Union and Nationhood* (Farnham: Ashgate, 2012), p.66. Cullen highlights how this would have been the first time Corkonians were exposed to such a potent mix of iconography and theatrics.

11 Maguire, *The Industrial Movement in Ireland*, pp.349–68.

12 See Cullen, *Ireland on Show*, pp.20–4. The 1853 Exhibition in Dublin had almost three times the amount of works in Cork the previous year.

13 J. Turpin, 'Exhibitions of Art and Industry in Victorian Ireland: Part 2: Dublin Exhibitions of Art and Industries 1865–1885', *Dublin Historical Record*, 35, 2 (March 1982), p.43.

14 See Cullen, *Ireland on Show*, pp.20–4.

15 See P. Murray, 'Art Institutions in Nineteenth-Century Cork', in P. O'Flanagan and C.G. Buttimer (eds) *Cork: History & Society* (Dublin: Geography Publications, 1993).

16 *Cork Constitution*, 7 June 1902.

17 *Cork Examiner*, 9 May 1902. The Galleries opened a month after the main exhibition.

18 *Irish Builder*, 19 June 1902.

19 Anon., *Official Catalogue of the Fine Art and Archaeological Section, Cork International Exhibition, 1902* (Cork: Guys, 1902).

20 Female artists were almost totally absent at the Glasgow Art Exhibition of 1901. P. and J. Kinchin, *Glasgow's Great Exhibitions; 1888–1901–1911–1938–1988* (Bicester: White Cockade Publishing, 1988), p.65.

21 See Cullen, *Ireland on Show*, p.24.

22 *Belfast Irish News*, 28 April 1902.

23 *Cork Examiner*, 2 July 1902.

24 Ibid.

25 A Government report quoted in Cullen, *Ireland on Show*, p.9.

26 This portrait was a copy of one by Von Angeli.

27 There was a long tradition of the South Kensington campus (including the V&A) lending art to Irish expos. See Cullen, *Ireland on Show*, pp.9–15.

28 *Cork Examiner*, 2 July 1902. The picture showed at Cork was a copy by the artist from his original executed in 1893 and is currently in the collection of the Manchester municipal gallery.

29 The PRB were well represented at Glasgow. See P. and J. Kinchin, *Glasgow's Great Exhibitions; 1888–1901–1911–1938–1988* (Bicester: White Cockade Publishing, 1988), pp.64–5.

30 The Studio, quoted in L. James, *The Middle Class; A History* (London: Little, Brown, 2006), p.381.

31 It is likely that this small (27in, 0.68m) bronze is now in Leighton House, London.

32 *Irish Builder*, 19 June 1902.

33 *Cork Constitution*, 5 July 1902.

34 J. Sheehy, *Walter Osborne* (Dublin: National Gallery of Ireland, 1983), p.31.

35 *Cork Constitution,* 20 May 1902.

36 *Irish Builder*, 19 June 1902.

37 *Cork Constitution*, 17 June 1902.

38 *Cork Constitution*, 16 June 1902.

39 Pearse was struck by the potency of this portrait when he saw it: 'the pose of the head, the fire of the eye, the hollowness of the cheek, all this is unmistakably O'Leary – student and revolutionary'. 'The National Salon', *An Claidheamh Soluis*, 11 August 1906.

40 Sheppard's enthusiasm for Irish names was not matched by his faithfulness to the language.

41 J. Turpin, *Oliver Sheppard, 1865–1941* (Dublin: Four Courts Press, 2000), p.25.

42 Pearse visited Cork city and county in autumn 1902, but makes no mention of the Exhibition at all in his report. *An Claidheamh Soluis*, 4 October 1902.

43 'The National Salon', *An Claidheamh Soluis*, 11

August 1906. Quoted in Turpin, *Oliver Sheppard*, p.70. Although this article is unsigned, we agree with Turpin's assessment that it is the work of Pearse.

44 See Cullen, *Ireland on Show*, pp.14 & 166.

45 Admittedly over the two seasons, but this was more than the estimate of the cost to build the Industrial Hall.

46 J.P. Cunningham and R. Fleischmann, *Aloys Fleischmann (1880–1964) Immigrant Musician in Ireland* (Cork: Cork University Press, 2010), p.67. His biography appears in R.J. Hodges, *Cork and County Cork in the Twentieth Century: Contemporary Biographies* (Brighton: W.T. Pike & Co., 1911) published as part of a wider study on Cork City and County. Gmür composed one opera entitled *Edelweiss*, as well as many church, vocal and orchestral music throughout his career. He was also the organist at City Hall. He would serve as director of the Cork Amateur Operatic and Dramatic Society, founded in 1883, performing light operas every year until 1911. He would get involved in the Munster Society of Arts founded in 1924, two years after the foundation of the Free State.

47 Leopold De Prins was organist at Cork's St Mary's Cathedral and teacher at School of Music until 1889; Hans Conrad Swertz, a native of Dachau, began as organist of St Vincent's Church and eventually appointed to the Cathedral in 1890. He was also professor of harmony at the school of music. His daughter would eventually marry another famous Dachau native, Aloys Fleischmann, whose union produced another important generation of immigrant musicians in the city. Heinrich Tils came to Cork as organist and Choirmaster for St Mary's in 1870s. He founded the Cork Choral Union in 1902 and successfully conducted the choir until 1906.

48 See Cunningham and Fleischmann, *Aloys Fleischmann*, p.5.

49 S. O'Regan, 'Concert performers in Cork from 1710 to 1840', *Journal of the Cork Historical and Archaeological Society*, 114 (2009) pp.39–50.

50 Ibid., p.43.

51 The Barrack Street Band (or 'Baracka') was originally founded as a temperance band by Father Mathew. The Butter Exchange Band (or Buttera), though formed in 1878, has its roots in a pre-Famine working-class band that frequented the area around Shandon. Both bands are still in existence and continue to offer much to the city's musical life.

52 See Maguire, *The Industrial Movement in Ireland*, p.445; W.K. Sullivan, J. Brenan, and R. Day, *Cork Industrial Exhibition 1883, Report of Executive Committee, Awards of Jurors and Statement of Accounts* (Cork: Purcell & Co., 1886), p.280.

53 They were won by the Barrack Street Band and Oxfordshire Light Infantry respectively. For a full report on the day and the music of the 1883 Exhibition, please see Sullivan et al, *Report of the 1883 Exhibition*, pp.280–3.

54 The term quadrille came to exist in the seventeenth century, within military parades, in which four horsemen and their mounts performed special square-shaped formations or figures.

55 See Sullivan et al, *Report of the 1883 Exhibition*, p.283.

56 See Cunningham and Fleischmann, *Aloys Fleischmann*, p.5.

57 A copy of this programme is in the collection of the Cork Public Museum.

58 *Cork Examiner*, 22 May 1902.

59 *Irish Times*, 16 July 1902.

60 The Barrack Street Band caused uproar in Anglo-Irish political circles after first refusing to take part in a piece of music entitled the 'British Army Quadrille' and then they

10

The Legacy of the 1902 and 1903 Cork Exhibitions

Tom Spalding

Some Unexpected Developments

In relation to the legacy of Ireland's Victorian exhibitions, the generally held view, as expressed by Dr John Turpin, is that they 'failed in their primary aim of reviving Irish industry. ... [But in] the field of art and culture they were considerably more successful.'[1] It is also claimed, with justification, that another side-effect of these nineteenth- and early-twentieth-century events was that they provided a new way for people to consume goods and provided retailers with a new and exciting forum for their promotion. Do these assertions apply to the Cork Exposition?

Returning to the analyses of Turpin and others, it is safe to say that in national terms, our cultural landscape would have developed in a very different way (or at least, it would have been severely retarded) without the holding of national exhibitions.[2] Many of our significant national cultural institutions owe their existence to the exhibition movement. This is true across the fields of music, the arts and sciences. For example, the National Concert Hall is situated in a building on Earlsfort Terrace which began life at the heart of the 1865 Dublin Expo.[3] This building in turn became the Royal University of Ireland. In a modified form, it maintained a link to technical education as a home for part of University College Dublin (UCD) until 2007. Although the glass-and-iron main exhibition hall of 1865 was removed long ago, the entrance gates and pillars still stand.[4] The National Gallery of Ireland was founded in 1854 as 'a direct result of the 1853 exhibition'[5] and 'as a memorial to [William] Dargan', the great railway entrepreneur who was the leading light behind this exhibition, and whose likeness still stands on the lawn outside

the gallery.[6] The National Portrait Gallery can likewise trace its roots to these exhibitions. The founding of the Natural History Museum and the National Museum of Science and Art also has exhibition links. These museums were an outcome of the passing of the Dublin Science and Art Act (1877), which encouraged the 'exhibiting [of] antiquities, ornamental art and natural history', and was itself a result of the 1872 Dublin Exposition,[7] as mentioned earlier. On a less academic note, Dublin's Iveagh Gardens maintain a living link with the Victorian exhibition tradition. Although their use as 'pleasure grounds' pre-dated the exhibitions, their retention today for social use can in part be put down to their popularity as an element of several of Dublin's nineteenth-century expositions, and later of UCD. In Cork, the effects of the 1902 and 1903 Exhibitions may not be so obvious, but were nonetheless significant and long-lasting. Firstly though, we must examine the industrial legacy.

Industrial Development and the Cork IDA

It was perhaps too much to think that a single event would lead to the revival of Cork's economy, let alone Ireland's, although it seems that the organizers were hoping it might. The Exhibition was seen by many at the time as a step in the path to recovery, and by some as evidence of the rosy future ahead after the eventual dawning of Home Rule. It is very difficult from this distance of time to prove cause and effect, and we should be cautious of ascribing too much of what happened later in Cork's history to the Exhibitions. With that in mind however, some conclusions seem clear.

10.1
The Original Irish Trademark from a Table.
The Munster Arcade's workshop provided office furniture for the British and US Navies during WWI, and made tables, glass display cases for the Crawford Art Gallery and other furniture using the Irish Trade Mark. By 1919 there were over 380 companies registered for this trademark, and at least 680 by the 1920s. (© Tom Spalding, Courtesy Cork City Libraries, Local Studies)

In the decade after the Cork Exhibition there was indeed a large increase in industrial activity in the country as a whole, and in the imports and exports moving through Irish ports. Irish export trade in general increased in financial terms by 55 per cent between 1904 and 1914, and the value of exported manufactured goods increased by nearly 100 per cent.[8] These are national figures which include Dublin, Belfast and the north-east. Unfortunately, Cork's export trade only contributed about 7 per cent to the national total, and had remained static for half of this decade (between 1908 and 1913) at a time when Ireland's export business boomed. In addition, and against the national trend, Cork's port remained a net importer. However, the official figures for Cork may have understated the situation. It was noted by D.J. Coakley in 1919 (unfortunately for our purposes, without supporting evidence) that 'the Trade through the Port of Cork forms only a part of the City's … Trade. A very large additional trade is carried through the ports of Waterford and Dublin.' Given the lack of clarity about the city's industrial production, it is hard to determine whether the Exhibition had a positive influence on Cork's industrial development in the medium term, but it seems possible. However, it would be foolhardy in the extreme to ascribe Ireland's Edwardian 'boom' to Cork's Exhibitions.

We are on firmer ground when we consider the existence of the Cork Industrial Development Association (CIDA). Inspired by the 1902 Exhibition, this group was founded in early 1903 by a group of Cork's leading businessmen, and as mentioned in Chapter 7, it played a significant role in that year's show, arranging an exhibit of fifty Irish manufacturing firms under their aegis. From 1904, they led a campaign against imported goods which they claimed were masquerading as being made in Ireland. According to the CIDA, this effort to deceive Irish consumers was evidence of the success of their 'buy Irish' campaign, and they called on the Department of Agriculture and Technical Instruction to apply the rigours of Merchandise Marks Act to stop foreign (and Irish) firms marking their goods with Irish names and branding when the goods contained were imported.[9]

The Cork Association held a number of annual exhibitions from 1904 on,[10] and hosted two early national industrial conferences, in 1905 and 1910. Also in 1905, they spawned a National Industrial Development Association (NIDA) which continued in existence until at least the mid-1950s. The CIDA provided information to those wishing to 'buy Irish' and, in 1910, published a directory of Irish manufacturers which ran to 200 pages.[11] Aside from all this good work, they would also write to companies they identified as not supporting Irish goods, cajoling them to source alternatives in Ireland instead. This tactic may not have endeared them to everyone.[12] The organization was severely under-funded in its early years: its Secretary E.J. Riordan reported in 1911 that its total subscriptions since 1903 'would not exceed the sum received by our local Opera House Company during two good weeks of their season'. Despite debts of £300 in 1911, the CIDA survived the crisis and prospered. From 1904, and through the First World War, the CIDA held annual 'Irish Weeks', where stores were encouraged to create 'all-window displays of all-Irish goods'. It seems these weeks coincided with St Patrick's Day each year.[13] However, the idea of prioritizing local goods was not new. One of the Gaelic League's first contributions to the field of industrial development in 1902 was that members buy Irish and persuade others to do so too.[14] Considerably earlier, in the summer of 1720 Dean Jonathon Swift felt moved to respond to a pamphlet which suggested that Irish buyers in his day should 'prohibit every Thing in *Ireland* that is WEARABLE, that comes from *England*'.[15] Somewhat later (1810) Cork Corporation passed a resolution that they 'wear garments of Irish manufacture' and recommended that the citizenry do as well.[16]

At a national level, the NIDA devised an Irish Trade Mark, '*Déanta i nÉirinn*' [sic] to be used on these goods,[17] a forerunner of today's 'Guaranteed Irish' scheme (10.1). The first firm to be certified to use it was Hicks, Bullick and Co. of Belfast, who (coincidentally) had exhibited their cotton threads at the Cork Exhibition, and apparently had no problem supporting the association's agenda.[18] This scheme is believed to be the first such in the world, and it became the first trade mark to receive legal protection in Ireland with the advent of the Irish Free State.[19]

After the First World War, the tone of the CIDA's publications became more explicitly anti-English (previously the euphemism 'cross-channel' was used to describe products which patriots should avoid). The group continued to hold exhibitions, such as the '*Tír na n-Óg*' Irish Industries Fair held in Cork during Easter 1919. The group's Women's Committee took a leading role in the running of this event, but unlike their predecessors from 1902, there were no peers of the realm on this committee. An example of the shift in the attitude of the organization is that prior to February 1918, Liam de Roiste, a Sinn Féin activist and MP, became the Co-Secretary of the CIDA. However, he shared this post with Michael A. Ryan, a constitutional nationalist whose business, the 'Blackthorn House' on St Patrick's St, supplied insignia to the British military.[20] Nonetheless, their Annual Report for 1918 had been strongly critical of the 'English' [*sic*] government's industrial policy towards the south of Ireland during the war, pointing out that the only new industries to come to the area were Furness, Withy & Co., who took over the dry docks in Cobh and Passage West and (Ford's) 'tractor making on the banks of the Lee'. Furthermore, it was claimed that the only pre-war industry which had benefited was margarine production. The Annual Report did note however that agriculture had 'prospered exceedingly in the past four years' adding that 'the prosperity of our agricultural community permeated all other classes in the nation'. The CIDA, with a little help from British PM David Lloyd George, could take a lot of the credit for attracting Ford's to Cork, and this factory continued to operate until 1984. One could even say that while it lasted it was a part of the legacy of the 1902 Exhibition. The present Industrial Development Agency (IDA Ireland) has separate roots to the National IDA mentioned above, but our present County Enterprise Boards and Enterprise Ireland owe a lot to this forerunner.

Aside from the CIDA industrial shows, the events of 1902/3 had been followed by smaller exhibitions in Limerick and Dungarvan in the summer of 1904.[21] In the case of Cork, her tradition of expositions continued into the Free State period in the form of the 1932 Irish Industrial and Agricultural Fair. In its overall format (Industrial Hall, Machinery Hall, etc.) this event was based on the 1902 festival, but was very much more modest, almost domestic in scale. It took place beside the Carrigrohane Road to the west of the city and its story is beyond the scope of this book, but it illustrates the enduring affection the city has with industrial exhibitions, regardless of whether the city was part of the Union or Free State.

The Park, Public Museum and Surviving Exhibition Buildings

The 1902 Exhibition has left a lasting physical legacy on its site. Prior to 1900, the lands on either side of the Mardyke Walk were primarily open space, with gardens, water-meadows and a cricket club. In the years since, the south side of the Walk has been completely developed, and the elms which had lent so much to its ambience had to be removed when they became diseased in the 1980s. Fortunately, the north side of the Mardyke is still predominantly open space. It is as if, after the Expo, Cork people, who had always been aware of the place as a promenade, wanted now to preserve and protect it as a public space in perpetuity. Prior to the Expo, piecemeal development of the north side of the Mardyke had begun,[22] but this halted almost completely after 1902. The western fields eventually became the property of University College Cork (UCC). The cricket and tennis clubs to the east remain, and the central part of the exhibition site became a public park, appropriately named after Lord Mayor Fitzgerald.

Immediately after the Exhibition, a private company, the Fitzgerald Park Association, acting on the public's behalf, took control of the grounds and the remaining smaller buildings (Lord Mayor's Pavilion, main bandstand, Normandy Cottage and one or more of the little kiosks). As mentioned in Chapter 5, the lands and Shrubbery House had been purchased by the Corporation in 1902, and the park was opened to the citizens in 1904, at first only on Sundays, and under private management.[23] This arrangement was intended to be temporary, and it entered public hands in 1907.[24] A fine set of railings were set up along the boundary the following year,[25] and the park settled into a peaceful retirement after the excitement of the Exhibitions.

The other major public facility in the area today, is of course, the Cork Public Museum (10.2). Given the absence of a municipal museum until this point, and the strong educational element of the Exhibitions, it was entirely natural for the Corporation to consider the establishment of such an

10.2
Cork Public Museum, 2012. The Museum and surrounding Fitzgerald Park are the most obvious part of the legacy of the 1902/03 exhibitions. The museum has had a chequered career opening three times; in c.1909 & 1945 before becoming permanently established in 1963. The old 'Shrubbery House' is to the right, the modern extension opposite. It is owned and operated by Cork City Council. The park was established in 1904.
(© Tom Spalding)

enterprise. In line with this, plans for a museum in Shrubbery House were being discussed by the Corporation from as early as January, 1904.[26] The Minutes of the Corporation's Park Committee reveal that, over the years, they sought advice on running and equipping the museum from Marcus Hartog, who had been involved in assembling the exhibition of archaeological objects for the Art Gallery in 1902. He was also the Professor of Natural History in UCC for many years and was one of the College's greatest scientists.[27] The Corporation also approached the National Museum in Dublin, as well as the Victoria and Albert Museum in London. The latter was requested to help in making reproductions of 'ancient Celtic works of Art … such as the Cross of Cong, the Ardagh Chalice'[28], illustrating a clear aim on behalf of the City Corporation to promote Irish national culture. In 1908, the Department of Agriculture and Technical Instruction set aside £1,250, provided by the Board of Education in London, for the purchase of items for the museum. It is unclear whether either of these initiatives came to anything.

The items from New Zealand which constituted their exhibit in 1902 had remained on site for over six years in the Lord Mayor's Pavilion, as had some of the glass exhibition cases, and it was intended to put these on permanent display. The museum did not open immediately, however; its gestation was more convoluted than that of the park. It first opened in 1909 or 1910 and was curated by Mr John Paul Dalton, who had been agitating for its foundation since at least 1907, and (like Hartog) had been involved in the Exhibition's archaeology exhibit.[29] It remained open after his early death in 1912, but appears to have fallen out of use during the troubled decade which followed. After the burning of the Civic Offices in 1920, the museum building was requisitioned as a temporary home for the Corporation and during 'the Emergency' (Second World War) it acted as a home for Cork's Air Raid Precaution unit. A permanent exhibit on the site was not established until the end of the war in April 1945, by Professor M.J. O'Kelly of UCC.[30] Incidentally, many of the early private sponsors of the museum were Cork companies involved in the 1902 Exhibition. The building eventually returned to the control of the Corporation in 1963. When the museum was extended in 2005, Dalton's contribution was remembered and one of the new galleries was named in his honour.

The establishment of the park and museum in Cork have to be seen in the light of two related late-Victorian phenomena: so-called 'municipal socialism' and the general desire to create a permanent legacy for exhibitions. Municipal socialism was the provision of public services in the form of 'People's Parks', social housing, public swimming baths and libraries by local authorities.[31] It could also include the establishment of utilities: gas, electricity and water. In some cases, pre-existing, privately owned utilities were absorbed by the local authority. Cork Corporation has operated a good public water supply since the 1850s, but it never became involved in gas-making (as in Limerick), electricity (like Dublin), the running of public transport (as happened in Belfast) or telecommunications (like Hull in East Yorkshire). Whilst these services had been available for a number of years, at least in the larger cities, they were privately owned, and not previously considered as part of a local authority's remit. However, towards the middle of Queen Victoria's reign, public space and services began to be run on a municipal basis. This phenomenon occurred across the then-United Kingdom, but Cork was a late adopter of the movement, partly due to its relative poverty. A public park was first suggested c.1813, but it wasn't until 1836 that a site was chosen to the east of the city, south of the Marina.[32] It finally opened as a park c.1846, but it had been run as a privately-owned racecourse since the 1860s. As explained in Chapter 8, it was also used for military manoeuvres and parades and for team games from the 1870s. In addition, it was set on reclaimed slob-land and does not appear from the map evidence to have ever been landscaped or to have included any of the features of a public park (benches, bandstand, paths, etc.). Aside from this, rather bleak, space and the streets, there were no open public areas in the city for the recreation of working people before 1902. Another example of Cork Corporation's expanding role at the turn of the century is the establishment of the city's first public library in 1892. In time, a purpose-built library premises on Anglesea Street opened in 1905, primarily due to the munificence of Andrew Carnegie.[33] In 1901, public swimming baths (now demolished) on Eglinton Street had been opened.

The second phenomenon is the strong link, world-wide, between exhibition sites, public parks, gardens and museums. Once again, the Crystal Palace set an example which has been followed since. It was erected in Hyde Park and when it was removed and re-erected (with modifications) in south London in 1852, it became the centrepiece of a large public park at Beckenham. Although the Palace burnt to the ground in 1936, thankfully the park remains. The pre-eminent example of the link between International Exhibitions and museums is the complex of British national establishments in South Kensington, London. After 1851 the area was developed as a hub of education including the Natural History Museum, the Victoria and Albert Museum, the Royal Colleges of Art and Music, and of course, the Albert Hall and Imperial College. In north London, another later exhibition building, the Alexandra Palace, sits today in 196 landscaped acres. The various Paris exhibitions were all held on the Champs de Mars, and the south Chicago lakeshore still shows traces of the 1893 Exhibition in what is now Jackson Park, which also contains a Museum of Science and Industry housed in the only remaining exhibition building. As explained in Chapter 6, the 1901 Glasgow show was held in a public park in the city's West End,[34] and included the Kelvingrove Art Gallery, itself a permanent legacy of Glasgow's 1888 Expo. This phenomenon was not unique to English-speaking countries. The key building of the 1929 Expo in Barcelona now houses the Museu Nacional d'Art de Catalunya, and as in the case of the other exhibitions, the expo site on Mt Juic, remains a public park.[35] Returning to Ireland, the existence of Herbert Park in Dublin 4 is primarily due to its being the site of the 1907 Exhibition.

Whilst the Fr Mathew Memorial Fountain and the President and Lord Mayor's Pavilion are the only remaining elements of Cork's Exhibition *in situ* today,[36] some of the other Exposition buildings continued in use on the site for a number of years after 1903. The Normandy Cottage was transported, it is said in one piece, and was relocated immediately to the east of the main park gates in early 1904. With an eye to his legacy, Edward Fitzgerald said that 'it would be an interesting feature in time to come to remind people of the exhibition'. [37] When this building was eventually destroyed (probably in the early 1920s) its replacement was also given the name 'Normandy Cottage'. It is still so-called, although it bears no resemblance to the original. The Chalet Restaurant was purchased by Cork County and Cork Constitution Rugby Clubs in 1904, disassembled and re-erected about 100yds (91m) downstream of Wellington/Thomas Davis Bridge (10.3).[38] It served as a sports pavilion for the clubs for many years, disappearing in the late 1920s. It was replaced by the present brick pavilion, which was extended in 2012.[39] The main exhibition bandstand stood for at least a decade after the Exhibition. The smaller Western bandstand was moved to the grounds of the Cork County Cricket Club. These structures and some small kiosks can be identified *in situ* in several Lawrence Collection photographs of the area datable to *c.*1912.

Sporting, Entertainment, Technical and Social Influences

The extensive programme of sports events during 1902 and 1903 previously discussed, the trophy presented by the Leander Rowing Club to the city and the re-using of the old Chalet Restaurant were not the Exhibition's only contribution to sport in the city. It seems that the Lee Boat Club used recycled material from the Expo to build a new club-house on the Marina after the event closed.[40] The Sunday's Well Tennis and Rowing Club, whose grounds had been included within the exhibition site, built a new headquarters in 1907 on the site of a temporary one provided by the Exhibition Committee. It shares some features with the Industrial Hall, which has led some to consider it a leftover from the show, but this is not the case.[41] However the greatest effect of the Exhibition on sport in the city was the acquisition and development, from 1911 onwards, of the western half of the site as sports grounds for UCC. Whilst the Cork County Cricket Club had been based in the centre of the Mardyke since 1874, the potential for this part of the city to be used for watching and playing sports had been strongly demonstrated during the Expo, and the area has primarily been reserved for this use ever since.

The Cork Exhibitions were the largest and most successful exhibitions held in Ireland to this point. They were also the most successful in terms of visitor

10.3
The Chalet Rest in its New Location.
This Poole photograph, taken from the parapet of Wellington Bridge, shows the Chalet Restaurant in its new guise as a sports pavilion for Cork rugby. The photo was probably taken during the course of re-erection in 1904. It stood here until the late-1920s. (© NLI, with thanks to Local Studies, Cork City Libraries)

numbers: the attendance in 1902 of 1.5 million easily exceeded the next most successful by this time.[42] In international terms they were not hugely innovative (apart from the involvement of the DATI) or influential. Having said that, what the Exhibition Committee had excelled at was the organization of the events which made up the social element. In an editorial written prior to the opening of the Exhibition *The Times* sensed that this was going to be a key attribute of the show. They commented on the 'southern temperament' of Corkonians and presciently noted that 'the genius of Cork is well disposed towards great public displays. The sprightly habit and intellectual aplomb of the Munster man will endow the coming exhibition with a brightness and artistic finish which might not be found in Dublin, and certainly would not be found in Belfast.'[43] It may be stretching an analogy, but at night the site must have felt to its patrons a little like a 'boutique festival' to us today. With coloured lights dancing in the trees, live music from the bandstands and the concert hall drifting through the evening air, plenty of places to eat and drink to suit every pocket, as well as the side-shows and souvenir stalls, there would have been a notably festive atmosphere. It was this mood that captured the imagination of many of the visiting journalists and commentators, many of whom were jaded veterans of Paris and Glasgow. In the years immediately after 1903, the site was used extensively for bazaars and band concerts. Today this spirit continues in the summer festivals held in the park. In recent years the 'Mad Pride' day promoting mental health, 'A Taste of Cork' food festival and a Street Performance World Championships have been held there. A new bandstand was built in the park as part of its redevelopment in 2013/14, and it is fitting that it stands on the site of the 1902 Concert Hall. The original organ, the prize element of the Concert Hall, was also intended to be part of the event's legacy. It cost £2,500 (more than many of the individual buildings)[44] and was gifted to the City Council by the Exhibition Committee. It stood in the old City Hall on Albert Quay until 1920, when it was burnt by British forces, along with the rest of the building.

The 1926 Ordnance Survey map shows a building marked as a 'Hall' on the current site of the Corporation yard, adjacent to the Mardyke. This was a large building, and would have been more than capable of hosting the small shows and exhibitions mentioned in contemporary sources.[45] These included charity bazaars and a roller-skating rink.[46] In addition, it seems that circuses (perhaps including Duffy's) were occasionally allowed to use a part of the site.[47] These events did not always go as planned. In 1909, a Mr Arnold of Lancashire offered to run a summer season of entertainments suitable for ladies and gentlemen. Within days of opening, he ran afoul of the Corporation who had heard reports of damage to park property, 'late hours and disorderly conduct'. Arnold and his troupe were ejected.[48] Despite these incidents, public events continued to be held in Fitzgerald's Park right through the First World War and beyond; examples include the 1918 'Stella Maris' Bazaar in aid of sailors' widows and orphans[49] and the '*Caed Mile Failthe* [*sic*]' Bazaar in Aid of the Poor in 1919, where the first Cork-built 'Fordson' tractor was demonstrated. As well as this contribution from Cork's newest industry, this event reprised elements of the 1902 festivities including the aerial railway and 'four band promenades each day'.[50]

As we hope we have shown, the applications and potential of electricity took a central place in the 1902 Exhibition. It was used to provide power, illuminate buildings inside and out and to display goods. Switzer's department store went to the trouble of creating a 'passage behind the stand which enables visitors to inspect some very beautiful gowns by the artificial light in which they are destined to be worn' (7.5).[51] (Light from electrical sources was felt to be less flattering than that from traditional means, and buyers wanted to preview their purchases, and be sure their clothing would look good whatever the light source.) Electricity ran the rides and powered the great organ in the Concert Hall. Given all of this, one would expect there to be a significant uptake of new connections to the local electricity grid after the Exhibition. Judging by the available evidence, this seems not to have taken place, aside from the increase in electric street lighting mentioned in an earlier chapter. In fact, in the year after the first exhibition season, the number of new customer connections was lower than it had been in 1902, which in turn had been less than in the previous year. However, in 1904, business picked up and there were 114 new subscribers, nearly twice the number as compared to 1903. This was maintained in 1905, but the rate fell back to about seventy-five connections per annum for the next five years.[52] If the exhibitions had an effect on promoting electric power, the influence was deferred and limited in scale. The conservatism of the market, plus the expense of the new power source, may have initially put off new customers.[53]

There was also a 'human' legacy of the exhibition. We have seen how the 20-year-old Harutun Batmazian was attracted from his hometown of Urfa, on

10.4
M.A. Ryan and staff, outside his temporary premises, c.1921.
The political consensus characteristic of the 1902 exhibition was long gone by the time this photo was taken. Ryan's business on St Patrick's St was burnt by elements of the security forces on 29 November 1920. The 'traditional' costumes and Celtic brooches of the shop-girls suggest where their allegiances lie.
(© CCCAI/ Ryan family)

the modern-day Turkish/Iraqi border, to move to Cork. He and his Turkish wife settled in 1902 and set down roots, trading as Hadji Bey et Compagnie. They raised a family and remained in the city. Another migrant was Michael A. Ryan, previously mentioned in connection with the CIDA. Born in Dover Castle of an Army family, Ryan was one of the staff in Johnson's Umbrellas (10.4, 7.13). After the Exhibition, the firm set up a Cork store and he decided to remain. He enticed a Protestant girl (Elizabeth Nixon) from the Belfast branch, they married and their descendants remain prominent in business in Cork today.[54] William Herlihy, Assistant Secretary of the 1903 expo, met his wife, Bridget Harrington, during the second season of the show, and they married in 1904. One of his grandsons is Bill O'Herlihy, the RTÉ journalist. These are surely only three of many, many cases of human relationships being formed during those two remarkable summers.

Architectural Influence

The 1902/3 Exhibitions left their mark on the architecture of the city in three different ways, and this has been poorly appreciated until now. These were: (a) in the physical remains at the original site, (b) in a number of 'second-generation' and even 'third-generation' buildings around the city and county, and lastly (c) in promoting the English Vernacular 'half-timbered' style.

Mention has already been made of a number of structures which remained on site, in some cases for a few decades and in two cases until the present day. The issue of the 'second-generation' buildings is harder to establish in detail, but quite as concrete. Whilst claims have been made that this or that building 'came' from the Exhibition, it is often hard to prove this is the case. The situation is complicated by the fact that there are no reliable images of some of the larger buildings, such as the Art Gallery or Temperance Restaurant. Had these been relocated in whole or in part, it would be hard now to confirm or deny whether any current buildings were really related to the original structures as we have nothing to compare them with. Some buildings, such as Gordon's Hotel and the Portable House had disappeared by early 1903 and were not even present for the second season.

There were at least ten auctions in 1903 and 1904 relating to the former expo buildings and their contents. The auctions were held by Joseph Woodward

& Sons (who are still trading today). The goods offered were elements of the buildings, especially sheets of glass and corrugated iron and lengths of timber. Entire kiosks were also offered for sale as being suitable for re-use as summerhouses, as well as all of the sanitary fittings, pipes, etc. In addition, it seems that the committee made gifts of small amounts of material to 'good causes' such as monasteries.[55] It is clear that material from the Exposition was extensively reused, which has led to confused claims about the provenance of some later buildings. Some smaller exhibition buildings appear to have been moved in their entirety. It appears the DATI's Poultry Section from their model farm was auctioned for £100 and moved to the Cork suburb of Blackrock, where it served as the parochial hall (known as the 'Green Hall') of St Michael's Church of Ireland for over a century.[56] It is also likely that a small dwelling facing the old railway station in Blarney contains elements of Expo buildings, or at least was built shortly afterwards in the style of the *Tír na nÓg* tearooms.

It has been written that the Atlantic Golf Links Hotel, built in 1903/4 at Harbour View, near Kilbrittain, was the former Chalet Restaurant.[57] However, as we have seen above, this is not the case. Despite some similarity between this hotel and some exhibition buildings, the Chalet was not relocated there. It seems the new hotel was assembled like a giant 'Lego' set from components (window casements, sheets of corrugated iron, etc.), some of which were used at the Expo. Furthermore, it is likely these components were mixed with non-expo elements to create the new buildings. Since there was $c.80,000\text{ft}^2$ of corrugated iron on the roof of the Industrial Hall alone, and perhaps $150,000\text{ft}^2$ $(14,000\text{m}^2)$ in the Exhibition altogether, it is not too facetious to say that half the barns in Co. Cork probably have (or had) components from the Exhibition on them![58]

The Atlantic Golf Links Hotel closed in 1922, but a second, smaller building, the Horse Rock Hotel, which apparently also contained elements of the exhibition buildings, remained in use nearby until 1973 (10.5).[59] There was a further link between the hotels and the Exhibition, as they had been built on land belonging to Dominic J. Daly, whose relative M.D. Daly had operated the Chalet at the event.[60] He purchased the larger hotel building after it closed and moved elements of it, possibly by sea, to Currabinny, Co. Cork (10.6). It was presented as a wedding gift to his son and served as a holiday home for the family for many years.[61] It has an unusual 'Y'-shaped floor-plan,

From top;

10.5 **Horse Rock Hotel, Killbrittain,** *c.*1970.
The Horse Rock Hotel stood for over fifty years near Killbrittain, Co. Cork. It shared several details with the Chalet Restaurant and other exhibition buildings, but was not built from components of the Chalet. It burned down in 1973. (Courtesy Adie & Paddy McKeown)

10.6 **Daly House, Currabinny, 1922.**
The details of the veranda, windows and half-timbering are very similar to known exhibition buildings, but nothing exactly like this stood on the expo site in 1902. It appears that expo building materials were recycled widely. (© Tom Spalding, Courtesy Dominic Daly & Arnaud Disant)

which had been pioneered by Arts and Crafts architects like C.F.A. Voysey at the close of the nineteenth century. The present interior includes elements such as the Art Nouveau electric light fittings which could conceivably have originated in an exhibition building (10.7).[62] This 'third-generation' building also contains elements which certainly had not come from the Exhibition, such as an unusual bathtub with three taps: one for hot, a cold one and one for seawater, which had come from the Atlantic Golf Links Hotel.

The Half Timbered Revival in Cork

A brief examination of images of the various buildings mentioned above will quickly reveal one of their defining characteristics – the presence of exposed timber framing (or half-timbering) on their external walls. This was a feature of a number of the smaller exhibition buildings, as well as the Chalet Restaurant and the Normandy Cottage, and was to become an unexpected legacy to housing in Cork. It is our thesis that the Expo promoted and popularized the style, as well as the suburban ideal of detached buildings in sylvan settings, which heretofore had only been within the means of the very wealthy. The fact that large suburban properties with exactly these attributes stood facing the exhibition grounds from Sunday's Well only served to underline the point. The Exhibition in Dublin in 1907 made the promotion of this model more explicit. Here, visitors could view a number of 'ideal suburban homes' which were built and exhibited on or near the exhibition site.[63]

Wooden-framed 'cage-work' buildings were common in the medieval city, so in a sense, we can rightly call the new 'half-timbered' houses a 'revival'. For example, the well-known engraving of the Exchange published by Charles Smith in 1750 shows a terrace of houses on the North Main Street with projecting timber bays. However, unlike many English or French towns and cities, there were no genuine timber-frame buildings of any size left in Cork by the turn of the twentieth century and the last 'cage-work' house in Dublin had been demolished in 1812.[64] What we see today in Cork was not the revival of any native Irish style, but buildings inspired by a fashion with its roots in Southern England. That the desire to own a home in the English style became an aspiration of citizens of the newly independent Irish Free State is remarkable and contrasts strongly with the anti-English rhetoric of the new political parties. However, a full analysis of this is beyond the scope of this book. We may speculate that, as genuine timber-frame homes

10.7
Electric light & interior detail, Daly House, Currabinny.
On grounds of style this electric light fitting and panelling are certainly of the correct period to have come from the Cork Exhibition. The ceiling and cornicing are tin-plated steel.
(© Tom Spalding, Courtesy Dominic Daly & Arnaud Disant)

were effectively absent from Ireland by this time, the imported half-timbered designs represented to some Irish people a generic 'olde worlde' home at a time when there was uncertainty about the future and a general nostalgia for an idealized rural life free from the cares of the modern world. Perhaps the new homeowners weren't conscious of, or concerned about, the roots of this style. These buildings were designed in a 'New-Old-Fashioned Way' and the clients and residents may merely have seen the style as novel, or *à la mode*, rather than specifically English.

We have seen in a previous chapter how the Portable House and Lord Mayor's Pavilion incorporated strong elements of the English Vernacular. Indeed, the designer of the latter, Arthur Hill, was an early advocate of the style in the city. Around 1900, Hill chose to build his home, 'Redgarth', on the Douglas Road in this fashion, complete with projecting gables and multi-paned windows. The mode had also been actively promoted at previous expos, such as at Chicago (6.21) and Paris (where Edwin Lutyens had built a replica Jacobean stone manor house as Britain's pavilion, 'amongst all that art nouveau').[65] Glasgow in 1901 had also included two model homes built in the revival style to represent the best of modern housing. Given all of this, it is not hard to see the propaganda in the quasi-English buildings shown at Cork.

Needless to say, the full situation is not as simple as suggested above. There were a variety of other architectural styles on display at the Exhibition of 1902 and early twentieth-century buildings in Cork are by no means all in this style. It is also important to note that the 'half-timbered' style was popular across the English-speaking world. Frank Lloyd Wright even dabbled with it in Oak Park, Chicago, in the late 1890s. It would have arrived on these shores regardless of our exhibition. Furthermore, the exhibition buildings were not the first in Cork in this style. Perhaps not coincidentally, a large stable building for Beamish & Crawford with Vernacular influences was completed only one month before the Exposition opened in a prominent location beside St Finn Barre's Cathedral (6.13).[66] On the other hand, it must be admitted that the exposure of nearly two million visitors (mostly Irish) to buildings in the style over the two seasons, would not have hindered its promotion nationally and locally either, nor would the glowing reviews of them in the press.

Initially, the style became particularly popular with the upper middle class, and this was also the case in Britain.[67] By the middle of 1903, two large English Vernacular revival houses, 'Leeholme' and 'Crossleigh', were completed on the

new Donovan's Road, within sight of the exhibition grounds.[68] The following year, 'Gillabbey House' was built on Connaught Avenue. This building has strong links to the Exhibition. The builder was Sir Edward Fitzgerald, the railings and gates were by Benjamin Watson (who supplied the main gates of the Expo) and the client was Alderman William Phair, Vice-President of the Cork Branch of the Gaelic League and a key member of the Executive and Building's Committees. Other good early examples include the housing on Perrott's Avenue, near UCC, and 'Ellerslie' on the Well Rd, near Douglas. Later examples include the Endsleigh Estate (Douglas Road, 10.8) and Menloe Gardens, (Ballintemple). It is notable how the style followed the electric tramlines to Douglas, Blackrock and along the Western Rd, which had helped facilitate the 'flight' of the middle classes from the city centre. It is also notable how many of the new developments had English-sounding names to accompany the architecture. The new style was not confined to domestic architecture; the Counting House for Beamish & Crawford was built on the South Main Street in 1919 (10.9) and the Winthrop Arcade was opened on Oliver Plunkett Street in 1926.

As time passed, the style filtered down to more modest homes such as those built in Sidney Park, off Wellington Road (mid-1930s) and Donovan Rossa Avenue. These were very similar to the standard 'Tudor-bethan' semi-detached houses of the same period which can be found across the UK. The

10.8
Housing, Endsleigh Park, Douglas Road.
Homes in this style became popular with middle-class Corkonians during the Free State period, especially in the growing suburbs of Douglas and Ballintemple and near UCC. Their popularity can partly be traced back to the Expo. Compare with (7.14). (© Tom Spalding)

10.9
The Counting House,
South Main Street.
The Counting House
was built for Beamish &
Crawford to designs of
the Irish/ Scottish duo
Chillingworth & Levie in
1919. It is the largest and
most prominent English
Vernacular revival building
in Cork. The company also
designed the Winthrop
Arcade and many other
buildings in the city.
Coincidentally, it shares its
twin-gables over loggia
design with the Chalet
Restaurant.
(© Tom Spalding)

popularity of the style diminished over time, but it continued unbroken throughout the life of the Free State and beyond. For example, it was adopted in the development of Montford Park, built beside the exhibition site on the Mardyke a half-century after the event. Of all the pseudo-historical styles available to house-builders (Neo-Georgian, Irish Vernacular, Gothic, etc.) English Vernacular could be said to be the most popular during the twentieth century. Middle-class housing in this vein continues to be built to the present day across the suburbs of Cork and other Irish cities too.

Other Influences from the Exhibition

Whilst it seems that the 1902 Exhibition did not achieve its primary aim of a significant revival in Ireland's industrial fortunes, it did have other positive, if less measurable, influences beyond the city. The prominent role played by the Department of Agriculture and Technical Instruction highlighted the potential of vocational, technical and agricultural education to develop skills throughout Ireland, as well as presenting approaches to solving some of her woes. Horace Plunkett certainly regarded the demonstrations at Cork as crucial in the early days of his Department.[69] Aside from the present-day Department of Agriculture, the work of the DATI eventually led to the establishment of the Vocational Education Committees, influenced the disparate technical schools which were to become the Institutes of Technology in Dublin, Cork

The Cork International Exhibition

and elsewhere, and provided the historical basis for the setting up of the training bodies Solas (Fás/AnCO), Teagasc, and so on.

A more immediate result was the Cork Expo's influence on Ireland's next great exhibition, that which was held in Dublin in 1907. The planning for this exhibition began during the Cork show's second season, but it was a more ambitious undertaking. This, combined with significant opposition from nationalist elements and the Gaelic League,[70] and arguments about balancing the promotion of national industries versus importing ideas and products from abroad delayed the project for a number of years. Earlier Dublin exhibitions had been held in Kildare Street, Earlsfort Terrace and near the Rotunda Hospital. Instead, this exhibition was to be held on the fringes of the city in Ballsbridge. Its setting was suburban and served by an electric tram line[71] and it was the first Dublin exhibition to abandon what we have called the 'one building' model. The range of entertainments offered comprised: a water chute, exotic bazaar, baby incubators, etc., and the layout included an Industrial Hall, an Art Gallery and a Canadian Pavilion. As we have shown, these were well-established features of foreign expositions by this point, but in terms of Ireland, were first introduced in Cork. In addition, as explored in Stephanie Rains's book *Commodity Culture and Social Class in Dublin*, some of these features had previously appeared in indoor bazaars in Dublin in the 1890s. However, given the recent success of Cork, it is hard to avoid the conclusion that the organizers in the capital were heavily influenced by the events in the southern city.

Conclusion

In 1902, Cork was a city of about 80,000 souls. This figure made the city somewhat smaller than, for example, Norwich in England, Strasbourg in France or New Haven in the US state of Connecticut and, to our knowledge, none of these cities ever attempted to hold an exhibition on this scale. In 1902 an expo was also held in Düsseldorf and great exhibitions were held in Turin in 1902 and 1911. However the population of each of these cities at the time was over 300,000. In comparison with the host cities of major exhibitions such as Paris and Glasgow, these places were still small. Although Dublin held a successful exhibition in 1907, it would not be until 1951 that Belfast attempted something like this. In that year they held a predominantly agricultural show, the Ulster Farm & Factory Exhibition, as part of the

Festival of Britain. It attracted about 157,000 visitors, a small percentage of the number which came to Cork in 1902. The only British town vaguely comparable to Cork which attempted to hold a significant exhibition at the time was Wolverhampton (population 145,000 in 1902), and this show was not a success. It is with this in mind that we must assess the scale, scope and success of our exhibition; it was a brave and confident thing to attempt for such a small city. No doubt her earlier experience in organizing exhibitions in the nineteenth century encouraged Corkonians that they could go one better in 1902. Whatever its shortcomings (and these were many and recognized by the more sentient commentators at the time) the holding of a large exhibition by a small community was a great achievement. [72]

In respect to the legacies of the Cork Exhibition, these fall into two main categories: the ephemeral and the concrete. The latter are various if generally unintended by the organizers and are predominantly related to sport, culture and leisure, and domestic architecture and sadly not on the whole to industrial development. Of the former, the most important are the memories of the millions of men, women, boys and girls who visited the events and which lived with them for the rest of their lives. For example, when William Levingston Cooke sat down in his late 60s to recall his early days in Cork, of all the things which could occur to him, his mind immediately fell upon a memory, as a three- or four-year-old, of 'being on the River on a lovely sunny afternoon, with my father rowing us. He used to take us out on the summer evenings too, to see the people coming down the water chute at the Exhibition.' He can't have been the only person to hold such cherished memories.

Notes

1   J. Turpin, 'Exhibitions of Art and Industry in Victorian Ireland: Part 2: Dublin Exhibitions of Art and Industries 1865–1885', *Dublin Historical Record*, 35, 2 (March 1982), p.51.

2   See also the work of Turpin, F.E. Dixon and Nellie O'Cléirigh, all in the Dublin Historical Record.

3   See Turpin, 'Exhibitions of Art and Industry, Part 2', p.49.

4   N. O'Cléirigh, 'Dublin International Exhibition, 1865', *Dublin Historical Record*, 47, 2 (Autumn 1994), p.170.

5   F.E. Dixon, 'Dublin Exhibitions: Part 1', *Dublin Historical Record*, 26, 3 (June 1973), p.95.

6   J. Turpin, 'Exhibitions of Arts and Industries in Victorian Ireland: Part 1,' *Dublin Historical Record*, 35, 1 (December 1981), p.9.

7   See Turpin, 'Exhibitions of Art and Industry, Part 2', p.47.

8   D.J. Coakley, *Cork: Its Trade and Commerce* (Cork: Guy & Co, 1919), pp.89–90.

9   *Cork Examiner*, 23 July 1904.

10 'Cork Industrial Development Association – Council Meeting', *Cork Examiner*, 23 July 1904.

11 Cork Industrial Development Association, *Eighth Annual Report* (Cork: Shandon Printing Works, 1911).

12 Cork City & County Archives Institute (hereafter CCCAI), Cork, ESB Holdings, U620, Box 39, Letters from CIDA to Cork Electric Tramway and Lighting Co, 28 August & 22 September 1905.

13 *Cork Examiner*, 8 April 1904.

14 'Irish Ireland!', *Ulster Herald*, 27 September 1902, p.15

15 J. Swift, A *defence of English commodities; Being an answer to the Proposal for the universal use of Irish manufactures* (Dublin: 1720), p.3.

16 J.J. O'Shea, *A Transcription and Extension of an Index to the Council Books of the Corporation of Cork from 31 October 1710 to 25 October 1841*, 3 (Cork, 1955?)

17 Cork Industrial Development Association, *Monthly Bulletin* (Cork: April 1919) and Cork Industrial Development Association, *Extracts of Annual Report for 1918* (Cork: 1919).

18 Cork Industrial Development Association, *Catalogue of 'Tír na n-Óg' Irish Industries Fair* (Cork: 1919), p.11.

19 Registered in 1927 by the Irish Industrial Development Association, http://www.patent soffice.ie/en/student_tradmarks.aspx, available 6 January 2014.

20 In conversation with Michael and Declan Ryan, grandsons of M.A. Ryan, 11, 19 September & 17 October 2013.

21 'Cork Industrial Development Association', *Cork Examiner*, 23 July 1904.

22 'Illen Villas', two pairs of semi-detached houses were built c.1898, probably to designs of William H. Hill.

23 *Cork Examiner*, 8 April 1904.

24 Cork City & County Archives Institute, Cork, Minutes of Fitzgerald Park Committee, 4 March 1907.

25 Cork City & County Archives Institute, Cork, Minutes of Fitzgerald Park Committee, 19 June 1908.

26 *Cork Examiner*, 9 January 1904 & 27 May 1904.

27 'Death of Professor Marcus Hartog', *The Times*, 28 January 1924.

28 Cork City & County Archives Institute, Cork, Minutes of Fitzgerald Park Committee, 25 January 1910.

29 Anon., *Obituary of J.P. Dalton*, Journal of the Cork Historical and Archaeological Society, 19, 98 (1913), p.103,.CCAI, Cork, Minutes of Fitzgerald Park Committee, 14 May 1907, reference to letter from J.P. Dalton, re: museum.

Cork Industrial Development Association, *Catalogue of 'Tír na n-Óg' Irish Industries Fair* (Cork: 1919)

F. Cullen, *Ireland on Show; Art, Union and Nationhood* (Farnham: Ashgate, 2012)

E. Cullinan, *Building a Business – 150 Years of the Sisk Group* (Dublin: Associated Editions Ltd, 2009)

J.P. Cunningham and R. Fleischmann, *Aloys Fleischmann (1880 – 1964) Immigrant Musician in Ireland* (Cork: Cork University Press, 2010)

D. Dwan *The Great Community – Culture and Nationalism in Ireland* (Dublin: Field Day, 2008)

T.J. Edelstein, (ed.) *Imagining an Irish Past – The Celtic Revival 1840-1940* (Chicago IL: Chicago University, 1993)

T. Farmar, *Privileged Lives – A social history of middle-class Ireland 1882-1989* (Dublin: A. & A. Farmar Ltd, 2010)

J.E. Findling and K.D. Pelle (eds), *Encyclopaedia of World's Fairs and Expositions* (Jefferson NC: McFarland & Company, 2008)

K. Finley, *The Biggest Show in Town* (Dublin: Nonsuch, 2007)

J. Fischer and G. Neville (eds.), *As Others Saw Us*, (Cork: The Collins Press, 2005)

P. Greenhalgh, *Fair World, A History of World's Fairs and Expositions from London to Shanghai 1851-2010* (Winterbourne: Papadakis, 2011)

B. Griffin, *Cycling in Victorian Ireland* (Dublin: Nonsuch, 2006)

J. Hannavy, *The Victorians and Edwardians at Play* (Oxford: Shire Publications, 2009)

D. Harkness and M. O'Dowd (eds), *The Town in Ireland: Historical Studies XIII* (Belfast: Appletree Press, 1981)

L. Harrington, *An Introduction to the Architectural Heritage of Cork City* (Dublin: NIAH Publications, 2012)

J. Helland, *British and Irish home arts and industries, 1880-1914: Marketing Craft , Making Fashion* (Dublin: Irish Academic Press, 2007)

R. Herlihy, *Tales from Victorian Cork 1837-1859,* (Cork: Red Abbey Publications, 2012)

R.J. Hodges, *Cork and County Cork in the Twentieth Century: Contemporary Biographies* (Brighton: W.T. Pike & Co., 1911)

Irish Industries Association, *Guide to the Irish Industrial Village and Blarney Castle, the Exhibit of the Irish Industries Association at the World Colombian Exposition, Chicago* (Chicago IL: Irish Village Bookstore, 1893)

L. James, *The Middle Class; A History*, (London: Little, Brown, 2006)

J. Jonnes, *Eiffel's Tower and the World's Fair where Buffalo Bill beguiled Paris, the Artists quarreled and Thomas Edison became a Count* (New York NY: Viking, 2009)

D.V. Kelleher, *James Dominic Burke; A Pioneer in Irish Education* (Dublin: Irish Academic Press, 1988)

K. Kenny (ed.), *Ireland and the British Empire* (Oxford: Oxford University Press, 2010)

P. and J. Kinchin, *Glasgow's Great Exhibitions; 1888-1901-1911-1938-1988*, (Bicester: White Cockade Publishing, 1988)

B. Lawlor, *The Irish Round Tower* (Cork: Collins Press, 1999)

B. Lawlor, *Rosenheim and Windermere* (Bantry: Somerville Press, 2011)

S. Lee, *King Edward VII, A Biography Vol 2* (London: Kessinger Publishing, 1927)

M. Lenihan, *Pure Cork,* (Cork: Mercier Press, 2011)

H. Long, *The Edwardian House,* (Manchester: Manchester University Press, 1993)

W. McGrath, *Tram Tracks Through Time* (Cork: Tower Books, 1981)

N. McMillan (ed.), *Prometheus's Fire – A History of Scientific and Technological Education in Ireland* (Cork: Tyndall Publications, 2000)

J.F. Maguire, *The Industrial Movement in Ireland as illustrated by the National Exhibition of 1852,* (Cork: John O'Brien, 1853)

B. Montgomery, *The 1903 Irish Gordon Bennett; the Race that Saved Motor Sport,* (Witney: Bookmarque Publishing, 2000)

F. Mulligan, *William Dargan –An Honourable Life 1799-1867* (Dublin: Lilliput, 2013)

J.A. Murphy, *Where Finbarr Played - A concise Illustrated History of Sport in University College Cork, 1911-2011* (Cork: Cork University Press, 2011)

J. Murphy, *Abject Loyalty, Nationalism and Monarchy in Ireland During the reign of Queen Victoria* (Cork: Cork University Press, 2001)

J. O'Connell, *North Mon 200* (Cork: Echo Publications, 2010)

P. O'Flanagan and C. G. Buttimer (eds) *Cork: History & Society* (Dublin: Geography Publications, 1993)

D. Ó hOgain, *Myth, Legend & Romance, An Encyclopaedia of the Irish Folk Tradition* (New York NY: Prentice Hall Press, 1991)

P. Oliver, I. Davis and I. Bentley, *Dunroamin; the Suburban Semi and its Enemies,* (London: Pimlico,1981)

C. O'Mahony, *In the Shadows –Life in Cork 1750-1930* (Cork: Tower Books, 1997)

S.M. Parkes, *A Guide to Sources for the History of Irish Education 1780-1922* (Dublin: Four Courts Press, 2010)

H. Plunkett, *Ireland in the New Century,* (London: J. Murray, 1904)

P. Poland, *For Whom the Bells Tolled,* (Stroud: History Press Ltd, 2010)

M. Potter, *The Municipal Revolution in Ireland,* (Dublin: Irish Academic Press, 2011)

S. Rains, *Commodity Culture and Social Class in Dublin 1850-1916,* (Dublin: Irish Academic Press, 2010)

J. Ridley, *Bertie: A life of Edward VII* (London: Chatto and Windus, 2012)

K. and E. Rockett, *Magic Lantern, Panorama and Moving Picture Shows in Ireland, 1786-1909* (Dublin: Four Courts Press, 2011)

R.W. Rydell, *All the World's a Fair',* (Chicago IL: Chicago University Press, 1984)

R.W. Rydell, J. E. Findling and K. D. Pelle (eds), *Fair America: World's Fairs in the United States* (Washington DC: Smithsonian Institute, 2000)

C. Rynne, *The Industrial Archaeology of Cork City and its Environs,* (Dublin: Stationery Office, 1999)

A. Service, *Edwardian Architecture,* (London: Thames and Hudson, 1977)

J. Sheehy, *Walter Osborne,* (Dublin: National Gallery of Ireland, 1983

J. Sheehy and G. Mott, *The Rediscovery of Ireland's Past,* (London: Thames and Hudson, 1980)

B. Siggins, *The Great White Fair: The Herbert Park Exhibition of 1907,* (Dublin: History Press, 2007)

T. Spalding, *Cork City, A Field Guide to its Street Furniture* (Cork: Finchfortune, 2009)

R. Storry, *A History of Modern Japan,* (London: Penguin, 1982)

J. Swift, A *defence of English commodities; Being an answer to the Proposal for the universal use of Irish manufactures*, (Dublin: 1720)

V. Toulmin (ed.), *The Lost World of Mitchell & Kenyon-Edwardian Britain on Film*, (London: BFI, 2004)

F. Tuckey, *Cork Remembrancer* (Cork: Tower Books, 1837 (1980))

J. Turpin, *Oliver Sheppard, 1865 – 1941*, (Dublin: Four Courts Press, 2000)

E.A. Wright, *Irish Industries, their promotion and development - A lecture* (Cork: Guys, 1883)

WEBSITES

Irish Census 1901 & 1911, http://www.census.nationalarchives.ie.

Dictionary of Irish Architects, www.dia.ie.

Hadji Bey Turkish Delight, http://hadjibey.ie/history.html

Gordon Bennett Races, http://www.gordonbennettroute.com/1903race.html

Shandon Boat Club, http://shandonboatclub.com/about-sbc/history.html

http://archiseek.com/tag/werburgh-street-dublin/

Irish Film & TV Research Online, website at www.tcd.ie/irishfilm

Appendices

Contents

Appendix 1: List of Participants at the Opening Day Procession, 1 May 1902

Trades Unions
Bakers Society (200 strong)
Stonecutters
Pork Butchers
Builders Labourers
Book Binders
Boot and Shoe Operatives
Iron Moulders
Tailors
Painters
Masons
Irish National Foresters
Glen Workingmen
Upholsterers
Mill sawyers
Typographical
Boot makers
Solderers and Preserve Purveyors
Coopers (120)
St Joseph's Society (Passage West)
Cabinetmakers and Polishers
Carpenters
Plumbers
Corporation Labourers (about 200)
Engineers (90)
Ancient Order of Foresters (150)
Printers' Machine Assistants
Irish Pipers
Coach makers (120)
Farriers
Electricians
Shop assistants and Industrial League
Plasterers
Gas Workers
Musicians
Brewery Workmen
Coal Porters
Harbour Board Employees
Hackney Car Association

Marching Bands
Butter Exchange
Carpenters
Barrack-Street (No. 1)
Parnell Guards
Workingmen's
St Nicholas
Blackpool
Douglas National Band
Father Mathew Temperance Band
The St Joseph's Society Band
House Painters
Passage West
Irish Pipers' Club

The Irish National Foresters
The Irish National Foresters were represented
by the following Branches:
Bryan Dillon Branch (Cork)
J.P. Leonard Branch (Queenstown)
Gerald Griffin Branch (Cork)
Captain Mackey Branch (Passage)
Branch Brothers Sheares

❧

Appendix 2:
**List of Important Committee Members
in 1902/3 Seasons**

**Incorporated Cork International
Exhibition Association, 1902**
Patron: Earl Cadogan
(Lord Lieutenant of Ireland)

President: The Earl of Bandon

Chairman of the Executive Committee:
Lord Mayor Edward Fitzgerald

Vice-Presidents:

The Earl of Mayo

Horace Plunkett, DATI

Lt-Col Sir John Arnott

Henry O'Shea

Captain Loftus Arnott

Alderman William Cave

A.H. Smith-Barry

Henry Shanahan

Alderman Henry Dale, JP

Col William Johnson, JP

R.M.D. Sanders, JP

Augustine Roche, JP

Honorary Secretary: Richard Atkins

Honorary Treasurers: M.D. Daly,
    J.P. and W.B. Harrington

Honorary Architect: Henry Cutler

Honorary Solicitor: Maurice Healy

Honorary Auditor:
    Michael Stapleton

Secretary: Herbert Honahan

Executive Committee:

J. Ahern

W.J. Fitzgerald

M. Ahern, JP

Joseph Firmo

Lt-Col Sir J. Arnott

Barry C. Galvin

R.A. Atkins, JP

George Georgeson

W. Ringrose Atkins, JP

W.B. Harrington

R. Barter, JP

Benjamin Haughton

P.D. Buckley

Prof. Marcus Hartog

Patrick Cahill

Maurice Healy

William Carroll

Sir Daniel Hegarty, Alderman, JP

William Cave, Alderman

C.J. Hemsworth, Alderman

George Crosbie

Arthur Hill (Architect)

A.M. Cole, JP

J.H. Hogan, (Manager
    Hibernian Bank)

Prof. H. Corby

D.J. Horgan

Henry Dale, Alderman, JP

Daniel Horgan, Alderman

Maurice D. Daly, JP

Thomas Jennings, JP

James Dwyer, JP

E.J. Julian

C.J. Dunn, JP

J.J. Kelleher, Alderman

Thomas Farrington, JP

I.S. Kelly (Manager of Provincial
    Bank)

Edward Fitzgerald

W. Kinmonth

Jeremiah Lane

M.J. O'Riordan, Alderman

T.B. Lillis (Manager Munster
    & Leinster Bank)

James Long

L. O'Riordan

John Lynch

Henry O'Shea

Francis W. Mahony

William Phair, Alderman

R.G. Maunsell, (Manager
    National Bank)

P.H. Meade

Michael Roche

Charles E. Murphy

R.M.D. Sanders, JP

Francis J. Murphy

Sir J.H. Scott, Alderman, JP

W.A. Mulligan

Henry Shanahan

Edward V. McCarthy, JP
Lt-Col Shuldham, JP
Florence F. McCarthy
D. Swiney, US Consul
David McDonnell
R.U.F. Townsend, JP
Henry McFerran
H.L. Tivy, JP
Alex McOstrich, JP
Robert Walker, JP
James F. McMullen
E. Walsh, Alderman, JP
J.R.B. Newman
W.T. Macartney-Filgate, DATI
T. O'Connor, Alderman

1902 Women's Section
Patroness: Countess Cadogan

President: The Countess of Bandon

Vice Presidents:
The Lady Mayoress
Lady Colthurst
Mrs Henry O'Shea
Emily Lady Arnott
Lady Carbery
Mrs Smith Barry
Lady McCalmont
Mrs R.M.D. Sanders

Chairman: Lady Mayoress
Vice-Chairman: Lady Colthurst
Deputy Vice-Chairman: Mrs Stanley Harrington
Honorary Treasurer: Emily Lady Arnott, Woodlands,
Secretaries: Miss L. Fitzgerald, Miss T. MacKenzie

Greater Cork International Exhibition, 1903
Patron: Earl of Dudley (Lord Lieutenant of Ireland)

President: The Earl of Bandon

Chairman of the Executive Committee:
Lord Mayor Edward Fitzgerald

Vice-Presidents:
The Earl of Mayo
William J. Goulding
Lord Barrymore
Henry O'Shea
Captain Loftus Arnott
Alderman William Cave
Alex McOstrich, JP
James Long
Alderman Henry Dale, JP
Revd P.J. Dowling

Secretary: Count Plunkett
Assistant Secretary: William N. Herlihy
Honorary Treasurers: Alderman Phair, H.L. Tivy
Honorary Architect: Henry Cutler
Honorary Solicitor: Maurice Healy
Musical Director: Herr Theo Gmür

Executive Staff:
Accountant: Michael S. McGrath
Ass. Accountant: S.J. Dorman
Assistants: Misses B. Harrington and N. Brennan
Superintendent of Press Department: W.N. Herlihy
Superintendent of Entrances: Ed Donovan
Superintendent of Grounds: J. Kinsella
Superintendent of Water Chute: W. Henderson

Executive Committee:
J. Ahern
E.J. Julian
R. Barter, JP
J. Kelleher, Alderman
P.D. Buckley

W. Kinmonth

James Byrne, JP Coroner

Jeremiah Lane

Patrick Cahill

James Long

William Carroll

John Lynch

William Cave, Alderman

Edward V. McCarthy, JP

J.L. Copeman

Florence F. McCarthy

Prof. H. Corby

F.W. McCarthy, Town Clerk

E.J. O'B. Croker

James F. McMullen

George Crosbie

Alex McOstrich, JP

Henry Dale, Alderman, JP

P.H. Meade

R. Dalton

H. Nalder

John Dinan

T. O'Connor, Alderman

W.J. Dunlea

Capt. O'Driscoll, JP

C.J. Dunn

L. O'Riordan

Thomas Farrington, JP

M.J. O'Riordan, Alderman

Joseph Firmo

Henry O'Shea

Edward Fitzgerald

William Phair, Alderman

W.J. Fitzgerald, (Clerk of the Crown and Peace)

Barry C. Galvin

Michael Roche

W.B. Harrington

R.M.D. Sanders, JP

Prof. Marcus Hartog

Sir J.H. Scott, Alderman, JP

Maurice Healy

Henry Shanahan

C.J. Hemsworth, Alderman

Lt-Col Shuldham, JP

Arthur Hill

Abraham Sutton, JP

Daniel Horgan, Alderman

H.L. Tivy, JP

D.J. Horgan

Women's Section 1903
Patroness: Countess of Dudley

President: The Countess of Bandon

Vice Presidents:
The Lady Mayoress
Mrs Roche
Lady Mary Aldworth
Lady Fitzgerald Arnott
Lady Carbery
Lady Barrymore
Lady McCalmont
Mrs R.M.D. Sanders

Chairman: The Lady Mayoress
Vice-Chairman: Mrs Stanley Harrington
Honorary Secretary: Miss L. Fitzgerald
Assistant Secretary: Miss Patton

Sub-Committees of the 1902/3 Seasons:
Finance
Poultry (1903 only)
Industrial and Textile
Bee (1903 only)
Fine Arts and Archaeological
Raw Materials and Minerals
Machinery
Buildings and Arrangements
Music and Amusements
Agricultural and Horticultural
Appointment and Control of Staff
Fisheries

Appendix 4: Exhibitors
Origin of exhibitors at the 1902 Exhibition
As one would expect, the majority of the 510 exhibitors came from within the then-United Kingdom. However, there was a sprinkling of traders and manufacturers from much further afield.

Country	Quantity	%age	Country	Quantity	%age
Ireland	322	63.1%	Belgium	2	0.4%
England	122	23.9%	Italy	2	0.4%
Scotland	28	5.5%	Australia	1	0.2%
France	5	1.0%	China	1	0.2%
Germany	4	0.8%	Croatia	1	0.2%
Wales	4	0.8%	Japan	1	0.2%
Canada	3	0.6%	New Zealand	1	0.2%
Russia	3	0.6%	Poland	1	0.2%
USA	3	0.6%	Syria	1	0.2%
(Unknown)	2	0.4%	Turkey	1	0.2%
Austria	2	0.4%			

Origin of Exhibitors (Ireland)
Of the 322 Irish exhibitors the majority were from the Province of Munster, although there was a strong showing from the northeast too. Of the thirty-two counties in Ireland, only twenty-two were represented, and many counties produced only one or two exhibits.

Origin of Exhibitor	Quantity	%age	Origin of Exhibitor	Quantity	%age
Cork	116	36.0%	Co. Louth	4	1.2%
Dublin	78	24.2%	Co. Armagh	3	0.9%
Belfast	34	10.6%	Co. Clare	3	0.9%
Co. Cork (excl. Cork city)	22	6.8%	City & Co. of Kilkenny	3	0.9%
City & Co. of Limerick	8	2.5%	Co. Leitrim	2	0.6%
Co. Antrim (excl. Belfast)	6	1.9%	Co. Tipperary	2	0.6%
Co. Kerry	6	1.9%	Co. Westmeath	1	0.3%
City & Co. of Wexford	6	1.9%	Co. Meath	1	0.3%
City & Co. of Galway	6	1.9%	Co. Carlow	1	0.3%
Co. Donegal	5	1.6%	Co. Down	1	0.3%
Co. Tyrone	4	1.2%	Co. Mayo	1	0.3%
City & Co. of Waterford	4	1.2%	Co. Offaly	1	0.3%
(Unknown Irish exhibitors)	4	1.2%			

Breakdown of Business sectors represented

In total in 1902 there were about 510 individual exhibitors in the main Industrial and Machinery Halls, and in the various other pavilions. Breaking them down by industry sector yields the following information. Nearly half of the exhibitors came from the top four industry sectors.

Sector	Examples of goods displayed	Quantity	%age
Food & Drink	Whiskey, brewers, cereals, bacon, ham, mustard…	72	14.1%
Construction	Turnstiles, sanitary-ware, slate, brick, prefabs,…	67	13.1%
Textiles	Lace, silk, poplins, linens, dyeing, tweed, fashion…	63	12.4%
Homewares	Lighting, furniture, bog oak, quilts, screens, rugs…	52	10.2%
Transport/Tourism	Bicycles, train & ferry co's., coachbuilders, tour Co's.	34	6.7%
Energy	Coal, mining, steam engines, dynamos, pulleys…	32	6.3%
Chemicals	Candles, soap, fertilizer, perfumery, laundry products	29	5.7%
Printing & Allied	Books, postcards, souvenirs, framers, newspapers	25	4.9%
Fashion Accessories	Umbrellas, sticks, jewellery, fancy goods, hair combs	22	4.3%
Leather goods	Boot and shoemakers, tanners, saddlery, harness…	22	4.3%
Manufacturing	Weighing machines, gas heating, motors, arc lamps…	20	3.9%
Farm/Garden	Lawn mowers, studs, machinery, milking apparatus	18	3.5%
Tobacco & Allied	Cigars, pipes, cigarettes, snuff	14	2.7%
Scientific Instruments	Microscopes, optical goods, cameras	11	2.2%
Education	Secondary and tertiary educational institutions	6	1.2%
Sporting Goods	Fishing tackle, guns, rifles, sports goods	6	1.2%
Musical Instruments	Pianos, sheet music, organs, other instruments	5	1.0%
Fire safety	Fire engines, alarms, pumps	3	0.6%
Charitable	Sailors and Soldier's Help Society, Temperance…	3	0.6%
Healthcare	Artificial limbs, baby incubators	2	0.4%
Solo Inventors(?)	Models of fishing and sailing innovations	1	0.2%
Toys	Toys	1	0.2%
(Unknown)	(Unknown)	2	0.4%

Surviving Businesses

A large number of the firms which presented exhibits at the 1902 show are still in business (in one form or another) at the time of writing. These include (from the UK): Chubb & Son Lock and Safe Co., Doulton & Co. (sanitaryware), Bryant & May Ltd (now owned by Swedish Match), Price's Candles, Quaker Oats, JS Fry & Sons Ltd and Van Houten (chocolate), W & T Avery Ltd (weighing scales), Crompton & Co. (lighting), Merryweather & Sons (fire engines), Thomas Cook & Son, Goodall, Blackhouse & Co. (pickles), Colman Ltd (mustards), Young's Paraffin Light & Mineral Oil Co and the Broxburn Oil Co. Ltd (both now part of British Petroleum), Isaac Braithwaite & Son (laundry equipment), Slingsby (factory equipment), British Schuckert Electric Co. (later subsumed into Siemens) and the Expanded Metal Co.

Dublin firms still trading since 1902 include: Easons, W & R Jacob & Co. Ltd (biscuits), MH Gill & Son (publishers), Kapp & Peterson (pipes), Paterson & Co. Ltd (matches), A Guinness, Son & Co. Ltd, Fannin & Co. Ltd (healthcare), J Tyler & Sons Ltd (shoes), JG Rathborne candles (now Rathborne Lalor Church Supplies), JW Elvery & Co. (sporting goods), IS Varian & Co. (brushes), Boileau & Boyd Ltd laboratory supplies and the Irish Independent newspaper.

Cork businesses which survive include Murphy & Co. and Beamish & Crawford (the brewers), Denis O'Sullivan brushes (now DOSCO Ltd), Cash and Company (now Brown Thomas), Charles McCarthy plumbers (now Charles McCarthy Services), Guy & Company (printers), Cork Distilleries Co. Ltd (now part of Irish Distillers Ltd in Midleton), R and J McKechnie (cleaners), Fitzgerald & Sons (menswear), McKenzies (now incorporated in Atkins garden machinery), Central Shoe Stores (then the Central Boot Stores), WHM Goulding Ltd (fertilizer), Hilser Brothers (jewellers). The Cork (now Irish) Examiner was present as were the Cork Gas Consumer's Co. (now subsumed into Bord Gáis).

Henry Denny & Sons (meats) and E. Smithwick and Sons, Ltd (the Kilkenny brewers) were also present. The Belleek pottery of Fermanagh was represented by Daniel Sheehan of St Patrick St and Schweppes Mineral waters were represented by JS Dudley of Belfast. Other northern firms which have survived include: The Old Bushmills Distillery Co of Antrim and from Belfast, Joseph Braddell & Son (guns), Davidson and Co. Ltd (now part of the Scottish Howden Group) and Harland and Wolff, W & G Baird Ltd (printers) JP Corry and Co. Ltd, (builders' merchants). From Germany: Eduard Seiler (pianos) and Lahmeyer and Co. (power generation) who showed in 1902 and are still in business.

Appendix 5: List of Mitchell & Kenyon Films shot in Cork during the 1902 Exhibition Season

Twenty-two films filmed in Cork city and county during 1902 have survived. Twenty of these films are attributed to Glaswegian showman, George Green while two of the films were shot by an Irish company known as Edison's Electric Animated Pictures. All these films are available to own on the British Film Institutes DVD – *Mitchell & Kenyon in Ireland.*

Edison's Electric Animated Pictures
M&K 785: Preparation of the Exhibition Grounds and Erection of Buildings
This was most likely filmed a month or two before the official opening in May 1902.

M&K 703: Panorama of Exhibition Grounds
This was filmed from the top of the Water Chute a few days before the opening.

George Green
M&K 704–5, 712: The Grand Procession
This was the first filming project undertaken by George Green showing the parading politicians, dignitaries and trade unionists marching on the Western Road on their way to the exhibition grounds.

M&K 702, 717: Opening of Cork Exhibition
The first scene shows the arrival of the Lord Mayor and the Earl of Bandon at the exhibition grounds amidst the chaos of carriages, visiting dignitaries and National Foresters. The second film is incorrectly linked to the official opening day and actually seems to show the arrival of the Duke of Connaught at the exhibition grounds a week later on 8 May 1902. The film shows a detachment of the Royal Irish Constabulary presenting arms and lowering a flag in salute. All the records of the opening day events do not mention the involvement of the RIC in such a manner.

M&K 715–16: Visit of the Duke of Connaught CIC Forces in Ireland and Prince Henry of Prussia
The royal party are seen passing through the grounds as well as climbing to the top of the Water Chute to officially open the attraction.

M&K 708: Albert Quay
This scene shows Albert Quay and surrounding environs. The quay is not particularly busy which would indicate that it was possibly a Sunday when this film was shot. This quay was named after Prince Albert following the royal visit to Cork in 1849.

M&K 706: Boat Race Cork Exhibition

M&K 707–8: Oar Boat Race

M&K 714: Sports Day at Queen's College
Sports form a significant portion of the M&K collection of Cork films. One of the films shows a race on the Mardyke between two small row boats. Another film shows crews practising on the water at the Marina in preparation for the Cork International Regatta held on 21, 22 and 23 July 1902. The highlight of the boating footage is the final of the International Cup between Leander and the Berlin Rowing Club. The sport's day held adjacent to the exhibition grounds on 7 June is also captured showing a variety of sports including running and cycling.

M&K 709–10: Illustrated Tram Ride over Patrick's Bridge and Grand Parade
The camera was placed on the upper deck of one of the city's trams and captures a journey from King Street (now MacCurtain Street) onto Patrick Street via Bridge Street. In the second part of this sequence, the camera is static shows the hustle and bustle of the Grand Parade and St Patrick's Street. These particular films are invaluable for historians as they provide us with a fascinating view of everyday life for the ordinary people of Cork going about their business.

M&K 711: Lee Boot Factory – Dwyer & Co. Ltd
This 'Factory-Gate' type film was set up to capture as many of the factory's workers leaving. The aim was to entice these workers to 'come see themselves' at the Cinematograph in the Concert Hall on the Mardyke.

M&K 721: Congregation leaving St Patrick's Roman Catholic Church

M&K 722: Congregation leaving St Mary's Dominican Church
Similar in style to the Lee Boot Factory film, a camera was set up opposite the entrances to both churches in an effort to film potential cinematograph customers. The contrast between both congregations is particularly striking as the poorer members of Cork's society seemed to attend St Patrick's (Lower Glanmire Road) while the more affluent citizens attended St Mary's Church (Pope's Quay). This is yet another example of how informative and illuminating the M&K collection is on early-twentieth-century Cork.

M&K 713: Regiment Returned from Boer War to Victoria Barracks, Cork
This film has been incorrectly labelled. It actually is footage of a regiment of the Munster Fusiliers leaving Victoria Barracks on route to their home barracks in Tralee. Judging by their equipment and the tanned complexion of many of the soldiers, it is clear that these men had just returned to Ireland from the Boer War and had decamped at Victoria Barracks before making the journey to Tralee.

M&K 718-720: Cork Fire Brigade Turning Out
This film shows the Cork Fire Brigade (formed in 1888) taking part in a re-enactment of a 'serious' fire and how the firemen contain it while also rescuing occupations from the 'burning' building. It would seem that the scene was shot near the Cornmarket and was probably filmed using two cameras.

M&K: 243 and 723: Train Drive from Blarney
These films were taken on the narrow-gauge Cork & Muskerry Light Railway, which ran from 1897 to 1934 between the Western Road Terminus in Cork to Blarney, Donoughmore and Coachford. These films are part of the wider sequence detailing a trip from Blarney (showing Blarney Castle and Blarney Station, via Leemount Station, Carrigrohane station and terminating at the Western Road station).

Appendix 6 : Music Played on the Exhibition Grounds on 24 September 1902

Visitors to the exhibition grounds on this day would have been treated to concerts from the Band of the 2nd Battalion Royal Scots Fusiliers, the No. 1 Barrack Street Band and an organ recital by Mr Frank Muspratt. Below is a list of the music each would have performed.

The Band of the 2nd Battalion Royal Scots Fusiliers
Bandmaster: W. Robertson

This band played four times that day at the Central Band Stand. Their repertoire changed between their afternoon and evening concerts but they illustrate the range of classical and popular music expected by Edwardian audiences.

Afternoon Concerts 2 to 3pm and 4 to 5pm
1. March – 'Wiener Kinder' – Krimmling
2. Overture – 'Les Dragons de Villars' – Maillart
3. King Henry's Song and Graceful Dance from Henry VIII Music – Sullivan
4. Grand Selection – 'Tannhaüser' – Wagner
5. Valse – 'A Toi' –Waldteufel
6. La Serenata – 'Der Engel Lied' – Braga
7. Cake Walk – 'Shuffling Jasper' – Scotton
8. Selection – 'Souvenir de la Russie' – Harris
9. Polka (with Whistling Trio) – Resi
'God Save The King'

Evening Concerts 7.30 to 8.30pm and 9.30 to 10.30pm
1. March – 'Bravoura' – Zillman
2. Overture – 'Crown Diamonds' – Auber
3. Chant Sans Paroles – 'Tschaikowsky' [sic]
4. Fantasia – 'Erin' – Basquit
Introducing the following Irish Melodies: 'Garryowen', 'Kathleen Mavourneen', 'The Shamrock', 'Tara's Hall', 'Barney O'Hea', 'Cruiskeen Lawn', 'Oh! For the swords of former time', 'Rakes of Mallow', 'Come Back to Erin', 'Sally shilly shally', 'Brien Boru March', 'Fairest put on a while', 'The Bottle of Punch', 'The Girl I left behind me', 'Fill the Bumper', 'to Ladies' eyes around', 'Let Erin Remember'

5. Valse – 'Sobre las Olas' – Rosas
6. Polacca (Piccolo Solo) – 'Picaroon' – Beckert
7. Song – 'The Wanderer' – Schubert
8. Selection – 'A Country Girl' – Monckton
9. American Sketch – 'By the Swanee River' – Myddleton
Regimental Marches of the Royal Scots Fusiliers
'God Save The King'

Organ Recital by Frank Muspratt
Conductor: Mr R.D. Howard
Concert Hall – 5pm
1. 'Fantasia in C Minor' – Berens
2. 'Meditation' – Gottschalk
3. 'Toccato' – Dubois
4. 'Air Varied' – Lemmens
5. 'Marche Cortege' – Gounod

No. 1 Barrack Street Band
Western Gardens 8–10pm
1. March – 'Right O' the Line' – Walker
2. Overture – 'Fra Diavolo' – Auber
3. Valse – 'Acclamations' – Waldteufel
4. Grand Selection – 'La Sonambula' – Bellini
5. Valse – 'Immortelle' – Gung'l
6. Selection – 'Irish Airs' – Elliot
7. Songs – 'Souls Awaking' – Haddock
8. Galop – 'Zephir' – Maire
Finale – 'St Patrick's Day'